Opining Beauty Itself

SUNY series in Ancient Greek Philosophy

Anthony Preus, editor

Opining Beauty Itself

The Ordinary Person and Plato's Forms

Naomi Reshotko

Published by State University of New York Press, Albany

© 2022 State University of New York

All rights reserved

Printed in the United States of America

No part of this book may be used or reproduced in any manner whatsoever without written permission. No part of this book may be stored in a retrieval system or transmitted in any form or by any means including electronic, electrostatic, magnetic tape, mechanical, photocopying, recording, or otherwise without the prior permission in writing of the publisher.

For information, contact State University of New York Press, Albany, NY
www.sunypress.edu

Library of Congress Cataloging-in-Publication Data

Name: Reshotko, Naomi, 1961– author.
Title: Opining beauty itself : the ordinary person and Plato's forms / Naomi Reshotko.
Description: Albany : State University of New York Press, [2022] | Series: SUNY series in ancient Greek philosophy | Includes bibliographical references and index.
Identifiers: LCCN 2022005497 | ISBN 9781438490458 (hardcover : alk. paper) | ISBN 9781438490472 (ebook) | ISBN 9781438490465 (pbk. : alk. paper)
Subjects: LCSH: Plato.
Classification: LCC B395 .R455 2022 | DDC 184—dc23/eng/20220706
LC record available at https://lccn.loc.gov/2022005497

10 9 8 7 6 5 4 3 2 1

*For my parents who taught me to inquire,
and for my children who confounded me with their inquiries.
To Terry Penner and Ruth Saunders,
who first introduced me to Plato's instruction on why inquiry is both
important and confounding.*

Contents

Acknowledgments		ix
Introduction: Tarrying on the Path to Knowledge		1
1	Recollection and the Beginning of Inquiry in the *Meno* and *Phaedo*	27
2	Another Look at the Beginning Problem	51
3	Nonphilosophers and Beauty Itself in the *Meno* and the *Phaedo*	67
4	Nonphilosophers and Beauty Itself in *Republic* V	85
5	Doxastic Structure at *Symposium* 201d1–212c3	111
6	*Doxa*, Ignorance, and False Judgment in the *Phaedrus* and *Theaetetus*	137
7	Opining Beauty Itself in *Republic* V	165
8	*Doxa*, Ignorance, and the Consolation of the Lover of Sights and Sounds	191
9	*Doxa* and Ignorance in the Cave and the Divided Line	209
Conclusion: What *Doxa* Opines and What Ignorance Is		223
Bibliography		237
Index Locorum		243
Subject Index		249

Acknowledgments

I have been working on the project that includes, but is not limited to, this book for so long that it is hard to have any confidence that I am thanking everyone who assisted me along the way. Of special note is Ruth Saunders, who read and gave me copious comments on a draft of a much longer manuscript that included what has ended up in this (shorter) book. The many discussions of this material that I have had with Ruth along the way to this book's publication have been a highlight of my engagement with these ideas. Special thanks also go to Hugh Benson and George Rudebusch, who read a much earlier draft of this entire manuscript and gave me detailed responses that (I hope they will agree) greatly contributed to its improvement. Numerous anonymous readers were enormously helpful in their comments and suggestions regarding versions of these chapters, whether they were made in the service of accepting them for publication or rejecting them. I am grateful to Nicholas Baima, who was the most recent colleague to go over the penultimate draft in detail and make useful comments and suggestions.

Scott Berman, Tony Chu, Robert Colter, Irena Deretic, David Ebrey, Michael Ferejohn, Mitzi Lee, Marco Nathan, Robert Pasnau, Terry Penner, Sarah Pessin, and Nick Smith read various drafts of papers and chapters over the last decade or so, and have been responsive to my queries and philosophical speculations regarding Plato's Epistemology, and many other topics, for many of those same years.

I benefited enormously from teaching a seminar that was inspired by the current incarnation of the manuscript in the spring of 2019. I learned greatly from all the students in that class. Mitchell Stewart and Jordan Watson gave me extensive written feedback on the manuscript after the class ended. I am deeply grateful to Jordan Watson, whom I was able to hire as a student assistant. I am lucky that this part of the project lasted exactly the four years of Jordan's undergraduate education and am even luckier that he is a person whose enthusiasm for philosophy is interwoven with strong capacities for writing, editing, understanding—and tracking and remembering—difficult ideas over many iterations of a manuscript. Phillip Banning also helped me a great deal with the manuscript, and especially as a consultant on the Greek. Still, any mistakes remain my own.

I also benefited from my audiences at the International Plato Society, Arizona Colloquium for Ancient Philosophy, West Coast Plato Workshop, Front Range Ancient Philosophy Workshop, The Greeks in the UW-Madison Philosophy Department, American Philosophical Association Symposia and Colloquia, Society for Ancient Greek Philosophy, Department of Philosophy at University of Wyoming, the University of Denver's Korbel School of International Studies and College of Arts Humanities and Social Sciences.

Michael Rinella, my editor at SUNY Press, was helpful and responsive. I am sure the timing of this submission, during the coronavirus pandemic, made his job harder than it would have been otherwise. I am also grateful to series editor, Anthony Preus, for his support of this publication.

My final year of preparation was supported by a sabbatical granted by the University of Denver, and a Dean's Meritorious Sabbatical Award granted by Dean Daniel McIntosh and the College of Arts Humanities and Social Sciences at University of Denver.

I make special mention of my late mother, Adina Venit Reshotko, whose interests in philosophy were always known to me, and who attended a full quarter's seminar on an earlier incarnation of these ideas. She supported me in many ways, including reading my work. She also inspired me to strive toward the same kind of detailed work in my scholarly writings that she invested in her wonderful artwork—especially her stone sculptures. A photograph of one of these sculptures graces the cover of this book. She named very few of her sculptures, but I would like to think she would have been happy for me to call this one "Opining Beauty Itself." The photograph was taken by PB Schechter.

I also am grateful for the emotional support of my father, Eli Reshotko, and my sisters, Deborah and Miriam. My children Sasha and Yevanit ReSchechtko, who have gone on to become scholars in their own right, have influenced my work in too many ways to count. My life partner, PB Schechter, has served in every capacity imaginable including model inquirer, interlocutor, technical support, editor, and best friend.

Introduction

Tarrying on the Path to Knowledge

In Plato's *Meno*, the attempt to figure out what virtue is gives way to the question of whether inquiry is even possible. There is also disagreement about whether it would be better to inquire about virtue's teachability before or after inquiring about what virtue is. In the *Theaetetus*, after Socrates and his interlocutors ask what knowledge is, they then berate themselves for trying to figure that out before attempting to understand true belief. They next decide that they cannot know what true belief is without figuring out what false belief is. Finally, they chastise themselves for trying to analyze false belief before they know what knowledge is.

I approach this project in a similar state of *aporia*: How much can we discern about Plato's understanding of knowledge without first clarifying his notions of inquiry, learning, opinion (or belief), reasoned belief, true belief, false belief, and ignorance? Can we really understand what Plato surmised about knowledge without first coming to terms with those epistemic states that fall short of it? Is it not especially difficult when some of these states are thought to be either pathways to, prerequisites for, or constitutive of knowledge? For example, inquiry is more primitive than, and prior to, knowledge without being a constituent of it. It is a doorway to knowledge. In contrast, our ability to refer to that which our knowledge is about seems like a prerequisite for knowledge. Many contemporary epistemologists think that belief—particularly true belief—falls short of knowledge but is either a pathway to, or a constituent of knowledge. Among Plato scholars there is considerable disagreement concerning the relationship between belief and knowledge.

My project in this book is to clarify how Plato conceptualizes the epistemic states that fall short of knowledge. A major step in this clarification will be to show that Plato takes all of them—including ignorance—to be *of* or *about* the same objects that knowledge is *about*. In other words, inquiry, learning, belief (or "opinion"), reasoned belief, true belief, false belief, and ignorance are all *of* or *about* the same objects as knowledge is *about*. I do not use *about* and *aboutness* as philosophical terms with a history in the philosophical lexicon. Rather, I use them colloquially and generically: whatever it is for any x to be about any y. For example, the relationship between my thoughts and my bed that allows my memories of making my bed this morning to be more or less accurate.

Thus, all of what Plato calls *doxa* is made true or false—or more or less accurate—by the same objects (the same truth-value-makers) that make knowledge true. I shall take the liberty of calling the objects that all of these states are equally about, "truth-makers." These truth-makers are things such as the diagonal itself, equality itself, and beauty itself, which are eventually associated with Plato's Forms. As my title suggests: Plato thinks that we opine beauty itself; belief—or opinion—is *of* (or *about*) the Form of Beauty. Plato demonstrates that these incorporeal truth-makers and their relationships to this wide variety of epistemic states make our belief-type states true or false and make our inquiries answerable. Wherever in the above paragraphs I have used terms such as *belief* or *opinion*, I am speaking about whatever it is to which Plato uses the Greek word *doxa* to refer.

Often, while on the road to saying something about what Plato says about knowledge, studies of Plato's epistemology are too quick to make assumptions about the many states that fall short of knowledge. Overlooking the possibility that Plato uses *doxa* to refer to something different from that which often gets associated with terms like *belief* today, scholars are quick to make claims about what Plato takes "belief" or "true belief" to be. Plato's contemporary readers assimilate his notion of *doxa* to contemporary epistemology's notions of belief.

Further confusion comes from the fact that Plato has Socrates speak about true *doxa* and knowledge at *Meno* 98a and *Theaetetus* 201d in a manner that, to the contemporary, analytically trained philosopher, evokes the thesis that knowledge is justified true belief. As a result, some scholars have assimilated Plato's views about both knowledge and true belief to that contemporary notion and moved on from there. This includes making several metaphysical assumptions about *doxa* and the objects of knowledge. However, these assumptions prove to be controversial when one looks at them in the light of other textual evidence in the dialogues.

For example, assimilation to the justified true belief theory carries with it the assumption that the content of *doxa* is propositional for Plato and that even the object of knowledge is a proposition. However, Plato appears to give us at least as many reasons to think that he takes the objects of knowledge to be abstract objects like his *Ideas* or Forms. I side with many others, particularly those who wrote before these more contemporary innovations in the theory of knowledge were developed, in arguing that Plato holds this latter view.

Anyone who has tried to sort out what Plato has to say about belief or opinion (*doxa*)—let alone true belief—in such dialogues as the *Meno*, *Phaedo*, *Republic* V–VII, *Phaedrus*, and *Theaetetus*, knows that this is no easy task. Many parts of these texts appear to contradict many of the assumptions that we make in our contemporary discussions of propositional belief and justified true belief even if textual evidence seems to resonate with these assumptions in other places.

This book contributes to the study of Plato's epistemology by examining texts where Plato's characters discuss the epistemological states that fall short of knowledge. Plato viewed the states that fall short of knowledge as pathways toward, prerequisites for, or components of, knowledge. Importantly, however, he always juxtaposes these variations of *doxa* with knowledge. I focus on texts that reveal Plato's thinking about these lesser kinds of epistemological states for two reasons. First, they are the kinds of epistemological states that Plato thinks *all* people entertain. Thus, to the extent that he thinks that ordinary people can inquire, learn, and improve their understanding of the world, they are important to his discussion of inquiry, learning, and the process of becoming a philosopher, or at least becoming as close to a philosopher as a human being can. I am making the—I think reasonable—assumption that Plato thought that most of his readers would fall into the category of those who entertain *doxa*. So, his efforts to communicate with his readers and manipulate their *doxa* (or *doxai*)[1] in order to improve it is also of interest. Second, I think that understanding these sorts of epistemological states will ultimately be instrumental to understanding how Plato thought about knowledge itself.

---

1. *Doxai* is the plural of *doxa* in Greek, as *beliefs* is the plural of *belief* in English. Throughout this book, I mostly use the terms *doxa* and *belief* in the singular as I use them largely to denote the abstract noun *belief*. I also argue (see the Introduction, 6, and chapter 5, 116–124) that in both Greek and English the term can serve as a "mass noun" even though it readily admits of a plural in ordinary speech and writing.

While this is a book about Plato's epistemology, it is not an examination of Plato's conception of knowledge. It lays important groundwork to aid in the exploration of how he conceived of knowledge, but does not discuss knowledge itself. I identify a "lowest common denominator" that it would behoove all interpreters of Plato's epistemology to bear in mind as they go on to develop their views of what knowledge is according to Plato. Understanding Plato's epistemology is a project of such complexity that it cannot reasonably be done in one book. I assume and hope that what I say here will be useful to others who go on to give divergent accounts of how Plato conceptualized knowledge. What I say here constrains some of what we can go on to say about Plato's understanding of knowledge; however, it does not determine exactly what he concludes about knowledge.

This study has two focal components. The first is an examination of what I think can best be characterized as generic *aboutness* and the role that it plays in inquiry, learning, and all manner of what Plato calls *doxa*. This part of the study revolves around two groups of texts. I first look at those passages in which Plato discusses the theory of recollection. Discussions of the theory of recollection let the word *knowledge* fly freely: for example, proposing that we have prenatal knowledge and even current knowledge of that which we recollect at the time when we recollect it.[2] There are those who argue that only prenatal knowledge, and not current (postnatal) knowledge, is needed for recollection.[3] However, even some of those who argue that knowledge itself is not necessary for recollection argue that either true belief is necessary or that some (unspecified) familiarity with that which is being recollected is necessary for recollection. Those who say that some kind of foreknowledge or current knowledge is necessary are making some foundational assumptions concerning what Plato thought knowledge was. Those who argue that only true belief is necessary must already have some views about what Plato thought true belief is like.

Even further, despite arguing for something weaker than knowledge or true belief as a prerequisite to recollection, at least one influential commentator has argued that Plato requires something weaker than

---

2. Grjic 1999, 24; Scott 2006, 84: White 1976, 139; Moravcsik 1971, 63; Matthews 1999, ch. 5; Dancy 2004, 228–36.

3. Fine 2003; 2014. Weiss (2001) is unusual in that she argues that there is no knowledge at any time (prenatal, current, or recollected) in the *Men*.

knowledge because of how she understands Plato to define knowledge at *Meno* 98a.[4] So even in this case, where we have found a commentator who analyzes recollection and inquiry without assuming that knowledge is present, her conclusion remains dependent on what she has already surmised or assumed about what knowledge and true belief are for Plato.[5] In attempting to analyze something as opaque as the theory of recollection, it behooves us to make as few assumptions as possible about what prenatal or current *knowledge* are, according to Plato. When we employ theory-laden notions of knowledge in analyzing Plato's discussions of recollection, we increase our risk of misunderstanding what he thought enabled us to inquire and learn.[6]

Plato uses recollection to solve a problem: the point of inquiry is to discover something we don't know. How can we begin an inquiry unless our inquiry is already *about* that into which we are inquiring? Further, how do we "point" our inquiry at something we do not know so that it can be about that thing that we do not know? My key finding in this case is one that continues to serve as a foundation for Plato's epistemology even after he ceases to write about recollection. Thus, the second group of texts that we look at with respect to aboutness are ones that show Plato assuming that all people are able to refer precisely to the things concerning which they take themselves to be inquiring or entertaining *doxai* about. Plato assumes that this reference succeeds even when a person is not entertaining any beliefs that are at all relevant to the object of their inquiry and even if their doxastic state contains misguided and false beliefs about its supposed object.

The second focal component of my project is an examination of *doxa* (often translated as *belief* or *opinion*) described in numerous places

---

4. Fine (2014) takes this moment in the *Men.* as a place where Plato defines knowledge as true belief that is tied down with reasoning. She then goes on to show that what Meno and the slave have at the beginning of their relevant inquiries does not amount to that. Thus, she concludes, Plato must not think that knowledge is a prerequisite for inquiry. Fine (2014, 16) claims that, in the *Men.*, Plato defines knowledge as true belief that is tied down with reasoning about its truth: one knows that p if and only if one believes that p, p is true, and one can explain why p is true.

5. And, in Fine's case, those assumptions are based upon prior assumptions about the propositional nature of belief and of knowledge.

6. Fine (2014, 33 n. 12, 33, 36 n. 19, 52, 130–31) herself provides evidence that knowledge in the *Men.* is more complicated than her simple gloss would suggest.

in the dialogues. While Plato, at times, appears to compare knowledge to ignorance (*agnoia* or *amathia* in Greek), I will show that *doxa* is most frequently contrasted with knowledge. In fact, I will argue that while it could be that *doxa* and knowledge are mutually exclusive, ignorance and *doxa* are not. Ignorance is composed of *doxa*—very low quality *doxa*. Thus, while I will not talk about Plato's conception of knowledge *per se* in this book, I will have something to say about how he conceived of ignorance.

I will show that Plato treats *doxa* as a bunch or mass of cognitive activity (what we would, generically, call "thinking"). Though our thinking contains many elements that can or cannot be mapped onto "what-is" to different degrees, it is always *about* "what-is," nonetheless (which, as I have already said, ultimately amounts to it being about the Forms). Plato shows that these doxastic states are as messy as they are rich. He also suggests that we can, through deliberation, individuate them into "judgments." He thinks of this individuation as artificial and context dependent, but still, it is only when we dissect these judgments out from our cloud or mass of thinking that we can start to see them as "true" or "false" or "well reasoned." I will argue that Plato does not find it as useful to deem individual judgments true and justified as he does to deem entire doxastic systems better or worse for deployment in a particular context. The expert sailor and the expert plumber have doxastic systems that are well suited to very different projects. If either had knowledge, we might be able to say that one is absolutely more knowledgeable than the other. However, if we imagine that they each have *doxa*—albeit very high quality *doxa* when it comes to performing specific tasks—we will only rank them with respect to one another with regard to how well each of their doxastic systems captures what-is regarding safety and navigation on bodies of water, or with respect to delivering water to a given location in a convenient and safe manner. Presumably, the sailor will rank higher than the plumber in the first case, but the reverse will be true for the second case.

Some aspects of my project involve some methodological practices that are worth mentioning. I will not focus on what we might think of as *arguments* made by characters in the dialogues who are trying to secure the definition of *reference, aboutness,* or *doxa*. I will, for the most part, examine some of Plato's dialogues in order to uncover the presuppositions that their author appears to make regarding aboutness and *doxa* in what are, at face value, discussions of recollection, inquiry, discovery, belief, true belief, true belief that is reasoned, and true belief that is not reasoned. I will also look at how Plato has his characters use terms such as *doxa* and *ignorance*. In some cases, I will even look at what is said about knowledge, but only in order to uncover presuppositions regarding aboutness and *doxa*.

Key to my conclusions is that we can understand all the epistemic states that fall short of knowledge in Plato's dialogues by understanding two distinct sets of Plato's assumptions concerning two distinct things and how they are related to one another. First, we need to understand Plato's assumptions about a type of referential connection that can be unwitting but is still cognitive in nature. Second, we need to understand the rich and varied way in which he makes use of (for lack of a sufficiently general English translation) *doxa*. Further, we must understand how these two mutually exclusive cognitive capacities are related: the first is a prerequisite for the second. I regard this specific type of reference (which I am also calling "aboutness") as the most primitive "epistemic" state that is evident in Plato's epistemology. Let me be clear that I do not think that Plato ever uses any Greek word that can be translated or understood as "reference." I am talking about something that I take Plato to be struggling to gesture toward in his theory of inquiry and recollection and that I think he assumes, with varying degrees of recognition, throughout his discussions of *doxa*.

These very specific theses regarding the referent of inquiry and the nature of what falls short of knowledge as theorized by Plato also offer up larger and more general conclusions for our overall understanding of Plato's epistemology. Interpreters often ponder the relationship between nonphilosophers and the Forms. There is a further concern that Plato is pessimistic about, or even dismissive of, the epistemological abilities of nonphilosophers. The focal theses of this book allow us to be optimistic. Nonphilosophers may never achieve what Plato deems knowledge, but they can investigate that which *is* rather than how things merely or deceptively appear. Further, *doxa* is an epistemological currency that can be improved and can make progress with respect to capturing what *is*. My conclusions support the notion that Plato thinks everyone can place realistic faith in inquiry and in the rewards of inquiry that is done well. Appropriate inquiry includes humility with respect to what human inquiry can accomplish combined with acknowledgment of, and respect for, its true object.

Reference as Unwitting Cognitive Contact

In the next chapter, I approach this specific notion of aboutness by engaging with Meno's paradox and isolating the "beginning problem."[7] This is the problem of how we focus an inquiry regarding something we do not know, since we do not know it. Plato is highlighting a problem with inquiry and reference that many philosophers since have also noted and endeavored to solve. A recent example is Michael Strevens (2019).[8] Both Strevens and Plato are describing a subject who is trying to refer to whatever x actually is, but, as that subject has perhaps either never conceived of x or misconceives of x, she can be clueless as to where her reference actually lands because she is clueless as to what x actually is (she is "unwitting," in my parlance). Strevens describes the referential problem that he and Plato are both trying to solve in several places:

> To be wrong about a category[9] we must be able to think about it—our concept must refer to the category . . . [in] a scenario in which we are abundantly wrong about the class of things to which we can successfully refer. (150)[10]

---

7. Following Benson 2015. I will expand on this in chapter 1.

8. Strevens's goal (2019, 153) is different from Plato's and those of the other, twentieth-century philosophers that he follows. He is developing a dispositional theory of reference that works for "inductive conceptual categories." Plato is interested in an objective truth that overrides any *conceptual* categories. Folks such as Kripke (1980) and Devitt (1981)—upon whom Strevens models his theory—were striving for this more objective target as well.

9. For Plato, the proper word would not be *category*, but *property*. In other words, something like virtue or triangularity.

10. Strevens speaks of the "reflexivity" of reference and identifies it as when "some of our beliefs about a category help to determine which category the beliefs are about" (2019, 143). He goes on to say,

> What is wanted is a variety of reflexivity [of reference] that allows for falsehood of any or all ordinary beliefs, while nevertheless establishing those same beliefs as a reliable starting point for philosophical analysis. (147)

This statement seems to imply that it is the *content* of the belief about the category that determines what the belief is about. This is a result of Strevens's goal of isolating inductive *conceptual* categories. It is important to note that, in this way, he diverges from Plato. Since I am advocating for Plato's concern that we refer to objective kinds

It is for this reason that Strevens celebrates the "causal historical" account (Kripke 1980; Devitt 1981) in which,

> [Reference] is fixed by the intention of the coiner that a term refer to a category exemplified by some baptismal specimen . . . whether or not [his] beliefs about that specimen are at that time or at any later time correct. (153)

Strevens notes:

> The great advantage of the causal-historical account, for the seeker of objective categories, is that it permits us to make profound and sweeping errors about the objects of our thought[11]—and in so doing it frees our categories to home in on objective worldly structure without running afoul of self-imposed semantic constraints. . . .
>
> Indeed, it has seemed to philosophers that the best theory of reference for basic natural kind concepts is *the least reflexive*: it is the theory that when determining the reference of a term or concept puts as little weight as possible—perhaps none at all?—on our beliefs, now or later, about the corresponding category. (153; emphasis added)

I have added emphasis in the above two quotations to underline the sympathy between what Strevens strives to provide and what I believe Plato is struggling to come up with: the ability to successfully refer to something just because we are trying to refer to it and because we want our reference to succeed in landing on whatever it actually is, notwithstanding any mistakes or misconceptions contained in our thoughts as we endeavor to make this reference. I use the term *unwitting cognitive contact* to get at the same referential phenomenon that Strevens says he

---

or Forms that are independent of our conceptual constructions of them, I will not use the term *reflexive* in my own voice and want to make clear that the notion of unwitting cognitive connection that I attribute to Plato is not a reflexive notion of reference. However, there is a great deal of resonance: looking forward to my final quotation from Strevens (from his page 153, below), it is worth noting that he is also trying to rely on content as little as possible and make it as "unreflexive" as possible.

11. I would add "inquiry" to "thought" on Plato's behalf.

and Kripke are trying to capture. However, I think Plato would disagree with Kripke on a number of critical points. I will discuss these after I have discussed the relevant similarities.

Like the Kripkean view, Plato attempts to solve the beginning problem by granting us an ability to refer that is successful regardless of any content contained in our beliefs about that to which we intend to refer, whenever we believe, think, speak, or inquire. That is why I will generally call it "unwitting," even though it can be "witting" on the part of the person making the contact. I will use the term *unwitting* generally because the important point is that it *can be unwitting*, and it usually is, in the cases that demand that we acknowledge the existence of this sort of reference. I call it "cognitive" because, just as Kripke assumes, it must be actualized by *thinking* on the part of the subject of this connection. It is referential contact with a truth-maker that is grounded in the *intentions of the subject of that referential cognition*.

It sounds awfully strange to say that someone is referring in a way that is both intentional and unwitting at the same time. Allow me to clarify the phrase "unwitting cognitive contact," which I will use frequently, especially in the next four chapters. I am describing a subject who is trying (which engages intention and, therefore, cognition) to refer to whatever x actually is, but, as that subject has perhaps either never conceived of x or misconceives of x, she can be clueless (thus unwitting) as to where her reference actually lands because she is clueless as to what x actually is.[12]

It might be that this kind of contact does not rise to the level of an epistemic state and it would be better to think of it as pre-epistemic, proto-epistemic, or a condition for possession of an epistemic state. Perhaps *cognitive* is not the best term to use; I use it to distinguish my view from the views of other scholars who claim that Plato thought that non-philosophers can have only an ontological—and not a cognitive—relationship with the sort of abstract object that is, for Plato, a Form.[13]

---

12. This mode of reference is not unfamiliar in Plato. He also uses it in a parallel manner regarding desire for the actual good, where agents do not know what the actual good is and, therefore, do not know what they actually desire even though they desire it. This thesis is common in much of the literature on Socratic moral psychology, which has sometimes been referred to as the "dominance" theory of desire. See Penner 1991, and those who follow that line of interpretation especially regarding *Gorgias* 466a–468c: Devereux 1995; Penner and Rowe 1994; Anagnostopoulos 2003; Berman 2003; Reshotko 2006, 24–56; 2011; Brickhouse and Smith 2010, 43–48.

13. Scott 1995, 68–69. We will look at this comparison view in the next chapter.

Plato would depart from Kripke's view that there needs to be a "coiner" of a specific "term" to whom, and a "baptism" to which, the person who makes the reference that overcomes the beginning problem must be historically connected. When Socrates asks, "What is virtue?" he is referring to whatever makes beliefs about virtue true (or renders them false)—it doesn't matter how the term came into being. Even less does it matter whether the earliest use of the term involved pointing to something, much less to something that was actually an instance of virtue. If Euthyphro and Socrates are trying to figure out what piety is and Euthyphro says, "It is what I am doing now," their inquiry is about piety even if what Euthyphro is doing now is far from pious (5d8) and even if no one has ever used the term to indicate an action (or any other perceptible thing) that is actually pious. Or even if they don't use the term *pious* (maybe neither notices that Socrates actually misspoke, saying "impious" where he meant to say "pious"—as so many of us often do).[14]

I argue that, whatever (else) he appears to hope to gain through his theory of recollection, Plato does presuppose unwitting *cognitive* contact with a truth-maker that is grounded in the *intentions* of the subject of that cognition in order to resolve the beginning problem. While I argue that the content of that cognition is independent of the object to which the cognizer becomes related, it is the fact that it is cognitive and intentional that I assume raises it to the level of an epistemic state. This notion of reference, however, is distinct from *doxa* (belief) and all other epistemic states. It is a non-doxastic subject/object relationship. It is a precondition of *doxa*: a pre-doxastic condition. All other epistemic states that fall short of knowledge are constituted by *doxa*. I find that belief/opinion and ignorance are all constituted by *doxa* (even if Plato at times seems to say that

---

14. There is another place where I would argue that Plato departs from Kripke, however, it is not relevant to my project in this book. It is a controversial claim for me to make concerning Plato's metaphysics and needs support. I will not be making any argument for it here, as none of the arguments that I am making require this issue to be settled one way or another. Kripke assumes that we are somehow pointing to the essence of a natural kind when we point to whatever gold is and name it. Plato would agree that gold has a "nature" (*Crat.*, 383a–390e) but not that it has the type of "essence" that Kripke (or Aristotle, see Berman 2020, 105, 130–33) assumes it does. In other words, Plato does not think that gold is characterized by a definition that consists of necessary and sufficient properties for what it takes to be gold. For a bit of an introduction to this controversial claim see Reshotko 2021. Others who argue for this kind of view are Penner (1987, 209–31) and Berman (1996; 2020, 105–22).

doxa and ignorance are mutually exclusive).[15] Reference—constituted in this case by a cognitive but unwitting connection to a truth-maker—is a prerequisite for these doxastic states and is also the prerequisite for inquiry and learning. Thus, contrary to most interpretations of recollection, which find some sort of knowledge or some sort of belief to be the prerequisite for inquiry, learning, and discovery, I find that only this contact, and not knowledge or *doxa*, is the prerequisite for inquiry and learning. In fact, as it is a prerequisite for all doxastic states, unwitting cognitive contact is a prerequisite for *doxa* (whether true or false) and (I assume) for knowledge as well.

Thus, our most minimal conclusion can be that Plato needed recollection to supply only this unwitting cognitive contact or content-independent reference. Without this contact, the theory of recollection is insufficient. Moreover, anything that Plato supplies through recollection that goes beyond this contact (like each soul having possessed all knowledge prior to birth only to forget it at the moment of birth) is implausible overkill with respect to solving the beginning problem. I argue that Plato appears to have gone beyond this "sweet spot" in articulating what exactly he needed from the theory of recollection in order to respond to Meno's paradox. This is probably attributable to his simultaneous and nonepistemological agenda of arguing for the immortality of the soul. Still, I find ample evidence that he is committed to this contact and that it is what is doing the work in allowing for inquiry and *doxa*. This unwitting cognitive contact can be the sole initiator of inquiry, learning, and discovery and is the most plausible candidate for this initiation. Thus, it is due to this unwitting cognitive contact that we can develop *doxai* that can be decomposed into true and false beliefs. I also show that Plato maintains a commitment to this sort of content-independent cognitive contact in many dialogues in which he does not discuss, and is probably no longer committed to, recollection. Plato needs this pre-doxastic theory of reference because more than one abstract object lends its character to the perceptible world. This reference is needed for inquiry and *doxa* so that the various candidate targets for inquiry, and objects of *doxa*, can be individuated and re-identified as we make and test our hypotheses concerning them.

---

15. Plato appears to say this at *Symp.* 200–12 and *Rep.* 475–79, but I shall argue otherwise in chapters 5 and 7–9.

Recollection versus *Doxa*

Most other treatments of recollection and inquiry find that whatever recollection provides that makes inquiry possible lies somewhere along a spectrum of epistemic states. This spectrum has knowledge, however construed, at one extreme and proceeds through partial knowledge,[16] various qualities of true belief (reasoned or not reasoned), and all the way to some kind of familiarity that is meant to reside on the weakest extreme.[17] In contrast, I find that recollection—if it is to solve the problem it is invoked to solve—must first supply an ability to refer that does not lie on this spectrum, but rather is a prerequisite to the formation of any of the epistemic states included on this spectrum. Our ability to refer is other than *doxa*, and is not reducible, even in part, to *doxa*. Furthermore, reference initiates the same spectrum of epistemic states mentioned above; ranging from full-blown knowledge all the way to the weakest epistemic state, which I shall say Plato regards as ignorance. I argue that Plato thinks that *all* epistemic states that fall short of knowledge are composed of *doxa*.[18]

Reference or Aboutness: A Prerequisite for any Epistemic State that Is a Stepping Stone

In *The Possibility of Inquiry* (2014: 12–15), Gail Fine, in addition to classifying the various views on what recollection supplies with respect to the strength of epistemic states (i.e., does it supply knowledge or something weaker?), examines whether it supplies a "matching" or "stepping-stone"

---

16. If there is such a thing (*cf.* Fine 2014, 90). Again, I leave this to those who form conclusions about knowledge but much of what I conclude regarding *doxa* militates against Plato recognizing such a thing in any rigorous treatment of knowledge.

17. Fine (2014, 70 n. 6) suggests this as something weaker than true belief, but it is hard to make sense of how she thinks about it if it does not amount to some combination of true and false beliefs (albeit unreasoned ones), given how closely she adheres to a propositional analysis of anything in the epistemic realm. However, she does refer to perceptions as non-doxastic appearances about virtue. She also refers to propositional beliefs about how virtue is misrepresented.

18. It makes sense to think that knowledge, if it is in any way "composed" of *doxa*, is *doxa* that has undergone some sort of essential transformation so that it is now knowledge and not "mere" *doxa*. See my comments on these sorts of views below (n. 23, chapter 9, n. 2, and Conclusion, 229).

version of that prerequisite.[19] Although Fine and Brown (2008a) cash these out with respect to knowledge (which I will not), I think these contrasting conceptualizations can still be helpful here. A "matching" prerequisite provides something like a template, or a blank, that must be filled in by *the thing about which* one is inquiring. Thus, matching requires that one put one's finger directly upon the object of inquiry.[20] On the other hand, a stepping-stone prerequisite is an "almost there" approach that can home in on and circle the object of inquiry; it can involve acquiring something that is relevant to, but indirectly connected with, the object of inquiry. If I need to catch Jesse's dog, I might not count myself as having made progress until I am holding that very dog (matching). Or, I might consider myself to have made progress if I manage to discover that the dog was last seen in the Jeffersons's yard and answers to the name "Saffron" (stepping-stone).

I believe it is informative to characterize my own findings by saying that Plato thinks that some sort of reference that fulfills, or replaces, the need for matching is a prerequisite to the acquisition of any epistemic state that can be used as a stepping stone. Reference provides this "matching" component and, in turn, allows for *doxa* that can be a stepping stone. The first thing any inquiry must have in order to have the potential for success is a relationship to an appropriate truth-maker that establishes when something is relevant to its target and when it is not. So, reference to the object of inquiry is the direct connection that allows the things related to the object of inquiry to get one closer to it. I might have trouble getting my arms around a particular dog, but if I manage to get hold of a leash that is already connected to the dog, that increases my likelihood of getting hold of the dog in a way that knowing the dog's name or where it was last seen cannot. Holding the leash is more akin to holding the dog than is having those other pieces of information. That is why this sort of connection fulfills or replaces the matching requirement. Still, the leash is not the dog, nor is it anything like the dog, whereas the dog's name and location might seem to have some important content, but only if that content is actually true of the thing on the end of the leash. A leash that is connected to the actual dog cannot lead me astray in the way that false content can. Once I establish that this sort of connection is part of Plato's pre-doxastic epistemology, I will go on to further examine the range of

---

19. Fine credits this terminology to Brown (2008a).
20. Although "matching" might not be the best name for it: see chapter 2, 64 n. 22, below.

doxastic states that fall short of knowledge and will figure out in what these states consist.

Reference as Unwitting Cognitive Contact without Recollection

I begin this book by showing how Plato employs recollection as a solution to the beginning problem as voiced by Meno's paradox. However, I go on to show that Plato's investment in unwitting cognitive contact and its necessity for any kind of inquiry or *doxa* goes way beyond, and is independent of, any investment that Plato has in the theory of recollection. I see the theory of recollection as Plato's attempt to come up with an explanation for this mysterious contact in a way that also fulfills another clear agenda that he has in the dialogues that contain it: arguing for the immortality of the soul.

Plato does not refer to recollection outside of the *Meno*, *Phaedo*, and *Phaedrus*. Furthermore, many have argued that there is no evidence that he commits himself to such a doctrine in any of the other dialogues. Some even cite evidence to the contrary.[21] For these reasons, I am more than content to say that my view is consistent with the view that Plato has dispensed with recollection in the rest of the dialogues. I will argue, however, that he has maintained a commitment to unwitting cognitive contact as a prerequisite for *doxa* throughout his epistemology.

It is helpful to think of the three dialogues that mention recollection as treating it the way Marco Nathan (2021) has recently identified as "Black Boxing." A black box is what allows a theorist to move forward without filling in every detail of an elusive part of their theory. Scientists such as Mendel and Darwin were able to make great strides in their contributions to the theories of genetics and natural selection without knowing what mechanisms accounted for the heredity of traits from one generation to the next.[22] According to Nathan, we can see them use black boxes to iso-

---

21. In fact, I believe that Plato offers arguments that contradict the theory of recollection and the assumptions behind his arguments for the immortality of the soul in the *Theaet.* and the *Tim.* However, I will not argue for these views here, as they are irrelevant to the thesis of this book. Everything I say is consistent with Plato abandoning recollection throughout the remaining dialogues.

22. Nathan (2021, 79) claims (controversially) that they postponed even trying to figure out what they were. This establishes an even greater parallel to my claim that

late the pattern of phenomena that they wanted to explain in a way that helped to isolate that pattern and hold it steady as it participated in the remainder of the theory (109). At some point, these thinkers themselves or others, who were working independently, focused in on the contents of the black box and tried to give a causal explanation that accounted for it as a "difference maker." That is, they tried to provide a model that made the mechanism in the black box transparent. Sometimes this eliminated the need for the black box.

In my narrative, Plato does this as follows: In the *Meno*, he isolates the beginning problem. The slave manages to think about something with which he was previously unacquainted and about which he had no true beliefs (the diagonal). Realizing everyone must have this capacity, Plato frames this pattern of behavior, calling whatever it turns out to be "recollection." In both the *Meno* and the *Phaedo* he attempts to produce a model that explains how it makes a difference—how it actually works. In both dialogues, he blends his explanatory model with his argument for the immortality of the soul. At times, he embellishes it with a view toward enhancing the argument for the soul's immortality, rather than simply using it to answer Meno's paradox.

Later, however, Plato no longer endorses recollection, but he still needs to frame whatever the solution to the beginning problem is. When he is not also thinking about the immortality of the soul, he does not think that recollection is necessary in order to account for the fact that everyone is able to overcome the beginning problem. There might be some other explanation. However, he is not going to spend more time on that explanation right now. He wants to assume that people can make this unwitting cognitive connection and move on to discuss *doxa* (and the rest of his epistemology). He frames unwitting cognitive contact with a "black box" and moves on.

When I discuss the *Theaetetus, Republic* V–VII, *Cratylus,* and *Phaedrus,* I aim to show that Plato is still committed to the thesis that everyone has unwitting cognitive contact with the Forms. He maintains this commitment even though he no longer explains how it comes about through recollection and, in fact, leaves how it happens unexplained in the rest of his work. While he might have given up on the plausibility and utility of recollection, he has not given up on the thesis that all human beings who can inquire and possess *doxa* have a mysterious and, as yet,

---

Plato eventually stops focusing on how this connection got established and simply makes use of it in his epistemology.

unexplained ability to make unwitting cognitive contact with the Forms. Based on this evidence, I conclude that Plato thought that everyone (his readers, lovers of sights and sounds, ordinary people, philosophers) have this sort of relation to his Forms and that everyone's inquiries, beliefs, and even their ignorance, are about the Forms.

Some Current Views on *Doxa* in Plato

In the twenty-first century, there has been a hum of argument in favor of Plato's "two world theory," where *doxa* and *epistêmê* have two different objects and are mutually exclusive.[23] These scholars complain about accounts of *doxa* in Plato that make it a component of knowledge. Some of these objections resonate with my own complaints about assumptions that are made regarding Plato's view of *doxa*. Some of the similarities between these views and mine will be hard to appreciate as I am reluctant to make positive claims about Plato's understanding of *epistêmê* or knowledge. I think it is plausible that Plato thought that one cannot have both *doxa* and *epistêmê* of the *same thing* at the *same time*, which is one way of summarizing the position of these proponents of a *doxa* that does not align with contemporary analytic uses of "belief";[24] whatever *doxa* is, it is overridden by, and is inferior to, *epistêmê*. If *epistêmê* is in any way *doxa*, then it is *doxa* transformed into *epistêmê*, it is not *doxa* and *epistêmê* at the same time.

However, in contrast to these views, the *doxa* that I find in Plato's dialogues must ultimately be *about* the Forms (which is also what knowledge and ignorance are about). *Doxa* might be inaccurate, misleading, confusing, and unclear. However, these properties would not make it inferior to knowledge unless it were inaccurate, misleading, confusing, and unclear *about* the *same* thing that knowledge is accurate and clear about, namely, what-is. So *doxa* must, somehow, be *about* the same thing that knowledge is *about*. This is contrary to Plato's so-called two world theory. Furthermore, I have no problem imagining that while knowledge will only be *about* perceptibles in a derivative way, knowledge of perceptibles will be unproblematic for one who knows the Forms and has time to adjust to the darkness upon returning to the cave (*Rep.* 516e3–6).

---

23. Gerson 2009; Vogt 2012; Moss and Schwab 2019; Moss 2021.
24. See Moss and Schwab 2019, 8.

Chronology

I take my project to make few if any assumptions about the chronology of Plato's dialogues. I assume that one can—and should—cross-reference textual evidence concerning Plato's use of *doxa* across dialogues more or less without regard to what others might say about their chronological relationships. The conjecture that Plato's views must have changed over the course of his writing makes sense to me. If I were analyzing Plato's view of knowledge itself, and, particularly, if I were discussing Plato's ontological theories concerning the truth-makers of beliefs and the objects of knowledge (which I—along with many others—would argue are what later came to be known as his *Ideas* or Forms), then I might have to take some hypotheses about Plato's development into account. However, here I focus on the presuppositions that Plato appears to have held (but leaves less than fully articulated) about *doxa* (belief or opinion) and what allows the *doxa* of the person who does not have knowledge to be true or false. Thus, I am treating the dialogues that I do mention as mutually reinforcing. That is, I am assuming that they contain similar assumptions about *doxa*, and that it makes sense to try to piece together a more complete and coherent view by taking their evidence to be mutually enhancing rather than isolated to an individual dialogue. I also assume that we should read different dialogues as consistent rather than contradictory whenever possible.

As it happens, apart from a few references to the *Apology* (a dialogue treated by developmentalists as "early" or "Socratic"), and the fact that the *Meno* is treated variously as "early," "transitional," and "middle," it is generally regarded as safest not to make strong developmental and chronological claims about the relationships among the other dialogues from which I collect evidence (*Crat., Phdo., Phdr., Rep., Symp., Theaet.*).[25] As a result, I venture that my exegetical project should be of interest to unitarians and developmentalists alike (and everyone in between) and also that these apparent assumptions that Plato makes about *doxa* need to be taken into account equally in any and all treatments of Plato's epistemology.

---

25. There are some individuals who make such cases for doctrinal reasons. One particular case has to do with in which dialogues Plato does or does not commit himself to the existence of Forms after criticizing the Theory of Forms in the *Parm.* See Cherniss 1957.

The Thread of Argument through the Chapters

Depending on the background with which a reader approaches this book, the various parts will hold different significance. The book falls into three parts: My two focal theses are argued for by the end of chapter 6, with my first thesis regarding reference or aboutness occupying chapters 1–4 and my thesis on *doxa* occupying chapters 5 and 6. Still, for some, chapter 7 will be the climax of the book, as it defends my conclusions in the first six chapters with a reading of *Republic* 475e4–479d5 that departs from both traditional and more recent interpretations of that passage. To most interpreters, in that part of the *Republic* Plato appears to be saying that neither ignorance nor *doxa* can be about "what-is." Clearly, this is contrary to both of my focal theses. I spend chapter 7 explaining what I find wrong with that reading and supplying my own. Chapters 8 and 9 reinforce my conclusions in chapter 7.

Chapters 1 and 2 discuss the prerequisite to all epistemic states for which Plato appears to search in his discussion of recollection, what I have called "unwitting cognitive contact." In these chapters, I focus on passages in the *Meno* and the *Phaedo*. This initial foray into recollection is not so much exegesis on my part as it is an attempt to look at the exegesis of others. I want to see if there is any way to move these debates forward in a manner that gives Plato that to which he appears to be committed regarding the brute evidence, from Socrates's demonstration with the slave, that we do manage to inquire and make—and then correct—false hypotheses concerning our object of inquiry. Plato appears to say that we once knew—before birth—all that we will later learn. According to his story, we then forget it all at birth. Clearly, Plato is indicating that he thinks we need something other than a *tabula rasa* to explain inquiry and learning. However, he leaves a clear description of what he thinks we need wanting. What marks are in this nonvirgin *tabula*? Does it contain *everything* in some compartment that is inaccessible until each individual idea is triggered by sense experience? This seems simplistic and extreme—mystical to the point of implausibility. Furthermore, as many have argued, it is hard to see how it answers the question of how we can begin to inquire.

Yet, it is hard to disagree with Plato that a *tabula rasa* seems inadequate to explain his realist view that the target of knowledge is an existent and unchanging abstract object, like beauty itself or the diagonal itself, that cannot be accessed by our senses. In the chapters on recollection, I go out on a limb and propose something that clarifies, and then satisfies, what I take to be Plato's intentions regarding recollection. I venture that our default should be to assume that what I propose is at least part of what he was seeking. It is what it behooves him to seek. Were he to venture only this modest assumption in order to solve the paradox of inquiry (the first—"the beginning"—question in Meno's paradox), he would succeed in resolving the beginning problem and allow inquiry to be about such things as the diagonal itself. Furthermore, I will argue exegetically in the remaining chapters that this is a supposition to which he is committed throughout the rest of his discussions of recollection and even in dialogues that feature hypothesizing and correcting hypotheses, without recollection.

Chapters 3 and 4 show that Plato assumes that all people (including ordinary people and his readers) are able to refer to, think about, and inquire into "what is" (such things as beauty itself and the diagonal itself) in the absence of any theory regarding why they are able to do so. In chapter 3, I use evidence from the *Meno* and from *Phaedo* 73c5–77b10 to establish that Plato believes that human beings can inquire because they are born with an ability to refer to the actual thing that will answer their inquiry, as opposed to their reference being restricted to what they presuppose will answer their inquiry. This is important because it shows that Plato thinks even those who start out believing that perceptibles are—and exhaust—what-is can be remediated through their inquiries, and can even come to have some appreciation for what he later comes to identify as his Forms.

I lay the groundwork for extending the thesis that this connection exists prior to inquiry and learning into the middle books of the *Republic* by examining Socrates's statement at *Phaedo* 72e3–77e5 that we come to see the inadequacy of particulars by comparing them to Forms. This passage was used by Scott (1995, 60–63) to justify his claim that Plato thought only philosophers could recollect. But Scott's claim has been challenged by Kelsey (2001), Williams (2002), Franklin (2005), and Harte (2006), and I use these latter interpretations (predominantly Harte's) to build the scaffolding upon which to develop my interpretation of both that particular claim and also of the general attitude that Plato displays concerning what relationship nonphilosophers hold to the Forms. In regard to the *Phaedo*, I argue against Scott's assessment of the intended audience for the sticks and stones argument (74b7–c5), showing that it is intended to make an impression on a more naive audience than Simmias and the others who are in Plato's inner circle and who already accept Forms into their ontologies. I show that in the slave demonstration in the *Meno*, the Slave is thinking beyond sensible particulars, and has beliefs about the square itself that are contrary to any perceptible experience he has ever had or might entertain.

Chapter 4 provides further evidence of the connection between the ordinary person and the Forms by interpreting the beliefs of the lover of sights and sounds in *Republic* V. I argue that Plato is treating the lover of sights and sounds as an ordinary person who makes use of a unitary abstract "beauty" while professing to believe that only individual beautiful particulars exist. I argue that this is evidence that Plato theorizes that lovers of sights and sounds can make cognitive unwitting reference to beauty itself. Plato has Socrates rely upon just such reference to show the inconsistency in the lovers' beliefs. Once this is done, Socrates exploits this inconsistency to make lovers of sights and sounds (or at least his readers) aware of their standing commitment to a unitary, abstract, beauty itself and to waken them from their dream state so that they can begin to use perceptibles as a means for investigating these unitary, abstract objects, such as beauty itself and ugliness itself. I believe that Plato's calculated exploitation of the inconsistency between what the lovers of sights and sounds *think* they believe, and their actual ontological commitments does give us a modicum of textual evidence regarding Plato's own recognition of his assumptions concerning the relationship between inquiry and unwitting—but intentional—reference.

After noting that Plato thinks all souls pursue the good despite their ignorance of it and so must be able to aim their seeking at whatever the actual good is (*Rep.* 505d11–e5), chapter 5 next finds further evidence for unwitting cognitive connection in the famous allegory of the cave. We see there that Plato assumes that even the most ordinary humans—the prisoners at the bottom of the cave—must already be in touch with these "things-in-themselves" that are beyond experience when they begin to ask questions about and investigate the patterns of perceptible shadows displayed on the walls of the cave. I close the chapter by pointing out that Plato has Socrates assert that the souls of ordinary people already have the tools to sort out the nonidentity of bigness itself and smallness itself, or thickness itself and thinness itself, when provoked by the question of whether an individual finger is properly characterized by one of these opposites or the other. Plato embeds this in a segment on the education of philosopher kings at 523e3–524a4.

In chapter 5, I begin to set my sights on *doxa*. I diagnose some assumptions regarding *doxa* that Plato appears to harbor when he has Diotima speak of *erôs, doxa,* beauty, and knowledge in the *Symposium*. In chapter 6, I go on to reinforce this picture of *doxa* by looking at Plato's more explicit discussions of *doxa* in the *Phaedrus* and the *Theaetetus*. It is in these two chapters that I discern that Plato sees *doxa* as everything that falls short of knowledge, including ignorance, and further, that *doxa* is dichotomous with knowledge.

My analysis of Diotima's speech yields a picture of *doxa* that is importantly different from the way belief, true belief, and justified true belief are deployed by some in contemporary epistemology.[26] Rather than speaking of *doxa* as naturally individuated into discrete units (such as propositions), the way to make sense of the pronouncements Diotima makes concerning *doxa* is to understand Plato as speaking of an interconnected doxastic structure (something like a "web of belief").[27] I find it most intuitive to speak of this as a "cloud" of *doxa*. Plato frequently uses *doxa* more like a mass noun than a count noun. Further, any given cloud of *doxa* might be a cloud of ignorance even if we can find areas of it that count as true and reasoned. In fact, "ignorance" is—etymologically in English—everything that is *not knowledge*.[28] And, in saying that he himself is better off than the craftspeople who "know" many useful things, at *Apology* 22d-e, Socrates seems to be acknowledging that some very useful clouds of *doxa* are ignorance and are, in fact, a worse kind of ignorance than is his own awareness that he knows nothing. Several other passages throughout the dialogues resonate with this as well.

I come to this conclusion by noting that Diotima appears to begin to construct a hierarchy of epistemic states. While there are other places in the dialogues where a similar hierarchy also appears to be constructed, Plato does not give us a way to make sense of a hierarchy of epistemic

---

26. Of course, "contemporary epistemology" is a vast and ever-growing field of study. Not all contemporary views are committed to the notion that belief is propositional and that beliefs can be individuated. However, the interpretations of Plato's epistemology that I think are most in danger of getting us off on the wrong foot force a choice between assimilating *doxa* to the contemporary theories that treat *doxa* as falling into natural units whose contents are describable as propositions and acquaintance theories of belief. I suggest a third alternative for Plato.

27. Compare with Quine and Ullian 1970.

28. The Greek word Plato sometimes uses, *agnôsia*, is, etymologically, "not-knowing."

states that entertains *individual propositions* that sit along a spectrum of false, true, and both reasoned and true, beliefs, that goes from ignorance to knowledge. Neither does he have Diotima do so in the *Symposium*. I argue that the text suggests that only entire doxastic structures can be evaluated as better as or worse than one another. Further, even then it is not clear that these can be placed into a unidimensional hierarchy. In later chapters, I will argue that Plato eschews any discrete, technical, notion of ignorance as a candidate for an analyzable epistemic state. All analyzable epistemic states that fall short of knowledge are to be identified with some sort of *doxa*.

At the beginning of chapter 6, I begin to support this view of *doxa* and its connection to what-is with evidence from the *Phaedrus*. Here Plato asserts that (1) all epistemic states that fall short of knowledge, are composed of *doxa*, (2) even those who have only ignorance (due to the nature of their *doxa*) have an unwitting cognitive connection to the truth-makers for their *doxa* (things such as the Forms), and (3), as a consequence, any *doxa*, even if it is false or constitutes outright ignorance, is about "what-is" (the same thing that true *doxa* and knowledge are about).

I go on to show that when Plato says that everything is either known or unknown throughout the middle of the *Theaetetus*, he is saying that everything is either *doxa* (unknown) or knowledge (known). However, he is also indicating that *doxa* comes in a wide range of qualities and configurations that cannot be ranked into a linear hierarchy. Of course, some *doxa* is so bad that it is useless and should be considered ignorance in any context. Some of what Plato says about *doxa* in the *Theaetetus* also reinforces what I have already argued for regarding unwitting cognitive contact between those who entertain *doxa* and "what-is" in my earlier chapters.

As I previously mentioned, chapter 7 is an analysis of the three-part distinction between knowledge, *doxa,* and ignorance in *Republic* V. This is where I show that, contrary to what some take Socrates to say there, there is nothing in the three-part distinction that dictates that we cannot opine beauty itself. Up until this point, all previous chapters have championed or reinforced the thesis that everyone can opine beauty itself. My correction regarding the three-part distinction involves distinguishing what Plato is describing when he says a capacity is "set over" an object (I call this the capacity's "primary object") from what the capacity is trying to capture (which I call the capacity's "secondary object"). Each capacity looks to (is set over) its own experience of perceptibles with a different attitude concerning the status of those perceptibles with respect to "what-is." The capacity of knowledge looks beyond the perceptibles to the Forms; this is what philosophers do. The capacity of *doxa* (opinion) assumes that perceptibles are all there is; this is what lovers of sights and sounds (I argue that lovers of sights and sounds also stand in for ordinary people and Plato's readers) do. The capacity of ignorance does not even use these perceptions as potential correctives to how things seem to it. Plato singles out the capacity of ignorance uniquely in the three-part distinction. There is nowhere else where he treats ignorance as distinct from *doxa*. I argue that he does this in order to "console" the lovers of sights and sounds and to warn them to steer clear of the ignorant practice that he associates with Protagoreans, who take whatever seems true to them to be true. These ignorant people have even worse epistemological practices than those of the lovers of sights and sounds. I argue that Plato consoles the lovers of sights and sounds because he thinks they are remediable—they are, in principle, capable of becoming philosophers.

Chapter 8 reinforces both chapter 7 and my two focal theses by filling out some of what I propose in chapter 7 regarding how we are to understand what the object of *doxa* as specified by the three-part distinction is. At *Republic* 477a6–b1, Socrates says that *doxa* is set over what both is and is-not—a confusing statement no matter what other epistemic theses one attributes to Plato! In this chapter, I theorize about how to make sense of this claim from both an ontological and an epistemological standpoint, once again emphasizing that it does not keep us from maintaining the view that *doxa* is also about those things that render our doxastic systems better or worse and our individualized judgments true or false. I also rehearse the three general strategies for interpreting the—seemingly ontological—claim that simultaneous being and not being is a possible condition of something related to *doxa* and conclude that my interpretation can be reconciled with any of the three. Thus, I leave any ontological concerns about this passage to one side as I continue with my epistemological project.

In the second part of chapter 8, I discuss what Plato could possibly intend by stating at *Republic* 477a9–b1 that ignorance is set over "nothing at all." I speculate that Plato, while saying that those with *doxa* are worse off than philosophers, is saying that they are better off if they refrain from adopting the Protagorean approach that what seems-to-be *is* what-is. I also defend the thesis that, while set over nothing at all, ignorance is still ignorance *about* what-is. I go on to argue that any strong distinction between *doxa* and ignorance that appears to hold them to be mutually exclusive is unique to this *Republic* V text and is a feature of the consolation of lovers of sights and sounds. In other epistemic passages in the dialogues, including *Republic* VI and VII, Plato's major interest is in the distinction between knowledge and *doxa*.

I corroborate my understanding of what ignorance is "set over" with comments made in the *Cratylus* about some ways that Plato advises against seeking knowledge or useful *doxa*; he advises against looking to perceptibles qua perceptibles and advises that we look to them to learn the natures of such things as weaving itself. We also return to the *Phaedrus* to see that even the most ignorant people are often described as entertaining—or possessing—beliefs. This further establishes the separation of the claim that knowledge, opinion, and ignorance are 'set over' mutually exclusive entities from any claim regarding what objects the one who deploys these capacities is endeavoring to capture with them.

Chapter 9 turns to Plato's images of the divided line and the cave in order to underline my contention that ignorance is nothing but *doxa*. I also show that when Plato wishes to contrast knowledge with some other epistemological state, it is most common for him to compare knowledge and *doxa*. It is not Plato's general practice to distinguish ignorance as a third (in addition to knowledge and *doxa*), distinct, epistemic condition outside of *Republic* V. The divided line's fundamental bisection is between *gnôsis* (knowledge) and *doxa*, leaving no segment that embraces neither of them. I propose that each of the sections of the divided line contains what each of their respective labels is "set over" (*epi*) in *Republic* V and not what each captures or tries to capture. That is, the divided line contains what I have called the "primary objects" of *gnôsis* and *doxa*, and not what I have called their "secondary objects." The line does not illustrate which metaphysical entities are the truth-makers for each epistemic state. Rather, it shows what can be looked to, and how those things can be used, to come up with epistemological attitudes of various qualities. The divided line confirms that the worst possible epistemic state is still a kind of *doxa*—*doxa* and ignorance are not mutually exclusive; they overlap. In the cave, even the prisoners in the worst epistemic condition—those who most deserve to be called ignorant—are not thinking about nothing at all, they are looking at shadows of puppets and conjuring up *doxa*. In fact, the text shows that some of these poor, deluded prisoners can organize their *doxa* better than others can; this relative veridicality is explained by the claim that their *doxa* is still connected to, and trying to capture, what-is.

My conclusory chapter reviews my key findings and how I arrived at them. I go on to place them with respect to the current debate between those who want to revive or maintain a "two world" or "distinct objects"[29] theory between the domain of knowledge and the domain of *doxa* and those—especially those more recent scholars—who see it as more permeable and assimilate Plato's views to some of the tenets of contemporary analytic philosophy's development of the "justified true belief" theory of knowledge.

For the most part, while I share sympathies with elements of each of these views, I show them to be orthogonal to my project. Those scholars are already discussing Plato's views on knowledge, and I am doing what I take to be the work on inquiry, aboutness, and *doxa* that I argue is propaedeutic to such analyses. I am tarrying along the path to knowledge and discerning what Plato thought about those states that fall short of knowledge. I am singling out what epistemic access Plato assumed ordinary people who seek to better their epistemic states possess and what resources he advises them to use. I am explaining how Plato shows Socrates eliciting from ordinary people the responses that allow them to improve their epistemic lots by taking advantage of their unwitting cognitive efforts to access such things as beauty itself. Furthermore, I show that Plato is giving the ordinary people who read his dialogues the tools to compel themselves to do so.[30]

---

29. This is Moss's descriptor for her own theory in her 2021, 20.
30. All unattributed translations of Greek in this book are my own.

Chapter 1

Recollection and the Beginning of Inquiry in the *Meno* and *Phaedo*

I will now isolate the "beginning problem" from what is often called "Meno's Paradox." In this book, I focus on the solution to the beginning problem (hence {B}). I never focus on the solution to what has been isolated as "the ending problem" (hence {E}), for reasons that I will discuss below. In this and the following three chapters, I focus on the question, "How is inquiry possible?" In later chapters (6–10), I will argue that all epistemic states—including false belief and ignorance—that fall short of knowledge consist in *doxa*. While the present chapter is about inquiry, it discusses a prerequisite for inquiry that is also necessary for false belief and ignorance. In fact, it is a prerequisite for all *doxa*. Inquiry, false belief, and ignorance all require that cognizers have an ability to refer to what their inquiries, false beliefs, and ignorance are *about* in a manner that is independent of the content of that cognizer's cognition. What each of those inquiries and beliefs is about is what distinguishes them from other particular inquiries and beliefs. Being about something determinate is what allows inquiries to have the potential for success or failure. It is what allows *doxa* of any kind to have a truth-value. Therefore, this connection is just as necessary for true belief as it is for false belief.[1] For now, let us put aside

---

1. As I mentioned in my introduction, I am sympathetic to those, such as Vogt (2012) and Moss and Schwab (2019), who claim that our current use of the English word *belief* is not in line with Plato's use of *doxa* and is a misleading and confusing translation of that word. These critics sometimes favor using only *opinion*, or *judgment* as a translation of *doxa* (see Moss and Schwab, n. 2). I will continue to use all three

doxa and start with the beginning problem and the very first step in its solution.

The Beginning Problem

At *Meno* 80e2–5, Plato has his characters discuss a paradox.² Meno introduces it and then Socrates reframes it. In this dialogue, Plato introduces the theory of recollection for the specific purpose of resolving this paradox.³ Having led Meno into *aporia* concerning the nature of virtue (80b–d), and having confessed that he doesn't know at all what it is (71a5–7), Socrates expresses the hope that, now that Meno and he agree that neither of them knows what virtue is, they might search for it together. Meno responds by challenging Socrates:

> And how will you inquire, Socrates, into something when you don't know at all what it is? {B}Which of the things that you don't know will you propose as the object of your inquiry? {E} Or even if you really do stumble upon it, how will you know that this is the thing you didn't know before? (80d5–8, Scott's translation, 2006, 76)⁴

Socrates restates Meno's challenge as follows:

---

where they seem appropriate in English. Sometimes *belief* seems more sonorous or grammatically correct. Sometimes *doxa* feels too awkward for those who are not familiar with classical Greek. I reserve *judgment* for use in places where it seems particularly appropriate to Plato's content, for example, in the digression on false judgment in the *Theaet* (187c–200d).

2. For a summary of the controversy over calling it a "paradox," see Fine (2014, 25–27).

3. Thus, he appears to introduce it for epistemic reasons. This is not always the case: at *Phdo.* 72–77, he uses it to bolster a theory of the immortality of the soul in addition to using it as an explanation for how we come to recognize equality and inequality. At *Phdr.* 249c, it is again introduced for epistemic reasons in that it shows how we can do something in thought: recollection is referred to as what allows humans to understand speech by bringing many appearances under reasoned unities.

4. καὶ τίνα τρόπον ζητήσεις, ὦ Σώκρατες, τοῦτο ὃ μὴ οἶσθα τὸ παράπαν ὅτι ἐστίν; ποῖον γὰρ ὧν οὐκ οἶσθα προθέμενος ζητήσεις; ἢ εἰ καὶ ὅτι μάλιστα ἐντύχοις αὐτῷ, πῶς εἴσῃ ὅτι τοῦτό ἐστιν ὃ σὺ οὐκ ᾔδησθα.

{B}[I]t's impossible for someone to inquire into what he knows or doesn't know: he wouldn't inquire into what he knows, since he already knows it and there is no need for such a person to inquire: nor into what he doesn't know, because he doesn't even know what he is going to inquire into. (80e1–5, Scott's translation, 2006, 77–78)[5]

I have inserted {B} and {E} into these quotations in order to introduce a debate that has arisen concerning this paradox: Meno appears to raise a problem for both beginning an inquiry {B} and ending an inquiry {E}.[6] Socrates responds by repeating only the beginning problem. Many interpreters have found reason to the resolve the two problems back into one. For example, Scott, noticing that resolution of {E} will also resolve {B}, says that recollection is introduced to resolve {E}. Benson notes that the discussion concludes with the statement that we ought to proceed on the assumption that {E} can be resolved (86b6–c2), even if Socrates only appears to mention {B} in his recounting of Meno's paradox, and so, agrees with Scott.[7]

I will suggest a different way of thinking about this—we need something very specific to resolve {B}. That is the ability to refer to the target of inquiry regardless of the content of one's thoughts about that target of inquiry. I will be examining Plato's theory of recollection to see if it provides this. Certainly, Socrates presents the theory of recollection as sufficient for, at least, resolving {B}. Still, even though Socrates concludes that we are better off if we do inquire and, therefore, should proceed on the assumption that we can resolve {E} (*Men.*, 86b7–c2), I will, not investigate Plato's attempts at resolving {E} in this book. However, I am confident that Plato suspects that his understanding of metaphysics and epistemology will enable us to do the best we can with respect to {E}.

---

5. ὡς οὐκ ἄρα ἔστιν ζητεῖν ἀνθρώπῳ οὔτε ὃ οἶδε οὔτε ὃ μὴ οἶδε; οὔτε γὰρ ἂν ὅ γε οἶδεν ζητοῖ—οἶδεν γάρ, καὶ οὐδὲν δεῖ τῷ γε τοιούτῳ ζητήσεως—οὔτε ὃ μὴ οἶδεν—οὐδὲ γὰρ οἶδεν ὅτι ζητήσει.

6. This point is perhaps made most forcefully by Scott (1995, 2006), who distinguishes {B} as the paradox of inquiry and {E} as the paradox of discovery. My terminology of beginning and ending is taken from Benson (2015), whose treatment of this debate I have found particularly clear and helpful.

7. Scott 1995, 30–31; Benson 2015, 62–63.

Addressing Plato's resolution of {E} would require addressing Plato's entire theory of knowledge—a task beyond my aim in this book. My more achievable aim is to make a useful examination of Plato's assumptions about epistemic states that fall short of knowledge.[8] Of course, the first step of a study that tries to answer {E} would have to be the effort to figure out how and whether recollection resolves {B}. In this chapter (and for the remainder of this book), I will focus on Plato's resolution of {B}, putting aside the question of whether recollection, or anything else that Plato does, resolves {E}. Still, for clarity's sake, on occasion, I will return to make suggestions about how what I am proposing relates to {E}.

My foray into recollection, in this chapter and the next, is not so much exegesis on my part as it is an attempt to look at the exegesis of others. I want to see if there is any way to move these debates forward in a manner that shows Plato telling a story that allows us to inquire by making—and then correcting—false hypotheses concerning our object of inquiry. Plato appears to say that we once knew—before birth, when we were not in human form—all that we will later learn (*Men.* 81c5–d5, 86a3–4; *Phdo.* 75c6–e8). According to his story, we then forget it all at birth (*Phdo.* 76d1–4). Plato indicates that he thinks we need something other than a *tabula rasa* to explain inquiry and learning. However, he leaves a clear description of what he thinks we do need wanting. What marks are in this nonvirgin *tabula*? Does it contain *everything* in some compartment where each idea is inaccessible until triggered by sense experience? This seems simplistic and extreme—mystical to the point of implausibility. Furthermore, as many have argued (and I will review below), it is hard to see how it responds to {B}.

---

8. At least, Scott (2006, 20, 181, 184–85) and Fine (2014, 16–17, 40, 166–67) suggest that *Men.* 98a shows, uncontroversially, that Socrates in the *Men.* holds that knowledge implies both knowing p and knowing why p is the case. However, the claim that someone knows why p is true is an incredibly vague claim and requires a large number of assumptions about what it is to answer a "why" question. Does it require a causal explanation? Does it require that one be able to explain how p falls under general laws? Any theory of explanation will rest on a body of metaphysical assumptions. There is some evidence in other dialogues that, for Plato, knowing why something is the case requires knowing law-like relationships among the Forms (Scott [2006, 87], hints at this theory). That is a lot to foist on the image of Daedalus's statues being tied down by "knowing the reason why" (*aitios logismos*) at *Men.* 98a. Weiss (2001, 158) emphasizes how stark and uninformative *Men.* 98a is regarding both knowledge and true belief.

In my discussion of recollection, I will go out on a limb and describe the minimal contents of the nonvirgin *tabula* it would behoove Plato to supply through something like recollection; a *tabula* that is marked at birth with something other than sense experience. I venture that our default should be to assume that this is at least part of what he gained. Were he to venture only this modest assumption in order to resolve {B}, he would succeed. Furthermore, I will argue exegetically in chapter 2 that this is a supposition to which he is committed throughout his discussions of recollection. In chapters 3–4, I will argue that he is committed to it in other dialogues that feature learning, hypothesizing, being mistaken, and correcting hypotheses, but not recollection.

Meno's Paradox and Recollection

Plato's strategy in introducing recollection as a resolution to {B} can be clarified by breaking what has just been isolated at 80e1–5 into four claims:

(S1) For any x, one either knows, or does not know x.

(S2) If one knows x, one cannot inquire into x.

(S3) If one does not know x, one cannot inquire into x.

(S4) Therefore, for any x, one cannot inquire into x.[9]

(S2) is not very surprising if one understands knowing x as knowing x completely. (S3) is more surprising. Into what could we inquire if not something that we do not know? We might explain (S3) better by restating "something I don't already know," as "something about which I am completely ignorant." Hence, (S3) explains why {B} asserts that I can't "point" my inquiry at something I do not know. If I do not already know what x is, not only will I not know when I am learning or when I have learned about it, I won't even know when I am wondering or inquiring about it.

---

9. I have adopted Fine's (2014, 9) formulation in order to facilitate a discussion of the comparison among several interpretations.

Making sense of (S3) by understanding "do not know" as "do not know at all" and (S2) by understanding "know" as "know completely" will lead to a specific interpretation of (S1). For (S1) must then be understood as "everything is either something I know completely or something I don't know at all." This reveals a problem with inquiring about something I do not already know since we have come to understand it as something about which I am completely ignorant. Scott and Fine characterize this as something about which I am "cognitively blank."[10] If not knowing x is being cognitively blank about it, then it is not clear what allows my inquiry to be about x at all. Nor is it apparent what allows it to keep on being about x as I arrive at various hypotheses—some of which are likely to be false—about x. On this reading (S1) treats a subject's knowledge of any x as an all or nothing affair. Either one knows x completely, or one is in a cognitive blank with respect to x.

If one reads (S1) this way, then, if one wants to try to avoid the conclusion that we cannot inquire, the key might be to reject (S1) and to imagine that there is a way of not knowing that does not require being cognitively blank. Many interpreters take this approach.[11] Some describe it as a search for something *in between* knowing and not knowing. Plato's characters never describe it this way when speaking of recollection and I will take pains not to do so either.[12] This is because I believe that when Plato's characters do speak about something in between knowing and

---

10. Scott 1995, 27; 2006, 76–77; Fine 2014, 12, 70–72.

11. Fine (1999, 8 and 2008, 3) argues this way. Scott (2006, 80) agrees that this is the logical way to solve the eristic dilemma but does not think this is Plato's strategy in introducing recollection. Dancy (2004, 226) doesn't quite take it this far; he says that we can only learn what we [have] already know[n], but that Socrates emphasizes that it is not known at the moment of recollection. Benson (2015, 51) points out that one alternative is to have a teacher who already knows but concludes that Plato is concerned about *de novo* learning.

12. Fine (2014, 176) is careful to say that she does not. She thinks that Plato uses true belief, and familiarity (which, I think, Fine might have to cash out as having true beliefs that are relevant to x but do not have the content "x is true") as what allows us to inquire and this, for Plato, is a way of *not knowing*. I shall be agreeing with Fine that these are all ways of not knowing for Plato. I shall also agree that Plato does not solve this problem by finding something in between knowing and not knowing. However, I shall not agree with her that these ways of not knowing are essential to what Plato thinks recollection—at least in its initial stages—provides.

not knowing, for example at *Symposium* 201e10–202a9, they are talking about something quite different from what is discussed in the recollection passages in the *Meno* and the *Phaedo*. In the *Symposium* passage (which I will address in chapter 5), they are talking about *doxa*. A key part of my thesis regarding {B} is that it cannot be resolved by using *doxa* and that this is not how Plato tries to resolve it. Therefore, in discussions of recollection, *doxa* is not being invoked to resolve {B}. For recollection, we need reference, which is a prerequisite for *doxa*. The prerequisite for *doxa* cannot be in between knowing and not knowing if *doxa* is what is in between knowing and not knowing. *Doxa* cannot be a prerequisite for itself; thus, the cognitive activity that resolves {B} must be other than *doxa* and also other than knowing or not knowing.

I do not claim that my distinction between these locutions of "*other than*" as opposed to "*in between*" is a literal translation of Plato's words. Plato's characters do *literally* say that *doxa* is in between knowledge and ignorance in several places (although not while discussing recollection). Further, no character says that what we recollect is *other than* knowledge and ignorance. It is my own philosophical assertions about what solves {B} in the theory of recollection (without overreaching), that lead me to encourage us to understand what recollection gives us as something *other than*, ignorance, or *doxa*, or knowledge rather than something that is *in between* ignorance and knowledge. Of course, to be perfectly clear, something that is other than x or y *can* be in between them. I am arguing that what recollection supplies is both *other than* knowledge or ignorance and is also *not in between* them. That is, many might suppose that *doxa* is other than knowledge and ignorance and *is also* in between them. I am asserting that recollection provides neither *doxa* nor something that is in between knowledge and ignorance. What we need is a prerequisite for ignorance, knowledge, and anything that lies in between them that is not itself identical with knowledge, or ignorance, or any epistemological state that has content that lies in between them (if there is one).

It is most enlightening to understand Plato's strategy as an effort to find something *other than* knowing or not knowing, or any epistemic state that is in between them, when he introduces recollection to defeat Meno's paradox. He claims that we knew x prenatally but have forgotten x at birth, and this allows us to escape both horns of the dilemma. The question is: What has been accomplished through our knowing and then forgetting x? I will argue that Plato would best answer this question by supposing that we, effortlessly and unwittingly, maintain a prenatally established relationship with *x*. I will argue that Plato does not provide the most plausible basis for his own epistemological project if he thinks that what was gained through recollection was some kind of true *doxa* (as some have claimed the text shows he does).

To resolve {B}, Plato needs us to have a cognitive postnatal relationship with *x*. Socrates claims that all learning (including everything that we experience as learning or discovery) is recollection (*Men.*, 81d). He also claims that all prenatal knowledge is forgotten at birth (*Phdo.*, 75e–76d). Any claim that we already have knowledge or true beliefs lurking in some part of our soul that is inaccessible until sense experience triggers our recollection of this knowledge, or these beliefs, sidesteps the problem that needs solving. Whatever true beliefs or knowledge we had prenatally were forgotten at birth. What is required is an account of how any knowledge or belief that is in our souls postnatally is *about* something extracognitive or perceptual. No one can come to possess, and then retain, knowledge or true belief at a time when they are out of contact with the truth-maker of this knowledge or true belief. If someone does come to possess knowledge or true belief postnatally, then they must have contact with its truth-maker at the embodied moment when they "recollect" it. If they cannot establish this contact once they are born, then they must have retained it from their preembodied state. There is no "holdover" of true beliefs or knowledge from the prenatal state (all is forgotten at birth). However, the retention of the connection to these truth-makers is not itself an epistemological condition, and is something that the soul continues to possess after its prenatal, disembodied, communion with them.

The claim that we are born with true beliefs about the things concerning which we inquire is also inconsistent with our experiences of learning and discovery. We often consider many non-intersecting and false hypotheses concerning *the same phenomenon*. When we override an altogether false hypothesis in favor of a more accurate one, we *assume* that the overriding one is *about* the *same* phenomenon as the overridden one. Advocates of natural selection claim that it replaces creationist theories of the fit between a species and its environment. These two inquiries cannot have the same target if that target is determined by the *content* of the cognizer's hypothesis. However, they can have the same target of inquiry if that target is determined independently of the content. The creationist thinks she is inquiring concerning the truth regarding how a species fits with its environment, where that fit is perfect. The advocate of natural selection seeks an explanation of a fit that is not perfect (where there is always going to be some environmental pressure). Both views are targeted toward whatever it is that explains how the characteristics of an organism help it survive in its environment.[13]

Furthermore, the idea that we had knowledge or true beliefs once, and that they now reappear, is simplistic and implausible.[14] If Plato really regards {B} as a problem and this as its solution, then his solution seems simplistic and underarticulated.[15] If he really wants to resolve {B}, then recollection should have our ability to refer to, to think about, and therefore to inquire about, an object that we neither know nor have true beliefs about, as at least one of its major concerns. As I have already said, I will focus on what is at least consistent with what Plato has described that might explain this ability.[16]

An Alternative Understanding of (S1)

There are other ways to interpret (S1–4).[17] Indeed, there are others that are consistent with what I propose. Rather than imagining that (S1) ("For any x either one knows or does not know x") is intended as a controversial

---

13. An unidentified reader pointed out to me that there might be cases in which the content restricts the target. There are debates about whether contemporary Christians and Muslims worship the same God. The argument that they do—that they have the same target—depends on the content of their beliefs. However, this suggests that worshipping requires the same externalities as inquiring. This is not the case. Not all who worship are realists about the God that is featured in their practices. I would argue that in the case where the worshippers are realists, it is their intention to worship whatever God actually is (even if the content of their beliefs about God are wrong), and not the content of their beliefs, that fix the target of the beliefs that undergird their religious practices. This is consistent with my view of inquiry.

14. Of course, Plato might have Socrates present a simplistic or implausible account for coercive (See Weiss 2001, 63–76) or literary (See Baima and Paytas 2021, 10–131) reasons. I am assuming that Plato is not—in defending recollection—making statements that are purely rhetorical in a manner that overrides our need to sort out what the account actually is. That is, I am rendering an interpretation that assumes that something about learning is truly puzzling to Plato and that he considered it beneficial to take some aspect of his proposal regarding recollection seriously.

15. See Fine 2003, 64.

16. For further compelling arguments against the attribution of true beliefs to the slave, see Rowett (2018, 71–73).

17. See Fine (2014, 81–136) for an erudite and illuminating discussion of the many different forms this argument can take and has taken in the literature.

all-or-nothing assertion, it could be taken as a straightforward statement of the law of excluded middle.[18] In that case, it would indicate that Plato is committed to a broad spectrum of epistemic conditions. Some range of these falls short of knowledge, while some count as knowledge.[19] None of them counts as both. Of those that count as non-knowledge, there might be epistemic conditions that have qualities that make some of them more epistemically useful to possess than others. I will argue that this is how Plato thinks of *doxa* at, for example, *Symposium* 202–212.[20]

A major thesis of this book, however, is that Plato assumes (even if he doesn't explain how it happens) that human inquirers have cognitive connections to things such as the diagonal itself, equality itself, and beauty itself even if they do not know them, it has never occurred to them that they exist, or they actively deny their existence. Plato regards these objects as the truth-makers of the inquiries and beliefs of every human being. This assumed cognitive connection *is not* grounded by any knowledge or by any epistemic state that falls short of knowledge and so, *does not lie on the spectrum of epistemic states the supposition of which allows us to understand (S1) as the law of excluded middle*. It is a further major thesis of this book that all epistemic states depend on this non-doxastic, referential, cognitive connection for their ability to be about something

---

18. I understand Fine's interpretation to be that Meno takes it the first way (ignorance is a cognitive blank) and Socrates reinterprets it as a statement of the law of excluded middle in his repetition of the argument (2014, 82–94). Since what I propose is consistent with both interpretations of S1, I see no reason to adjudicate this matter beyond agreeing with Fine that there are many ways of not knowing other than being a cognitive blank. I believe that I am alone in maintaining that Plato's argument might, in theory, still work even if we allow that a person's epistemic state can be a cognitive blank (I will discuss this in chapter 4), not that I think that it ever is. Again, I emphasize this because I plan to emphasize that Plato needs something like recollection to—at minimum—form a cognitive connection that is independent of the content of any particular cognition. Therefore, the connection might be formed with a content-free mental state (if there could be one). Thus, I join Fine in the claim that Plato thinks (S3) is false (2014, 124). One can inquire about *x* even if one does not know *x*.

19. I follow Fine (2014, 33 n. 11) in expressing it in this commonsense manner (that aligns with the way many express it in contemporary epistemology).

20. Interestingly, while Fine protests that the beliefs and other things that she claims Socrates sees as the key to being able to inquire are not *in between* knowing and not knowing (2014, 176), she never comments on Diotima's pronouncement at *Symp.* 202a9 that true belief that is not reasoned *is* in between knowledge and ignorance. I will compare this in-betweenness with what is supplied by recollection in chapters 5–6.

(they depend on it for their ability to refer) and for their possible truth or falsity.[21] Thus, there would be no epistemic states without this non-doxastic cognitive connection.

Recollection's Failures

Not many commentators think that Socrates's description of recollection (*Men.* 81c5–e2) alone resolves the paradox in the *Meno*. As Fine says in an earlier work:

> [T]he theory of recollection (in contrast to the elenctic reply) does not by itself provide a sufficient answer to the paradox—for if one once knew, but now lacks the ability to inquire, the prior knowledge is idle. We should therefore be reluctant to place the whole weight of Plato's reply on the theory of recollection; and on my account of its role, we need not do so. (2003, 64)[22]

The "elenctic reply" is Socrates's geometric demonstration with the slave. Fine points out that, in contrast to other instances of Socratic questioning, this *elenchos* does not end in *aporia*. Rather, Socrates brings the slave beyond *aporia* to true belief (2003, 56). Thus, the slave serves as a counterexample to our inability to inquire. He did not have the answer and was able to come to discover it anyway. The elenctic reply shows that the claim that one cannot inquire is false. Geometry is, presumably, not relevantly different from virtue, so we can inquire into virtue as well.

Therefore, even if Plato does not disarm Meno's paradox by reasoning against it, he does do so by providing a brute counterexample to

---

21. Of course, I am assuming that Plato regards things like the diagonal itself, etc. as the objects of knowledge as well. But, as I am not discussing knowledge here, I need not expound on that assumption. These sorts of objects—things such as equality itself—are what are regarded as Plato's Forms. I am assuming, here, that Plato takes some kind of abstract objects to be the truth-makers of our doxastic states. While the fullest argument for this would require a book-length foray into Plato's metaphysics, I believe that this is enough of a commonplace assumption in Plato scholarship that it will not offend my readers. Furthermore, I believe I cover enough evidence for the fact that Plato thinks these are the truth-makers of even the ordinary person's beliefs in chapters 2–4, to make this assumption viable.

22. See Fine (2014, 121) for an expression of the same sentiments.

it.²³ All that Plato needs is the brute fact that we obviously do succeed in inquiring into, and developing true beliefs about, things concerning which we were once ignorant. This alone lays {B} to rest.²⁴ It is safe to say that there is consensus, at least among a large number of scholars, that Plato thinks inquiry is possible.²⁵

In the *Meno*, brute evidence appears to lay {E} to rest as well. It seems the slave *recognizes* that the diagonal is that for which they have been searching. The slave's eureka moment marks the end of at least one stage of inquiry. But what degree of recognition is this brute evidence supposed to suggest and what degree of recognition is required for {E} to be accomplished? The slave recognizes the diagonal, but there is much disagreement about whether he has come to know it.²⁶ Further, if Socrates

---

23. Fine speculates in her 2003 that recollection is only supposed to explain our tendency toward the truth as we inquire. She continues to fill out this speculation in her 2014 (123). This appears to leave little for recollection to do or explain. Recollection ends up being a statement about human nature (even if it makes substantive claims about what was true of us prenatally). Plato, at least, thinks we have some unexplained tendency to make epistemic progress and he tries to give a description of learning that puts that tendency to one side more than he tries to account for it. I agree with Fine that Plato suggests that what we call learning can be reduced to recollection rather than that there is no such thing as what we call, and recognize as, learning (2014, 107, 117–18). I also agree with Fine that Plato assumes recollection as a way of taking certain phenomena for granted thereby putting any concerns about them to one side rather than accounting for them. I will, however, show that Plato adopts a substantive and philosophically sophisticated phenomenon that might only be able to be underwritten by something like recollection as an essential feature that must be assumed in the remainder of his epistemology. Still, I can only account for this mechanism's existence and role. I cannot account for the nature of the mechanism itself. I argue that, in the end, Plato finds himself in this same boat.

24. In fact, even the development of false beliefs proves that we have succeeded in *inquiring* (despite those inquiries having been *answered* poorly); if we hadn't inquired concerning the appropriate referent, our belief would have had nothing to make it false. I will clarify this position as I continue.

25. For examples of who falls into each group and a discussion of the manner in which, and the degree to which, they do, see Fine (2014, 10–12). She mentions Ryle (1976) as someone who thinks that Plato thought inquiry impossible. She counts herself (1992), White (1976), Moravscik (1971), and Sharples (1985) among those who hold variations of the view that Plato finds inquiry possible. Benson also holds that Plato thinks inquiry is possible (2015, 66–69).

26. This will be discussed below.

had not been able to produce it, or if the slave had been unable to recognize it as the line upon which the side of the square with twice the area of the original square could be drawn, then {B} would still have been resolved in the absence of {E}.[27] Any confirmation that {E} has been resolved requires sufficient understanding of Plato's epistemology to verify that the slave's recognition is sufficient for knowledge. Plato certainly acknowledges that we can *take* ourselves to recognize something in a situation where we do not have knowledge (for example, we can think that unequal sticks are equal). Thus, we might conclude that if the slave's recognition constitutes a resolution of {E}, then such resolution is not sufficient to show that the slave has *learned* anything. We will look at the complexity of {E} a bit further when we look at the sticks and stones argument in the *Phaedo*, but again, only to emphasize that determining whether recollection is a resolution of anything beyond {B} requires more understanding of Plato's epistemology than can be gleaned from the *Meno* and the *Phaedo*.

Recollection in the *Phaedo*

The *Phaedo* prefaces its discussion of recollection with some principles: the technical notion of *anamnêsis* specifies that it be of that which our souls learned at a previous time when they were not in human form (72e2–73a2).[28] Recollection is when, perceiving one thing—call it the *trigger*—a person comes to think of a further, distinct, thing (73c6–d1). Recollection can be occasioned by triggers that are either similar or dissimilar to the thing recollected. For example, a lyre reminds one of one's mother while being dissimilar to her, and a photo of one's mother reminds one of her due to similarity. In the case where there is similarity, one must necessarily bring to mind whether that similarity is complete or deficient

---

27. Perhaps this would be especially clear if they had continued to search for it by eliminating some false hypotheses and eventually accepting some that seem true but are not proven to be true (and maybe even turn out to be problematic), as we see with other inquiries in other dialogues.

28. If we had been in human form, then we would have been stuck in the same situation—beholden to all the same epistemological problems that we are when we are forced to recollect.

(74a5–7). For example, if the photo triggers a recollection in me, I will be able to say if the photo is a good or poor likeness of the thing I recollect.

Since Socrates says that sticks and stones fall short of equality, it makes sense to think of them as a trigger that is either different or is similar but deficient. They are supposed to draw us to think about how they are different from the thing that we are to recollect (the trigger is pairs or groups of sticks and stones and the recollected objects are equality itself and inequality itself). The argument is brief:

> Don't equal sticks and stones, the same ones, sometimes appear to one [man][29] equal, to another not?
>
> Yes indeed.
>
> What then, have the equals themselves ever appeared unequal to you, or equality [ever appeared to be] inequality?
>
> Oh never, Socrates.
>
> Therefore, they are not the same [thing], Socrates said, the equals and the equal itself.
>
> It appears to me they are not the same at all, Socrates. (74b7–c5)
> (This translation follows Penner [1987, 57–58])[30]

This argument is a nonidentity of discernibles; Socrates wants to show that equality itself is not identical to equal perceptibles (equal sticks and stones) but exists in addition to them. He does this by demonstrating that equal sticks and stones have a feature that equality itself does not have: one man will say of a pair of sticks that they are equal, while a second man will disagree, saying that they are unequal. In contrast—to follow the parallel

---

29. Something needs to be supplied to the Greek text here. It's also possible to supply *stick* or *stone* here, with ramifications for interpreting the argument (see Bostock 1986, 72–85). I won't address these issues here as I believe they force a choice that is more relevant to Plato's metaphysics than to his epistemology. See also chapter 2, n. 16, below.

30. ἆρ' οὐ λίθοι μὲν ἴσοι καὶ ξύλα ἐνίοτε ταὐτὰ ὄντα τῷ μὲν ἴσα φαίνεται, τῷ δ' οὔ; —πάνυ μὲν οὐντί δέ; αὐτὰ τὰ ἴσα ἔστιν ὅτε ἄνισά σοι ἐφάνη, ἢ ἡ ἰσότης ἀνισότης; —οὐδεπώποτέ γε, ὦ Σώκρατες. —οὐ ταὐτὸν ἄρα ἐστίν, ἦ δ' ὅς, ταῦτά τε τὰ ἴσα καὶ αὐτὸ τὸ ἴσον. —οὐδαμῶς μοι φαίνεται, ὦ Σώκρατες.

in a literal manner—it is not the case that one man will say of equality itself that it is equal while another man will call equality itself unequal.

Thus, we can restate the argument as follows:

Whereas,

(P1) equal sticks and stones have the property of sometimes appearing unequal,

(P2) equality itself does not have that property.

Hence,

(C) equality itself must be something other than equal sticks and stones.

Both the *Meno* and the *Phaedo* discuss recollection. Some scholars think that the exercise with the sticks and stones in the *Phaedo* requires access to the Forms in a way that the demonstration with the slave in the *Meno* does not.[31] This puts the two arguments in tension with each other, as Plato's use of a slave in the *Meno* seems to show that everyone (not only certain people with special access to the Forms) can recollect in the manner in which the slave does.

My project is to show how recollection alleviates {B} in both arguments while leaving {E} aside. I will show that both arguments require the same degree of access to the Forms in order for *inquiry* to take place. Furthermore, I will show that this access, which does not involve knowing the Forms or even knowing that they exist, is democratically distributed according to Plato.

A Chicken and Egg Problem

The following puzzle causes some people consternation over the extent to which Plato managed to use recollection to ameliorate the ordinary person's situation with respect to {B} and, in turn, {E}:

---

31. Franklin 2005, 295. Scott (1995, 69–70) reflects on this possibility, but it is not clear to me whether he thinks that geometrical Forms must be equally available to everyone in the *Men*.

If (1) x can trigger me to retrieve y from within myself

then, (2) I must already have y within myself, and

(3) I must already discern some connection between x and y.

But, (4) If I discern a connection between x and y, then I must already have concepts of both x and y.

So, (5) x can't be what triggers my first concept of y.[32]

Some commentators find this problem sufficiently obvious that they do not think that Plato ever intended for recollection to explain how ordinary people, as opposed to philosophers, form their own concepts of beauty, equality, and the like. They have endeavored to develop alternative readings that supposedly allow this shortcoming to have been apparent to Plato. On their readings, recollection resolves both {B} and {E}, but only for the philosopher.[33]

---

32. Bostock (who suggests that Plato takes us to be recollecting something like the meanings of words), argues that Plato's solution simply leads to further telescoping paradoxes, and concludes that "Plato, and the traditional account, are wrong about the only way of learning the meaning of a word" (1986, 110).

33. Scott argues that recollection cannot be used to explain ordinary concept formation as such an assumption would, in turn, result in further absurdity and paradox.

> Plato is right to point out that if we are to be reminded of x by y, then we must have a recognition of y that does not involve knowledge of x, otherwise we have the absurd result that in recognizing y we are already thinking of x, and so recollection of x is impossible. But if we insist that Plato is using recollection to explain concept formation . . . then we invite just that absurdity. (1995, 56–57)

Scott elaborates an alternative understanding of recollection for Plato upon which it does not explain ordinary concept formation, but only the philosopher's knowledge of the Forms. Thus, Scott takes recollection to resolve both {B} and {E}, but only for the philosopher (1995, 53–73). Several other commentators have followed Scott's suggestion. See chapter 3, n.14, below.

Recollection as Constitutive of Recognition

There is, however, a further alternative to this, more restrictive, reconstruction. Plato might have intended the (perhaps former) presence of equality in one's soul to provide a relationship with equality itself that is unwitting. If I can inquire into what I do not know by asking questions about it and be assured that the answers that I find, in the form of hypotheses to be tested, are *about* that particular thing concerning which I asked, then I might be able to seek that which I do not know. If I already—even without realizing it—have some sort of inner connection to the object of inquiry, then I might be able to grope at the truth through a bunch of beliefs all of which are unstable, unreliable, and maybe even false.

It seems that Scott (1995) supposes that when Socrates talks about comparing particulars to Forms, he talks about doing so *consciously*. Otherwise, his concerns would not arise. However, several scholars have responded that Plato may have thought that both the comparison and our contact with the Form take place unwittingly.[34] Kelsey (2001, 94) agrees with Scott that *Phaedo* 75b4–8 shows Plato committed to the view that we "cannot recognize equal sticks without having the Form of equality 'in mind.'"[35] However, since Plato must have assumed that everyday adults recognize equal sticks and stones, Kelsey counts this as "strong evidence" that Socrates thinks that recollection of the Form is required in order to explain ordinary, everyday, cognitive achievements. In Kelsey's view, this suggests that Socrates did not think that recognition of the Form of equality occurred *subsequent* to seeing equal sticks and stones, but rather that a grasp of the Form (whatever that amounts to) is *constitutive* of the recognition of the equality of perceptibles. The recognition of the equality of sticks and stones comes about by virtue of our having the equal itself "in mind." Thus, Kelsey takes it for granted that recollection is part of an analysis of everyday concept formation and does not require the kind of "articulate understanding" of the Form of equality that Scott implies it does.

---

34. Scott (2006, 84) recognizes that we must escape a "circle of belief" where recollection is concerned. But Scott thinks that the only viable alternative to belief is knowledge. I will be offering reference as an alternative (building on work by Franklin, Harte, and Kelsey).

35. This is Kelsey's way of tracking Plato's use of the Greek word *ennoein* in its various forms.

Franklin (2005, 295) agrees with Kelsey that recollection describes everyone's ordinary learning. However, he is sensitive to Scott's point as well: the exercise conducted at *Phaedo* 75b4–8 is designed to help philosophers *understand* what it is that all people do when they recollect. It is not intended to help them each, personally, recognize (i.e., recollect) the equality of sticks and stones. This is analogous to the way a theory of optics helps certain people with specialized educations understand what it is to see, but they come to understand how *everyone*—even the uneducated—are able to see. Franklin agrees with Scott that in order to *understand* what recollection is, one must already have an articulated understanding of the Forms (291).[36] However, understanding what recollection is and being able to recollect and, therefore, inquire are different. The former requires much more philosophical sophistication than the latter.

Recollection's Purpose and Results

Whatever recollection assumes about those who recollect, there is also controversy about whether Plato ever presents it as resulting in actual knowledge in those who do it. There are commentators who think that the text shows that the slave has both recollected and acquired at least some knowledge by the end of Socrates's demonstration. Unsurprisingly, those who think that recollection is reserved for the likes of Socrates and Simmias think that it results in knowledge for those who are philosophically inclined.[37] Others find the results more understated. I will here treat the results of the *Meno*'s slave demonstration as parallel to the recognition in the *Phaedo* that pairs of sticks and stones are equal. That is, I will proceed to discuss how recollection can result in epistemic states for individuals like the slave. I will not discuss whether the slave has an understanding

---

36. See also Williams (2002) and Harte (2006, 2007) for further support of the constitutive view. I agree with Franklin that a person must be aware of their commitment to the existence of abstract objects in order to understand the necessity of the connection for which I argue recollection stands. A relativist (or Protagorean) would not need to assume this connection.

37. Scott 1995, 45. One of the chief frustrations with Scott's view is that it offers no account of where the philosopher started in life (Do philosophers begin as ordinary people?) and how he or she became a philosopher (see Williams 2002, 150). Nor does it answer the question of whether or not ordinary people have immortal souls (see Harte 2006, 38).

of what Forms are that would enable him to understand that learning is recollection (Socrates is trying to convince Meno of this, not the slave). Thus, I will be looking at the elements of the sticks and stones argument that show ordinary people thinking about equality and inequality. I will note the places where the sticks and stones argument in the *Phaedo* is an argument addressed to people like Simmias who, unlike Meno, already acknowledge the existence of the Forms and that learning is recollection.[38]

Some think that at *Meno* 85c9–d1 Socrates states that recollection yields knowledge.[39] In contrast, in the *Phaedo*, just after the argument where he uses the equal itself as an example of something that is recollected, Socrates says that no one knows the beautiful, the good, the just or the pious, and he holds them parallel to the greater, the smaller and the equal (75c–76c).[40] While he does have Socrates call the entire process from initial grasping to gaining knowledge "recollection," Plato never indicates that recollection allows us to gain something knowledge-like any more quickly than we gain it through a slow process of empirical research and rational deliberation.[41] So, presumably, whatever Plato thinks about the possibility of human knowledge, he does not think that our first moment of recollecting results in knowledge. He suggests that recollection—at least to the point of knowing—requires and includes our many empirical endeavors. It does not replace them.

---

38. Thus, I put Scott's suggestions aside for the remainder of this discussion. The continuity between the two arguments for recollection is debatable in any case. A prima facie look at the text might indicate that the *Meno* shows recollection of "truths" and the *Phaedo* recollection of Forms.

39. See, for example, Fine (2003, 49), but she is far more nuanced in her 2014 (119–23).

40. I would argue that, particularly due to the infallibility requirement, Plato has, and believes in having, a very high bar for what counts as knowledge and that he does not count particularly well "tied-down" true beliefs as knowledge (*cf. Men.* 97c11–98b6). However, my intention is only to discount this moment in the *Men.* as conclusive regarding whether recollection always or ever results in knowledge. I am not claiming to have sufficient evidence that Plato thinks that knowledge is infallible (but see *Euthd.* 280a6–8, *Rep.* 477e6–7, *Theaet.* 152c5–6).

41. Hackforth (1955, 75) says that recollection is a long and gradual process. Gulley (1962, 13) has three explicit stages of knowledge acquisition, only the first of which is associated with recollection. Fine (2014, 110, 171) also describes recollection as a long, gradual, process.

Prerequisites for Recollection

In comparing the two versions of (S1), above (as an all or nothing statement versus a statement of the law of excluded middle), we have also foreshadowed an existing debate about the position that people are in prior to recollection: Does neither knowing nor not knowing itself constitute some kind of true belief or knowledge? While no one would dispute that we have beliefs prior to recollection, in the *Meno*, Socrates demonstrates that recollection typically begins after an experience of *aporia* (79e7–80b7, 84a3–b1). Whatever *aporia* amounts to, it is at least a profound lack of confidence concerning one's beliefs. When Fine and Irwin turn to interpret the text's suggestions of how we get to refer to that about which we are inquiring, they do it on the assumption that we have at least some true beliefs about it.[42] But Nehamas (1985) and White (1976) both use textual evidence to support the claim that Plato has the person who recollects begin from complete ignorance, which they take to preclude true beliefs; Socrates states that he does not know "in any way at all (*to parapan*) what virtue itself is" (71a5–7). Socrates, here, disclaims all knowledge of the nature of virtue, and he does so again at 71b4, again using *to parapan*.[43] Furthermore, Socrates continues, saying that not knowing at all what something is entails not knowing at all what qualities it possesses (71b4). He is ignorant of virtue and does not know how to answer any questions whatsoever about it (71a3–7). Socrates then questions Meno, who does profess to know something about virtue, and leads him into *aporia*. Subsequently, Meno arrives at his own confession of ignorance also using *to parapan*.[44] When Socrates prods Meno once

---

42. Irwin 1977, 138–39; Fine 2003, 222 n. 16. In her 2014 (132–35), Fine expresses the weaker position that we can have true beliefs or "familiarity." I am unsure how she would cash out familiarity in a way that does not involve beliefs.

43. See Nehamas (1999, 5) for his agreement with Bluck (1962, 209) concerning reading *to parapan* at 71a6 closely with *oude*.

44. Meno actually uses *to parapan* in reference to his complete inability to *say* what virtue is (*Meno* 80b4) but, since he claims to be numb in both his tongue and his soul, I think it is fair to take it as a profession of ignorance. Weiss (2001, 56–57) approaches this differently: Socrates can be completely ignorant about virtue and still say and believe things about it (even true things). I think Weiss's Plato would also need to assume and rely upon the unwitting cognitive contact that I describe in this book in order for her interpretation to be feasible.

again to say what virtue is, Meno asks how they can possibly go on with the inquiry and suggests the paradox, once again using *to parapan*: "How can you search for something when you are completely ignorant of what it is?" (80d5–6).

Much has been made of the fact that, in restating the paradox, Plato has Socrates eliminate *to parapan,* saying only that, "a man cannot search either for what he knows or for what he does not know" (80e1–5).[45] But others argue that if Plato were trying to have Socrates reduce the effect of complete ignorance in a philosophically significant way, one would expect him to be more overt about it: the real effect of Socrates's reformulation is to show that Meno has presented a dilemma, both sides of which are closed. If it really is a dilemma, then "the function of *to parapan* is important and ineliminable."[46]

---

45. Thomas 1980, 128–29; Moravcsik 1971, 57; Scolnicov 1976, 52.

46. Nehamas 1999, 9. According to Irwin (1977, 138–39), the paradox is resolved because it relies upon the assertion that I cannot inquire into an object if I know nothing about it whatsoever. Irwin thinks that Socrates rejects the assumption of complete ignorance and points to 85c6–7 where it is agreed that the true beliefs that blossom in the slave after the inquiry must have already been in him prior to the inquiry (316 n. 14). Nehamas responds,

> These true beliefs are recovered by the slave at the end of his examination by Socrates; they could not therefore play the identificatory role Irwin asks of them and that requires them to be there consciously at its very beginning. (1999, 14)

Nehamas goes on to point out that the knowledge the slave is said to be able to eventually recover is also said to be in him. So, there is no difference between the slave's access to his true beliefs and to his knowledge prior to recollection and, as a result, the true beliefs cannot serve as the hook for recollection of the knowledge. Scott (2006, 76) also states unequivocally that unless the inquirer described by Meno has a "total blank" with respect to the object of inquiry, the absurdity of {B} will lose its force. Gonzalez (2007, 277–79) defends attributing *to parapan* to Socrates on the grounds that if we grant (as Vlastos does) that we already possess known propositions about virtue from which other propositions could be logically derived, then there would be no occasion for Meno's objection. He also suggests that what Fine and Irwin attribute to the Slave at the beginning of the *elenchos* are the kinds of things Socrates says he has at the end of the *elenchos*. Dancy (2004, 221) also argues that comprehension of the interaction between Socrates and Meno requires that Socrates assumes that the paradox arises from not knowing at all. I would argue that the effects of interpreting *to parapan* as a complete blank are minimally different from the effects of understand-

The Chicken and Egg Problem, Again

It is important to note that, even setting aside any evidence concerning *to parapan*, there is a chicken and egg problem for the inquirer with any kind of belief, true or false. The true or false belief must be *about* the object that makes it true or false *in order* to have a truth-value. Therefore, unwitting cognitive contact must have been made with whatever makes one's belief true or false (which for Plato is such things as equality itself and beauty itself) *prior* to the belief's acquisition of that truth-value. Thus, it is the constitutive view that offers the most promise for resolving {B}. I, of course, grant that a piece of information that is known to be true—rather than only *thought* to be true—has an additional cognitive connection to its truth-maker. However, the ignorant person who has some true beliefs is not in this situation. Plato thinks that, in principle, we *can* inquire while having only false beliefs about our object of inquiry, because the prior unwitting contact required is the same for true beliefs as it is for false ones. Recollection, I would argue, is Plato's opportunity for an explanation for how that unwitting reference takes place.

Recollection, albeit mysteriously, resolves {B}.[47] Perhaps Plato feels comfortable doing this due to the brute evidence (as demonstrated with the slave) that we do manage to refer to things such as the diagonal when we inquire about them. He is not willing, however, to resolve {E} in a mystical manner, as there is no brute evidence that thinking and feeling we recognize a conclusion as the answer to our inquiry is always—or even often—justified (Meno thought he knew what virtue was). Thus, even if

---

ing the ignorant person to have both true and false beliefs, while being unaware of which are which (as I assume would be the case for someone who is ignorant but has some true beliefs). So, an interpretation that downplays *to parapan* does not really gain the ground upon which views such as Fine's and Irwin's rely. I will make this argument as I continue.

47. As mentioned in the introduction, I would compare this aspect of what Plato thinks we get from recollection to what Kripke (1980) and his descendants think we get from "direct reference" (see Caplan 2006). I might be departing from Kelsey and Franklin here, as they seem concerned with recognition (at least Kelsey says that ordinary people recognize equal sticks [2001, 94]). I think that this unwitting reference resolves {B}, but as the ordinary people might think the sticks they are looking at are equal when they are actually unequal, it does not resolve {E}. This alone does nothing to show that Plato thought {E} could not be resolved, just that this element of recollection is not Plato's vehicle for {E's} resolution.

some later stage of recollection takes place due to the possession of true beliefs, there is an earlier stage of recollection whose role is to explain how any person's belief—true or false—originally came to be about its truth-maker.

Knowledge by Acquaintance

Some might suggest that I am merely reprising the notion of knowledge by acquaintance. However, knowledge by acquaintance is too strong for, and cannot do the same work as, content-independent reference. It is too strong in that it asserts knowledge and acquaintance, neither of which captures the sort of minimal connection that Plato seems to think allows for inquiry concerning something with which one can only be ambiguously acquainted (I can't experience equality through my senses without also experiencing inequality and color and many other properties).

Here is one way to think about it colloquially. If I babysit for an infant by holding it and interacting with it in other ways, even for just a short amount of time, it makes sense to say that I am acquainted with the infant. However, suppose I arrive at the infant's home while it is sleeping. The parents ask me to go to the baby's room only if I hear the infant crying through a sound monitor that allows me to hear loud crying (it's not sensitive enough to hear breathing or little whimpers). I hear no identifiable baby noises during the thirty minutes or so that I am there. The parents return home and thank me, and I leave. Perhaps an even more apt (but bizarre) analogy would have me brought to the home and told that "something" is in the room being monitored. Further, I would be instructed that, if I hear any noise, I should try to figure out what is in the room and help bring about the best conclusion for my welfare with respect to it without going into the room that is being monitored.

I think most of us would hesitate to say that I am acquainted with the baby or with whatever is in the room. Content-independent reference is parallel to my connection by monitor to the contents of the room, not to my holding the baby. What I have is a conduit to the contents of the room through which acquaintance with the baby (or whatever is in the room) *might* pass were a triggering opportunity to arise. This conduit is limited, but it does afford me the opportunity to gain experience of the contents of the room. In this analogy, I acquire perceptual experience, the actual contact upon which Plato relies gives me some sort of cognitive conduit through which I can acquire some sort of contact that we do not describe as perceptual (perhaps at the same time as I acquire some perceptual experience).[48]

Russell (1912, 109–10) makes it clear that knowledge by acquaintance, unlike other kinds of knowledge, holds no room for error. Knowledge by acquaintance is *incorrigible* knowledge of the *content* of our sense data and conceptions. In contrast, Plato is counting on my *corrigible concept* of equality to connect me to equality itself, even if the *content* of my *concept* is erroneous *with respect to equality itself*.[49] Thus, Plato needs content-independent reference in order for the content that I entertain to be about the universal that it does not properly describe (the content of my concept will thereby be erroneous—it is certainly corrigible). Once I am embodied, my awareness of abstract objects must travel through this already available conduit. This conduit provides the opportunity for me to "touch" these abstract objects with my thoughts even if it is not a good enough conduit to allow me to capture them in the content of those thoughts and never—or seldom—results in my knowing them.

Now that we have ascertained something about the nature of the unwitting cognitive contact that I am claiming Plato needs to overcome the beginning problem, let us go on to see that it is the minimum that Plato needs recollection to do for him. I will now put this minimal cognitive contact into the context of what Plato says about recollection in the *Meno* and the *Phaedo*.

---

48. Thus, while I embrace many of her arguments against competing interpretations of *doxa* in Plato, I disagree with the positive theory set out by Rowett (2018) as I group it in the same family as acquaintance. This is seen most clearly in her arguments against propositional attitudes (107). Rowett acknowledges this (200, n. 12). Her view is that we have knowledge as a result of recollection, but not definitional knowledge. I am arguing that cognitive contact that falls well below the level of knowledge, belief, or what is traditionally described as "acquaintance" is sufficient for learning and is all Plato needs from recollection.

49. Strevens (2019, 125–30) stresses the importance of corrigibility of our concepts in any theory of reference that expects inquiry and investigation to be open-ended. I should note here that this says nothing about Plato's stance on whether or not I am corrigible with respect to the *content* of my concept. The corrigibility here is corrigibility about what my concept is a concept *of*—what it is trying to capture (*cf.* Penner 1987, 26–32).

Chapter 2

Another Look at the Beginning Problem

My proposal is that something like recollection could and *must* resolve {B} indirectly by resolving a preliminary problem. The solution to this problem is a prerequisite to—and is sufficient for—the resolution of {B}. Already knowing everything there is to know prenatally only to forget it at birth is insufficient for resolving {B}. It is also simplistic and seems overreaching as an explanation of what we call learning. Still, there is a role for something as mysterious as recollection in Plato's assumptions about what it takes to inquire in both the dialogues that discuss recollection and in those that do not.

Here is an illustration of this preliminary problem. Augustine begins the second paragraph of his *Confessions* by voicing a conundrum:

> "Grant me Lord to know and understand" (Ps. 118:34, 73, 144) which comes first—to call upon you or to praise you—and calling upon you is an act of believing in you. But who calls upon you when he does not know you? For an ignorant person might call upon someone else instead of the right one. But surely you may be called upon in prayer that you may be known. Yet "how shall they call upon him in whom they have not believed?" and how shall they believe without a preacher? (Rom. 10:14). "They will praise the Lord who seek for him" (Ps. 21:27). (Chadwick, trans.)

Realizing that he does not know the Lord, and believing that praying to the Lord is the appropriate vehicle for coming to know him, Augustine begins to pray. However, his prayers bring him to realize that he is caught in a paradox: how can I seek the Lord through prayer if I do not already know him? For how will I be sure to address my prayers to the right addressee?[1]

Note that Augustine's paradox is not {E}: the concern is not, I do not know God, and so, if I seek him, how will I know when I have found him? The problem is, I must pray to God in order to *come to know* him, but if I do not know God how can I address my prayers to him? It is as if I need to send God a text, but the only way to find his number is to ask him—via texting him at his number. Since this is impossible, I must just send off my text to some number that seems right, but certainly could easily be wrong and could place my prayers in the inbox of someone other than God or leave them wandering around in cyberspace. We have here a paradox of address. *A paradox of reference to that of which we are ignorant.* If, after accidentally addressing my prayers to a being other than the one I intend, I then come to know *that* being and think of it as God, my inquiry will have failed on many counts. I have to *think about* the Lord before I can pray to him and, so, *before* I can come to know him. In fact, I must think *about* the Lord before any of my beliefs can *be about* him and before any of my beliefs about him can be true or false. For it is the fact that they are already about God that will make my beliefs have the truth-values that they do. How can I be sure I am thinking about—and thus trying to get to know—the right thing?[2]

Augustine's problem requires a solution that is parallel to needing something that does not lie on the spectrum of doxastic states—he needs something that is other than a doxastic state, rather than a doxastic state

---

[1]. Note that in order to create this conundrum Augustine must assume that there are other possible things that he might accidentally address. In parallel, I argue that Plato has this paradoxical problem with reference because there is more than one Form.

[2]. Scott MacDonald also relates this Augustinian text to Meno's paradox. He notes that it is not the same as Meno's paradox. He calls it the "paradox of invocation" (2008, 24). He does not say that it is prior to {B}, nor would the solution that he finds Augustine to have proposed (which supposedly solves the problem for coming to know God) solve the problem at the heart of {B}. MacDonald (34–37) finds Augustine proposing that we can invoke God because we have gained a token of God through experience. In the case of recollecting *equality*, it is not clear how seeing sticks that *fall short of equality* counts as a gaining a *token* of it. Nor how it counts as gaining a token of equality rather than inequality. I will discuss this further, below.

that falls short of knowledge.³ Augustine needs something like having God's number—a conduit through which what is needed for *doxa* can pass. He needs some content-independent way to reach God *as he inquires* into what God is like. He needs to keep track of this thing he doesn't even recognize while he gets to know it. God must be the truth-maker for Augustine's beliefs. Only then will it be God that he is coming—or failing to come—to know.

Plato, in proposing recollection as a solution to {B}, might be trying to make the beliefs that I intend to be about equality be *about* equality "before" they are true or false, so they can become true or false when they are applied to my intended element of what-is.⁴ If Plato's theory of recollection was at least partly motivated by this concern, then he recognized and tried to solve a *problem of reference* {R}. It's solving {R} that allows {B} to be solved.⁵

Plato could thus use recollection primarily as what allows a person to continue to hold the same object before his or her mind while examining and discovering it. We need this relationship in order to begin and to sustain an inquiry because we need a way to ensure that our inquiry is about some particular x even if none of the content we are cognizing is true of—or even approximates—x. We need this especially because

---

3. It might be argued that a belief that is "known to be true" has a connection to its reference that is more secure than the connection found in the kind of reference discussed for doxastic states that are true but are not distinguished in one's own mind from those that are false (but are, of course, regarded as true). It is not clear to me that Plato has room in his system for beliefs that are known to be true. This sounds like belief that has gone through the transformation of becoming knowledge and it's not clear to me that Plato thinks this can happen to a single "belief" (I will discuss this in chapter 5). If we consider doxastic states that, even if true, are not distinguished by the one who believes them from those that, though regarded as true, are false, then we must still assume that there is some prior, non-doxastic, content-independent, connection that *all* doxastic states have prior to being made true (or false) by what is. This is because the ones that later become knowledge must *first* be true in order to become knowledge *later*.

4. I put "before" in scare quotes because we must understand this as a nontemporal priority. I use "what-is" to translate *to on*, Plato's term for "what exists," which I here use to loosely refer to the whole of reality. I would argue that this is consistent with Plato's use of this term.

5. Indeed, I see Plato relying upon something like "direct reference," where ψ can refer to μ even if ψ has no content, has no content that is relevant to μ, or has content that implies $\sim\mu$. This would make recollection solve {B}, but not necessarily solve {E}.

inquiry can fail, or garner misinformation. Plato appears to call the whole process, from initial grasping, to recognizing, to the (at least theoretical) acquisition of knowledge, "recollection." However, it appears that everything other than this initial contact takes place slowly and gradually in both the *Meno* and the *Phaedo*. Recognizing and knowing are not part of the resolution of {B}.

A further reason that Plato should have been working on a solution to {R} is the fact that, in the *Meno*, he has Socrates demonstrate that recollection is most readily triggered by an experience of *aporia* (79e7–80b7, 84a3–b1). The fact that being at a loss concerning the thing that one wishes to think and inquire about is a good way to begin recollecting it forces us to consider the relation between {R} and {B}.[6] My perceptual encounters with triangles or sticks and stones, and the inconsistency of my beliefs about them when I begin to try to answer questions about them, allow me to note that I am at a loss concerning some property such as equality. What it is for me to be at a loss concerning this property is for me to recognize that any beliefs I currently have about it could be false.[7] This motivates me to launch an inquiry concerning it. However, before I can be at a loss concerning it, and in order to begin the inquiry—I need to refer to it. How am I going to be able to do that with any confidence that I am indeed referring to the property concerning which I am at a loss and with respect to which I am motivated to inquire rather than some other property? Since, being in *aporia*, I recognize that I might have only false beliefs about this property, what guideline connects my inquiry—or even my false belief—to that particular property in such a way that my inquiry actually gets to be an inquiry *about* that particular property, or my false

---

6. I note here, for emphasis, that it makes no difference whether we are in a cognitive blank or whether we are entertaining content that is false concerning x, or is no truer of x than it is false, or is no truer of x than it is of many other things. Furthermore, happening to have some true beliefs, which we cannot discriminate from our false beliefs, also will not help.

7. To make clear something I have already tried to indicate: I am not insisting that the inquirer has to have only false beliefs or no beliefs at all, rather than some false and some true beliefs. I am insisting that neither true beliefs nor satisfied definite descriptions are necessary to overcome {R}. Recollection overcomes {R} by allowing our beliefs to refer independent of their truth or falsity. That something such as this is necessary comes to the fore when one tries to account for false belief and statement—as Plato suggests at *Theaet.* 187a4–199d8 and *Soph.* 259d–261e.

belief gets to be *about* that property (and therefore false)? With recollection, there might be some vestige of the idea of equality (a vestige that is not itself an idea and that has no content) of which we are incognizant in our soul. Plato could use this vestige of our soul's former, preembodied, contact with equality as the means for successful reference to it. Thus, he could use it as a means for successful reference to something concerning which we are ignorant. Thus, we can inquire, "What is x?" even while ignorant of x and still have our inquiry be about x.[8]

Now, why Plato thinks that having the vestige of the forgotten object in our soul allows us to refer to it remains mysterious. One might argue—as Bostock (1986) seemingly would—that just having its vestige in our soul does not make us any more likely to refer to it than to any of the other forgotten ideas of which we have vestiges in our soul.[9] Perhaps the analogy that I offer below makes a plausible, though speculative, suggestion. Still, what is important to my project is that Plato's positive epistemology relies upon this assumption: that it is possible to refer to an object of inquiry even while being ignorant concerning it. Somehow, just trying or intending to refer (even by making a mistake) to this thing concerning which one has a vestige results in our reference to it.[10] When I intend to launch an inquiry concerning x, even while ignorant and at a

---

8. This solution (the solution to {B}—I make no comment regarding {E}) commits Plato to prenatal knowledge, but not innate knowledge. Whatever was known is now forgotten. But it has left some kind of remnant or stain in the soul. The trace that remains does not count as knowledge and, in my view, need not have any content. Thus, I am not sure how much it rises to the level of what Fine (2014, 151–52) and Moravcsik (1971, 58) call "entitative." What remains is some sort of guideline or label. I will offer clarification with my analogy below (61–64). Fine (2014, 21) also finds Plato committed to something prenatal, but not innate. However, she deems it knowledge.

9. However, in the case of {R}, the paradox does not telescope and continue. There is no content to our reference to the forgotten object in our soul and, so, nothing for a second order "matching problem" to be about, either. Here, the notion of a guideline might better illustrate Plato's view. I am not *matching* two *entities*, but I, after birth, continue to hold one end of a string that remains attached to the object of inquiry. See my analogy, below (61–64).

10. In fact, when Plato endorses the theory of recollection, he appears to endorse the even stronger claim that such reference is unfailing. I speculate that Plato weakens the assumption that we are infallible in this respect in the *Rep.* and *Theaet*. Plato appears to assume this sort of unwitting cognitive connection, but does not discuss it in the context of recollection in those dialogues.

loss concerning *x*, I do incontrovertibly refer to *x*. Whatever Plato thinks recollection is, it needs to supply this guaranty in order to solve {B}, and it need do no more than refer successfully in order to make inquiry possible. When we emphasize {B} and, therefore, the possibility of inquiry, Plato need not prove anything about the mechanics of recollection. He sees that our ability to inquire requires some sort of explanation and he uses recollection to explain that ability.

Aboutness comes from that which a statement mentions.[11] An inquiry about an object concerning which the inquirer is ignorant and in *aporia* would have to come to be about its particular object in this same way. For those who are convinced that an inquirer will always have at least *some* true beliefs about the object of inquiry, let us take note that a belief must refer to what makes it true *"before"* and *in order* for it to be true. Therefore, the resolution of {R} needs to be assumed for true beliefs as well.[12]

Further Evidence from the *Phaedo*

I am suggesting that something like Plato's theory of recollection is needed in order to explain our capacity for inquiry. Plato realized that he needed our souls to have something going on in them when we were born. Still, I am also agreeing with others that Plato's articulated story, that every soul used to contain all knowledge of the Forms prenatally, and that this knowledge was forgotten in its entirety by every soul at birth, does not give us an understanding of what might make the soul fertile for inquiry. I am arguing that recollection must be at least partly focused upon fixing the reference of *x* in order to anchor the question, "What is *x*?" The point is to allow this sort of question to be about something concerning which one is ignorant. This ignorance can take several forms:

---

11. The statement's reference is independent of its utterer's beliefs. I am suggesting that Plato thinks its reference is, nevertheless, determined by the utterer's intentions. It is the fact that these intentions come into play that would make it unsatisfactory to describe the reference as *de re* (see Reshotko 2011).

12. Even if it is simply the—supposedly true—belief that equality exists. Plato's recognition of the problem of reference and false belief seem to have prompted his explorations of these topics in the *Theaet.* and *Soph*. I find those discussions to be further evidence that Plato thought we must somehow overcome {R} in order for our beliefs to have truth-values. I will discuss only the *Theat.* (chapter 6) in this respect.

It can consist of having no true beliefs or satisfied definite descriptions. Alternatively, it can consist of having both true and false beliefs but not discerning which among them is true and which is false. Finally, it can consist of having beliefs that are no truer of the objects of inquiry than they are of many other things.[13] In order to launch an inquiry concerning something about which I am ignorant, I must be able to—and have confidence in my ability to—refer to it despite my ignorance of it. I need my inquiry to be about the property I intend to investigate and not some other property.[14] Thus, recollection might not be necessary if there existed only one abstract object.[15]

In order to see that Plato is beholden to overcoming {R}, even if only under the guise of overcoming {B}, let us look more carefully at the sticks and stones argument for recollection in the *Phaedo*. The sticks and stones argument, however construed, is a nonidentity of discernibles showing that equal sticks and stones and the equal itself are importantly not the same thing (74c3-4), and that equal sticks and stones give misleading information about equality itself, yet it is due to equal sticks and stones that we grasp equality (74c7-9). This is a case where there is a considerable difference between that which we see and that which we recollect (74d4-8). In fact, we are using something other than, and inferior to, equality itself in order to come to recollect equality itself (74d9-e8); we are using something

---

13. I will (later) argue that—apart from *Rep.* V, where ignorance (*agnôsia*) has a special role to play, Plato thinks ignorance is composed of *doxa(i)*. Ignorance consists in having a network of true and false beliefs where one cannot discern which is which. Of course, ignorance is also consistent with being cognitively blank, if such a thing is possible.

14. Scott (1995, 57), acknowledging this problem with reference, uses it to promote the notion that the "traditional" interpretation of recollection is wrong, and that recollection was never meant to explain everyday concept formation. Scott says only an ontological relationship between ordinary concepts and Forms exists. I do not see how this ontological relationship (if it is purely ontological it is independent of the ordinary person's intentions) is established in the ordinary person given that these ordinary concepts would require radical reformulation in order to capture what-is. How did the ordinary conception of "the morning star" get to be about something that is not a star and is a significant feature of the evening sky? It had to refer to the planet Venus in ordinary usage in order for there to be anything that constituted a "correction." Williams makes a similar point against Scott (2002, 150). I will say more about this in the next chapter.

15. This would make it the case that we need understand only one abstract object in order to investigate the perceptible world and it would be easy to be unerring in our reference.

that can only be perceived through sense experience in order to bring to mind something that could not possibly exist in sense experience. We are recollecting equality itself by noting that these objects—which are so different from equality itself—strive to be like equality itself (75b1) but will always fall short of it. Plato has Socrates wonder how we might recognize them by what they strive to be like but are destined to always be unlike and suggests that it must be because we once had knowledge of that toward which they strive.

> Then before we began to see or hear or otherwise perceive, we must have possessed knowledge of the equal itself if we were about to refer sense perceptions of equal objects to it, and realized that all of them were eager to be like it, but were inferior. (Grube, 76b)

What exactly is this former knowledge supposed to be doing for us? Using the *Phaedo*, we can further diagnose the modest solution that recollection might offer for {B} and began to offer in the *Meno*.

The recollection argument in the *Meno* granted me access to two kinds of things—a collection of things-in-themselves on one side and a collection of sense experiences on the other. I seem to have *access* to these things-in-themselves, even though, once born in human form, I am ignorant of them. My access to them takes the form of some vestige of each one that remains in my soul. I must investigate them by investigating the sense experiences that both point me to them and fall short of them. However, nothing to which I have access tells me which thing-in-itself is which. In particular, if I am always at risk of mistaking equal stones for unequal stones, how are these sense impressions supposed to help me to distinguish equality itself from inequality itself? I need to investigate sticks and stones in order to recollect equality, but, if I am ignorant of equality, how can I know that it is equality (rather than inequality) that sticks and stones are helping me to investigate? In addition, if all sticks and stones are problematic examples of equality, how can I be sure that any particular sticks or stones are revealing equality to me? We might now put {R} as follows:

> (R1) I have a vestige of each thing-in-itself by which to group my sense experiences within me, and I have many sense experiences.

(R2) Every sense experience falls short of each thing-in-itself that it exemplifies.

(R2a) I have no (reliably) true beliefs about the things-in-themselves.

(R3) I need to associate the sense experiences with the appropriate things-in-themselves.

But performing the task indicated in (R3) seems problematic: if equal sticks and stones fall short of both equality itself and inequality itself, then how do I end up associating them with the appropriate thing-in-itself (equality itself) despite my possession of something that is only a vestige of it? Furthermore, if this vestige does not have content, or if it has no reliable content, how can I link any sense experiences to that of which it is a vestige?

My sense experience alone cannot guarantee that it is getting me to think about the things-in-themselves about which I take myself to be thinking. Whatever thing-in-itself I abstract from my sense experiences of equal sticks and stones, these sense experiences cannot all by themselves indicate to me that what I am abstracting is equality rather than inequality.

Let us look at the options for what Plato thinks the perceptual objects to which we do have access, and which cause us to recollect, are like. Either, they do not even have the property that they are presumed to cause us to recollect (mathematical perfection). Alternatively, they could both have and not have the property at the same time—every perceptible example of equality is also an example of inequality. A third possibility is that they are confusing examples of equality.[16] All of these are examples about which I could easily be wrong when I attribute equality to the objects of my sense experience in that they are all examples that fall short of equality in some way.[17] In any case, how does the property that

---

16. Mathematical perfection understands equality as purely mathematical and so not a feature of perceptible objects. Penner (1987, 44–55 and 181–90) calls this the "traditional approach." Some examples of this approach are Bluck (1955), Hackforth (1955) and Geddes (1885). Gulley (1962) might be said to follow this approach as well, but he does so somewhat self-consciously. See n. 18, below. Penner's reading is that the perceptibles are confusing but equality itself is not (1987, 184–86).

17. Plato emphasizes this even more at *Rep.* 475e4–479d5 and 523a–525a: the beautiful sights and sounds are also the ugly ones, the halves are the doubles, the larges are

I *take myself to be* thinking about, and therefore investigating, get to be the property that I intend to investigate? I need to get the identity of the property that I am actually thinking about from something other than sense experience. Plato needs me to be able to fix my thoughts upon actual equality even while looking at what are—at best—misleading examples of it. I need to be able to think about equality and differentiate it from inequality (and every other property) in the absence of any reliable beliefs about equality. I need to be unerring in *reference* despite the possibility that I err in my *beliefs*. I need to be able to think about equality, even if it is as a result of looking at *unequal* sticks and stones and believing them—falsely—to be equal.[18]

Plato wants to assume that I do not already have to know or be able to give an account of equality itself, or have true beliefs about equality itself, before I can safely assume that I am referring to it. This is because I need to refer to it in order to ask a question about it and seek the true answer. I need my reference to succeed without knowing equality itself. I need this from recollection so that I can begin the investigation that—ideally—ends in knowledge. Ideally, the sticks and stones argument leaves me with a notion that whatever equality is, it is not identical with equal sticks and stones, but it also does not require me to begin with *any* specific beliefs about the nature of equality. That is, my unwitting contact has no content relevant to equality; its content reflects only my ability to direct my attention to a specific, but unknown, abstract entity to the exclusion of all others.

What we need from our nonvirgin *tabula* is a way to track and individuate the various abstract objects about which we must inquire and

---

the smalls. Just as the same finger is an example both of thickness and of thinness. See chapter 4, 93–100 and 105–108.

18. Gulley (1962, 34–40) argues that Plato makes two implicit assertions. First (Gulley's iii), in *all* cases, sensibles are sufficiently approximate copies of the Forms to be able to give correct suggestions of them. Second (Gulley's iv), the senses are always to be trusted. Gulley supports this latter claim by pointing out that Plato does not show us how to distinguish between genuine cases and spurious cases of being reminded of a Form. I take Gulley's point to be similar to the one I am making here: if we can recollect equality by mistakenly attributing it to unequal sticks (and vice versa), from where does our confidence that we are recollecting equality rather than inequality come? This is why recollection seems much better at allowing us to ask a question ({B}) than at allowing us to know whether we have answered it correctly (which might be required for {E}).

learn in order to better understand our sense experience. We need this because there is *more than one* feature of what-is (there is at least one further abstract object from which we must distinguish the one we have chosen to investigate). Furthermore, each perceptible reflects more than one of these abstract objects, and often, a given perceptible reflects both of two opposite properties at the same time.

Consider the following three scenarios as an analogy to what recollection has to give us in order for us to break through {R} and resolve {B}:

Scenario 1 (here there is no need for recollection):

I am a hermit living off the land on my own and I seldom encounter other people. I have a shack. I would be unlikely to survive without my trusted dog, who was bred in such a way, and who I have trained on top of that breeding, to be a perfect complement to the survival of a person living as I do. The arrangement has worked very well since I acquired the dog eight years ago and we have now trained each other to the point where we are the ideal symbiotic pair. If this counts as knowing, then I know this dog.[19] Imagine that one day, while I am outside my shack doing one of my solo duties (the dog is off doing one of his), a huge branch falls on me and knocks me out. When I awake, I have amnesia. I have completely forgotten who I am, where I am, or how I got here. I stand and see a dog (my dog, but I do not recognize him) running toward me in a very friendly, happy way. Thinking the dog will lead me to someone who can help me, I join the dog and follow him back to a shack that I do not recognize. Over the next few months, I interact with the dog and figure out how he can help me live comfortably as a hermit, with only the dog for company and assistance, in this shack in the woods. If I knew him before, I know him again, now.

Scenario 2 (here, recollection is needed, but there is none):

I am a hermit living off the land on my own and seldom encountering others. I have a shack. I would be unlikely to survive without my three trusted dogs, they have been bred in such a way, and I have trained

---

19. In case you're worried, I have arranged with the breeder to bring me a clone of this dog every nine years or so, so that I can train overlapping dogs and survive the transition from one dog's death to the next complementary dog.

them on top of all that, to be perfect complements to each other and to the survival of a person living as I do. Unfortunately, the breeder could not accomplish this without making them look, and continue to grow to look, exactly alike. Luckily, the breeder delivered each one to me with a collar of a different color. Over time, I have been able to name them and teach them their names. They come unfailingly when I call them by the proper name, and otherwise indicate that I have called them by the right or wrong name in other situations in which I need to re-identify them. Thus, even though the well-worn collars fell off them long ago, this is not a problem. I have integrated their distinct personalities and complementary tasks with their names. So, by voicing their names, I can re-identify them by means other than how they look. The arrangement has worked very well since I acquired the dogs eight years ago and we all trained each other to be the ideal symbiotic foursome since then. If this counts as knowing them, then I know them.

Imagine that one day, while I am outside my shack doing one of my solo duties (the dogs are off doing theirs), a huge branch falls on me and knocks me out. When I awake, I have amnesia. I have no recollection of who I am, where I am, or how I got here. I stand and see three dogs (my dogs, but I do not recognize them) running toward me in a very friendly, happy way. Thinking the dogs will lead me to someone who can help me, I join the dogs and follow them back to a shack that I do not recognize. Over the next few months, I interact with all of the dogs. But, I can't tell them apart well enough to even give them consistent names and I have no way to mark them physically.[20] Despite how similar they look, they behave very differently from one another and I am never sure what to expect from any individual dog. I seldom make a good choice about which one to leave home while I take another one or two with me to do a chore. I never learn to distinguish them from one another and re-identify them. My life with the dogs is a frustrating struggle that sometimes works out okay but often leaves me in tragic and unsafe circumstances. This is a barrier to familiarizing myself with, or knowing, any of these dogs, and I die shortly thereafter.

SCENARIO 3 (THIS IS SCENARIO 2 PLUS RECOLLECTION):

Everything is the same as it was in *Scenario 2*. However, once delivered by the breeder, I brand each dog with a unique abstract symbol at the same

---

20. We must assume this for the sake of the analogy. This is supposed to be analogous to the way an embodied human interacts with abstract objects.

time as I name it. The brands are permanent and very distinguishable. When I come to, with amnesia, and return with the dogs to a shack, I do not recognize them, or the shack, or know their names. However, over time, I come to distinguish them from each other due to these brands and learn their individual strengths and roles. I even give them new names to which they eventually answer. After some time, we are [again] a symbiotic foursome and live comfortably together. I know them as well as I knew them before.

Now let us analogize *Scenario 3* to recollection using the sticks and stones argument. Recall that the argument is a nonidentity of discernibles, Sticks and stones have—or lack—at least one property that makes them "fall short" of equality itself. The property in question is not a feature of any particular sense experience that I have. Thus, the argument carries the underlying assumption that, somehow, the thoughts associated with my sense experiences are already *about* the thing-in-itself of which those sense experiences fall short. So it is not straightforward to associate the sense experiences with their proper things-in-themselves. This is true even if each sense experience is too ambiguous to be transparently associated with any particular thing-in-itself due to its content. Thus, the metaphorical thought behind {R} as a resolution of {B} is that at some point, before I was in human form, I knew the things-in-themselves and, at that time, I, so to speak, labeled them. Upon birth as a human being, I forgot my knowledge of the things-in-themselves, but the labels that function merely as arbitrary differentiators remained. It is as if I am born with my soul holding a separate guideline to each individual Form. When I tug at the guideline, I wiggle the Form to which it is attached even if I can't see it and don't know its identity at the moment when I wiggle it. So, I can now refer to, re-identify, and distinguish these things in themselves from each other. My nonvirgin soul contains nothing but these contentless labels that inevitably connect me to the object about which I am inquiring whether I realize that it is the object of my inquiry or not. To clarify scenario 3's analogues with recollection: The dogs' roles and personalities are the abstract objects I am investigating. The dogs' behaviors are playing the roles of perceptibles. The brand or label is the vestige in my soul. My life before amnesia is my life before I am embodied and my life upon waking with amnesia is my life as an embodied human being.[21]

---

21. I find this analogy helpful even though the dogs and their personalities are particulars and not universals. As it happens, Plato also analogizes the Forms to concrete particulars in discussing recollection (see *Phdo.* 73d–74a).

What has been given to me by recollection is exactly what was needed to resolve {R}. When I try to inquire or think about one of the many properties of a perceptible, I manage to think about that property and not one of the many others that also waits in my internal storage space. I succeed in thinking about the property I try to think about whether I think something true about it or something false about it. I even succeed if I just ask, and don't even try to answer, a question about it ("What is this?"). One might say that what recollection does is make me able to fix my reference upon that to which I wish to refer, when I wish to refer to it. I am able to do this even without there being any content to my thoughts that is relevant to, or true of, the particular referent about which I am thinking via its label or guideline. This ability to fix my reference allows me to investigate it or entertain a belief about it. No matter the results of my inquiry, I can count on my struggle being a struggle *about* that particular property (the equality of the sticks rather than their inequality), though I might remain confused concerning it and do not know, and might never come to know, where the guideline is leading me.[22]

Conclusion

If recollection allows one to think about the property that one is trying to think about, when one tries to investigate it, then recollection makes inquiry possible. Therefore, neither knowledge nor true belief is necessary for beginning an inquiry. This ability to think about the object of inquiry regardless of the content of one's thought is the only necessary first step to the acquisition of knowledge. It is the only prerequisite for inquiry. It is a prerequisite for having a belief *about* a specific thing and that is, arguably, the first step in asking a question *about* that particular thing where the answer has a truth-value. It is therefore the first step to coming to know that thing. This initial baby step toward knowledge is

---

22. Fine (2014, 168) appears wedded to the claim that discovery {E}—not inquiry {B}—requires "matching." I do not know if "matching" is the best term for what is required. It is *inquiry* {B} that must *already* contain reference to that which we seek. Discovery only requires inquiry if it is discovery that answers an inquiry. Many inquiries result in discoveries that are important but do not answer them. For example, we test drugs to see if they alleviate a symptom and find they do not, but find they do something else that is helpful for those who take them. See Fine (2014, 6, 79) on accidental discovery.

not handed to us by sense perception. We rely upon it in order to *attribute* properties such as equality—correctly or incorrectly—*to* our sense perceptions. This unwitting cognitive connection resolves {R}, which is a prerequisite to the resolution of {B}. The resolution of {B} is a necessary step toward any possible resolution of the "ending problem" from Meno's paradox ({E}). For if our reference to a property is incorrect or imprecise, we will be unable to entertain even false beliefs about either that property itself or about the sense experiences of which it is predicated (whether the predication be positive or negative).[23]

Whatever else Plato is hoping to gain from the theory of recollection in the *Meno* and *Phaedo*, he needs to assume that it allows us to refer to the specific property that is the truth-maker for any hypotheses that we generate as answers to our inquiry.[24] Whether Plato should feel comfortable assuming that recollection guarantees that we will make this reference even while ignorant is not altogether clear. It is clear that were embodied human beings to have this modest and subtle toehold, it would enable them to launch inquiries and pursue knowledge despite the fact that the only input they gain during their mortal lives is perceptual. It is also clear that only this kind of relationship can allow us to investigate an object about which we are ignorant so that we are no longer beholden to the problem of inquiry {B}.

---

23. Irwin (1977, 139) seems to think that we need to have at least some true beliefs about a thing before we can fix the reference of it and, therefore, before we can inquire into it. But how did the beliefs come to be true *prior* to referring to that which makes them true? Dancy (2004, 260) also seems to think that we cannot refer to, or think of, a thing without knowing it ("knowing what it is"). This notion that knowledge precedes reference is also hard to understand. Can an epistemic state be knowledge apart from being true? Can it be true *before* it refers to whatever makes it true?

24. While the text does seem to allow that all of learning, not just this moment of reference, is recollection, Williams (2002, 151) believes that "the theory of recollection was never meant as an account of the *logismos*; it merely explains how human beings can make the sorts of judgments that cry out for a *logismos*." I take Williams to be saying that recollection was never intended to account for more than {B}.

Chapter 3

Nonphilosophers and Beauty Itself in the *Meno* and the *Phaedo*

In this chapter, we will examine evidence for the thesis that Plato relies upon this unwitting but cognitive contact in order to make several assertions that relate both the slave in the *Meno* and nonphilosophers in the *Phaedo* to the diagonal itself and equality itself (Forms), thereby solving the beginning problem {B}. This will allow us to map out the way ordinary people relate to equality itself and beauty itself and the stages through which they presumably must move in order to develop beliefs about, or even knowledge of, these abstract objects. In later chapters, we will see that these early stages might even point to a strategy for becoming a philosopher.

Phaedo 74b7–c5

Socrates frames the sticks and stones argument at *Phaedo* 74b7–c5 with two remarks that have provoked diverse reactions from Plato's recent commentators. Before launching into the argument, he says:

> When the recollection is caused by similar things, must one not of necessity also experience this: to consider whether the similarity falls short in some way or is complete? 74a5–7 (following Grube's translation with modifications)[1]

---

1. ἀλλ' ὅταν γε ἀπὸ τῶν ὁμοίων ἀναμιμνῄσκηταί τίς τι, ἆρ' οὐκ ἀναγκαῖον τόδε προσπάσχειν, ἐννοεῖν εἴτε τι ἐλλείπει τοῦτο κατὰ τὴν ὁμοιότητα εἴτε μὴ ἐκείνου οὗ ἀνεμνήσθη;

After the argument, Socrates summarizes as follows:

> Whenever someone, on seeing something, realizes that that which he now sees strives to be like some other being, but falls short and can't be like that other thing because it is inferior, do we agree that the one who thinks this must have foreknowledge of that to which he says it is like, but deficiently so? 74d9–e4 (following Grube's translation with modifications)[2]

As discussed in the previous chapter, in his 1995 book *Recollection and Experience*, this framing motivates Dominic Scott to offer a novel interpretation of the theory of recollection as found in Plato's *Meno*, *Phaedo*, and *Phaedrus*. For Scott, these framing comments are a principal piece of evidence that marks off the discontinuity between the beliefs of ordinary people and those of philosophers. Scott thinks that Plato intends to communicate that only philosophers can have beliefs that appeal to the Forms. This is because Scott takes this framing to imply that, when recollecting, people compare sensible equal objects to the Form of equality in a manner that is transparent to the person doing the comparing, during recollection. From this, Scott gathers that Plato believes that those who recollect have transparent and conscious access to the Form prior to recollection. Therefore, Scott criticizes those who think this claim implies that recollection explains concept formation in the ordinary person. Scott argues that the theory of recollection explains only higher philosophical learning and not the ordinary person's possession of mundane concepts. He suggests that Plato thought that knowledge can come from two sources and that there is a discontinuity between beliefs arrived at through sense experience and beliefs arrived at via recollection of the Forms. According to Scott, the ordinary person has no cognitive relationship with the Forms:

> [D—the interpretation championed by Scott] seems to claim that all of the concepts by which we classify our sense experience are empirically gained, while our grasp of Forms is recollected

---

2. οὐκοῦν ὁμολογοῦμεν, ὅταν τίς τι ἰδὼν ἐννοήσῃ ὅτι βούλεται μὲν τοῦτο ὃ νῦν ἐγὼ ὁρῶ εἶναι οἷον ἄλλο τι τῶν ὄντων, ἐνδεῖ δὲ καὶ οὐ δύναται τοιοῦτον εἶναι [ἴσον] οἷον ἐκεῖνο, ἀλλ' ἔστιν φαυλότερον, ἀναγκαῖόν που τὸν τοῦτο ἐννοοῦντα τυχεῖν προειδότα ἐκεῖνο ᾧ φησιν αὐτὸ προσεοικέναι μέν, ἐνδεεστέρως δὲ ἔχειν;

well after we have accumulated sense experience. But this seems puzzling. If we have these two *distinct* sources, how is it that both our empirical concept and our recollected knowledge are of "equal." There must be some connection. There is. . . . [b]ut the explanation for this is not that information "leaks" from our innate source to our beliefs about particulars. . . . [Given that ontologically the particulars participate in the Forms] there will indeed be a resemblance between the contents of recollection and perception, but that stems from an ontological link and not a cognitive one. (1995, 68)[3]

Scott has influenced several interpreters;[4] he also has a number of critics.[5] According to Scott, the assertion that recollection is intended to explain concept formation is not only absent from the text, it is also the source of "acute difficulties." Pointing to the claim (*Phdo.*, 74d4–75a4) that recollection comes about because we notice the deficiency of the particulars as compared to the Forms, Scott says that this would imply that Plato believes that everyone compares particulars to Forms and has done so from birth and that is absurd (1995, 60–63).

Contrary to Scott, Harte has provided an interpretation of this framing upon which we can build to show that Plato *did* think that ordinary people compare particulars to Forms. This same foundation will also allow us to explore further the relationship that ordinary people have with the Forms, and to elucidate the textual evidence that supports and expands our understanding of this relationship.

---

3. I will discuss this claim of Scott's later in this chapter and argue that it cannot be an ontological relationship alone that allows both our mundane concepts based on our perceptions and our philosophical musings concerning the Forms to be *about* the same thing (82–83).

4. Scott's 1995 interpretation of recollection is partly rehearsed in his 2006. For its continued influence in the subsequent study of recollection in Plato see Dancy (2004, esp. 254 n. 2) and Fine 2003 (Scott credits her for making him think in this direction [see Scott 1995, 16 n. 4 and 54 n. 1]). Sedley 2006, n. 9; Bobonich 2002; Dimas 2003, n. 13.

5. I will focus on Harte 2006, but see also Kelsey 2001, Franklin 2005, and Williams 2002.

Comparing Particulars to Forms

An exercise conducted by Harte (2006) provides a point of departure for my demonstration that Plato assumes that the ordinary person has unwitting cognitive contact with such things as equality itself. In order to understand both her exercise and my extension of it, let us look at the even wider context for the sticks and stones argument, which is Socrates's argument for the immortality of the soul at *Phaedo* 72–77. Socrates's strategy is to show that we have knowledge that we could not have acquired during our lifetime as we could not have acquired it through our senses. The idea seems to be that we have some other kind of inborn access to equality itself and that certain of our sense experiences can trigger us to make use of it in some manner or other.[6]

Let us summarize the larger argument:

1. If anyone recollects anything, she must have known it before. (73c1–3)

2. Recollection happens when a person perceives one thing and not only comes to know that thing but also comes to think of another thing, the knowledge of which is different from the first thing. (73c5–d1)

3. Examples designed to demonstrate 2: These consist of both triggers that are dissimilar and triggers that are similar to that of which they remind us. (73e5–10)

4. When the trigger for recollection is similar to the thing recollected one also has in mind whether the trigger's similarity falls short or is complete. (74a5–7)

5. The sticks and stones sub-argument that leads to the conclusion that equality is other than equal sticks and stones. (74b7–c5) (See chapter 2, 40).

---

6. I am being vague purposefully here about what we do with this inborn access. What our "use" of the Form amounts to and requires is clearly a deciding factor between views such as mine and those like Scott's. The purpose of Harte's exercise is to show that whatever we are doing with it does not necessitate the kind of robust relationship (already knowing the Form) that Scott assumes that it does.

6. We have come to grasp equality itself from equal things that are different from equality itself, whether they are similar or dissimilar to it. (74c7–12)

7. But, we see equal things as being deficient as compared to the equal itself. (74d8–10)

8. In order to see this deficiency, we must already have knowledge of the equal itself. (74d9–e4)

9. We must then have knowledge of the equal itself before we notice this deficiency. (74e9–75a3)

The examples of being reminded of one thing by another, which constitute 3 above, start with a lyre triggering a memory of a lover, and end with a more similar trigger; being reminded of Simmias by a picture of Simmias. Harte concludes that it is this last example that is supposed to be most analogous to being reminded of equality by equal sticks and stones. I take it that this is because it seems appropriate to describe it as something "wanting to be like some other reality, but falling short," as Socrates declares is part of the experience at 74d10–e1 (7, above).[7] She takes this to partner with the next statement (8, above), which alludes to the comparison that is the focus of Scott's revised interpretation. In the case of the sticks and stones, one sees them as distinct from equality itself because one additionally has in mind that the sticks and stones are striving to be like equality but fall short of, and are inferior to, it.[8]

Harte then conducts the exercise that will be our entry point into the question of what the contact of ordinary people with the Forms consists in and how Forms allow us to gain an epistemological foothold.[9] Harte

---

7. Harte's translation (2006, 25) of this sentence is [it is necessary that] "one have in mind whether or not the [reminding thing] is lacking in respect of likeness to that of which it reminds one?" (74a6–7). ἐννοεῖν εἴτε τι ἐλλείπει τοῦτο κατὰ τὴν ὁμοιότητα εἴτε μὴ ἐκείνου οὗ ἀνεμνήσθη;

8. This is a paraphrase of 74e9–75a2 (34). ἀναγκαῖον ἄρα ἡμᾶς προειδέναι τὸ ἴσον πρὸ ἐκείνου τοῦ χρόνου ὅτε τὸ πρῶτον ἰδόντες τὰ ἴσα ἐνενοήσαμεν ὅτι ὀρέγεται μὲν πάντα ταῦτα εἶναι οἷον τὸ ἴσον, ἔχει δὲ ἐνδεεστέρως.

9. Harte follows a suggestion by Gosling (1965).

sketches out three scenarios to illustrate the position of the person who is—so to speak—comparing equal sticks and stones to equality itself.[10]

> E1 A person sees a lifelike wax statue of Simmias, but doesn't know that it is a representation of some person named Simmias. They are told "this is Simmias" and assume that Simmias is the name of this particular statue.
>
> E2 A person who knows Simmias and knows that Simmias is a person sees a lifelike wax statue of Simmias and, thinking it is Simmias, greets it and attempts to shake its hand.
>
> E3 A person sees a lifelike statue of Simmias and recognizes that it is a representation of Simmias the person and is reminded of Simmias by it.[11]

Clearly, the person who succeeds in distinguishing equal sticks from equality itself is supposed to be analogous to the person in E3. As Harte emphasizes, however, the person who mistakes equality for equal sticks and stones is supposed to be analogous to the person in E2, not E1. For the remainder of this book, I will call being in a position analogous to the person in E1 "being in E1" and will use the same type of locution to refer to anyone who is analogous to the person in E2 or E3. This person in E2 is supposed to understand that Simmias is a person and merely mistakes the statue for that person. Thus, *Simmias the person* is featured in the mind of the person who makes the mistake in E2, but not in E1. So, what does this imply about the person who mistakes equal sticks and stones for equality itself? That person—being in E2—assumes they are looking at equality itself; equality itself is featured in their mind. This person is different from the person in E1. The person who is in E2 in the

---

10. In a footnote (2006, 25 n. 10), Harte diagnoses Scott's own view (D). She suggests it is necessitated by his apparent supposition that if Plato commits himself to the claim that everyone compares particulars to the Forms, he must be thinking that people consciously focus their attention on, for example two sticks—either unequal or equal—and then consciously focus their attention on the Form of the Equal, comparing the two to see if the first falls short of the second. Harte goes on to suggest that this contact with the Form is unwitting, as do Franklin (2005, 295) and Kelsey (2001, n. 11).

11. I am here conflating a number of her examples so as to make her point as efficiently as I can.

wax museum understands that there is an actual person who is Simmias. So, by analogy, the person who is in E2 while looking at equal sticks and stones takes there to be an equality itself. Presumably, the person in E2 assumes the statue has all of the capacities of Simmias the person (this is why they try to shake his hand). Analogously the person in E2, who thinks equal sticks and stones are equality itself, assumes that the sticks and stones are equality itself, which includes the assumption that these particulars can do whatever equality itself can do. The person in E2 thinks that, as Simmias is an actual person, there could also be images of him that are not actual people. Likewise, the person in E2, while regarding equal sticks and stones as equality itself, thinks that equality itself can be represented by things other than equality itself. This person thinks that it is possible for equality itself to be represented by something other than it and that they at times look at something that only represents, but is not, equality.[12] Perhaps a painting that shows a pair of scales perfectly balanced with grain on one side and weights of stone on the other would be understood as a representation of equality by someone who thinks equality itself is identical to perceptible objects. The critical thing is that even though the person in E2 knows that there can be mere representations of equality, they think that in the case of the sticks and stones they are looking at equality itself rather than at a representation of it. Whether they realize it or not, this person is committed to the existence of an equality itself (whatever it turns out to be) to be looked at and represented. As Harte puts it, the person in E2 does not recognize their misidentification of two things with one another.[13]

---

12. This is my own explanation for why the second example represents the person who thinks equality is equal sticks and stones. Harte does not provide one.

13. This point can be confusing as the two situations are not analogous with respect to E2's background beliefs. The first E2 person was someone who "knows Simmias and knows that Simmias is a person." The exact correspondence in the case of equality itself might be: "The person in E2 knows equality itself and knows that it is an intelligible form." But that cannot be Plato's point in speaking of recollecting from things that do or do not fall short of equality. It would be absurd for someone who knew this to identify equality itself with equal sticks and stones (that is something like Scott's point). The disanalogy is that in the original case, we are not talking about "dormant knowledge" that Simmias is a person. The original E2 person's knowledge that Simmias is a person seems perfectly conscious. It seems to us that the person who identifies equality itself with equal sticks and stones is someone who is familiar with the *expression* "equality itself" but does not realize that it refers to something

The person in E2 takes themselves to be thinking about only one thing, but in order for their thinking to be true or false, and to be correctable through proper experience or instruction, they must, according to Harte, have equality itself in mind. I encourage us to interpret this relationship as I have in the last chapter: this person must at least have unwitting cognitive contact with equality itself. Thus, they somehow have equality itself "in mind" even while mistakenly thinking that it is identical with equal sticks and stones (2006, 29–30). It is the fact that they are in some sort of cognitive contact with equality itself that allows them to think this and—at the same time—to be wrong about what equality itself is when they identify it with sticks and stones.

Thus, Harte thinks that the person in E2 has the materials to make the comparison that Scott highlights, but does not come to make it.[14] She identifies the person in E2 with the ordinary person. There is much to be said for an interpretation like Harte's over Scott's: all philosophers are born ordinary people, and Scott's account lacks any explanation for how budding philosophers first come to agree that there is an incorporeal equal

---

other than equal sticks and stones and believes, wrongly, that it is just a way to refer to all equal particulars. Plato's point, however, is that this same person will admit that this use of the expression readily breaks down once the person is put in a situation where it becomes apparent that equal sticks and stones cannot play the role in the sentences in which he uses "equality itself" while maintaining the truth values of those sentences, just as the original person's assumption that this entity before him is Simmias cannot stay true once he tries to shake its hand. Thus, the E2 person assumes and readily admits that in using the expression "equality itself" he is trying to refer to whatever equality itself actually is and is more than happy to have it override any mistaken beliefs that he happens to have that render beliefs that are more important to him (such as equality ≠ inequality) false. I am grateful to an anonymous reviewer for pointing this out.

14. As for the third example above, Harte thinks it is a clear case of making a comparison between the statue of Simmias and Simmias himself, so that we both see it as a representation of him and do not mistake it for him. However, she is comfortable saying that this comparison is commonplace and needn't be the focus of our attention when we make it. So, she concludes—contrary to Scott—that this can also be true in the case of our noticing that sticks and stones fall short of equality (2006, 26). The comparison that Scott says is only made overtly is, according to Harte, made inattentively when we see that a picture is of Simmias, so we can also make it inattentively when we see that sticks and stones reflect, but are not identical to, equality. Kelsey (2001, 95–96) sees acquisition of cognitive contact and comparison happening simultaneously.

itself to use for comparison.[15] She also allows for an account of why all souls and not just those of philosophers will be immortal if the argument succeeds (2006, 38).

Plato resolves {B} by alluding to a resolution of the problem of reference. He is forced to do it this way because there is no route from E1 to E2.[16] If one does not begin with some sort of cognitive contact with equality itself—at least one that is unwitting—we are at a loss to explain how it comes into one's cognitive repertoire. Equality itself is not perceivable, and the only way into the cognition of embodied human beings is via perception. A perceptible that has never been experienced is cognized for the first time through nerves, light waves, motion, etc. However, none of these can allow our cognitive faculties to become aware of things that do not succumb to motion in the form of light waves, sound waves, or other kinds of motion that stimulate nerves.[17]

The person who starts in E1 could never become the person in E2 because a person who cannot refer to the actual Simmias and can only refer to the statue cannot think or talk about Simmias the person. Thus, such a person cannot question whether or not Simmias is identical to the statue. If someone were truly in E1, that is, if someone could only make cognitive contact with the perceptible sticks and stones or the wax statue, then that person would not be able to have the statements "Simmias is the statue" or "The sticks are equal" be false. They could not inquire into who or what Simmias actually is or what equality actually is.[18]

---

15. Williams (2002, 150) makes this point concerning Scott's lack of an explanation for how the philosopher evolves: on Scott's account, it is not clear that it is possible for ordinary people and philosophers to communicate (See also Franklin, 2005, 296 n. 11) or for the transition from ordinary person to philosopher to take place (Franklin 2005, 308 n. 33). Harte does not make this point.

16. If Plato has a solution to the paradox of discovery—to the ending problem {E} from Meno's paradox—that will align with some explanation of how we get from E2 to E3.

17. Although theories of perception have changed since Plato's time, he also conjectured that motion is necessary in order for perception to take place in an embodied human being. See *Theaet.* 156a-157c and Reshotko (1994, 145).

18. Kripke's (1980, 67-68) examples using the biblical characters of Moses and Jonah can be used to make the same point. If the person who thinks that Simmias *is* the statue manages to think about it by "defining" Simmias as the statue, then he thinks something like, "Simmias is necessarily the statue." As a result, this person cannot ask himself if he has maybe mistaken a representation of Simmias for the actual Simmias. This is what it is like to be in E1. The person in E1 cannot fathom the

Plato's point in introducing recollection is—at least—to show that inquiry is possible by showing that we are born in E2; we are born already in some sort of cognitive contact with those abstract objects, such as equality itself, that make our beliefs true and false. Thus, there is no need to account for a transition from E1 to E2. Of course, few people who believe that there is only the perceptible world give any thought to whether they are in E1 or E2. However, Plato shows that ordinary people can be assumed to be in E2 because their beliefs about such things as equality and beauty can be shown to commit them to the existence of things such as equality itself in addition to equal sticks and stones even if they mistakenly identify equal sticks and stones with equality itself. This commitment is inconsistent with any belief they have that equality itself is *necessarily* identical to, and exhausted by, perceptible objects. It is inconsistent with any prejudice they might harbor concerning the impossibility that things other than perceptibles exist or that equality itself might be one of those imperceptibles. It happens that Plato also shows that this inconsistency works in their favor when it comes to inquiry and learning. It is an inconsistency that can be exploited by interrogation; these inconsistent beliefs can be pulled apart and once the inconsistency becomes apparent it can prompt an inquiry. The hope is that the recognition of this inconsistency can motivate the person who held those inconsistent beliefs to journey from E2 to E3 and beyond. If an ordinary person believes that there are only perceptible objects, yet she assents to claims about perceptible objects that she herself can come to see could not possibly be true of them, this allows Plato to see, to show us, and to show the ordinary person, the extent to which they are already in touch with the Forms.

---

duality required to ask herself whether or not Simmias or equality itself are actually other than the thing she has taken them for. Someone might object to my claim that no one who can learn is truly in E1 and that nonphilosophers are thus in E2, by saying that E1 appears to be a common type of error and that it is problematic to have a theory that cannot account for it. However, it is only cases such as mistaking a lifelike wax figure for a person that are common. Cases that constitute being in E1 with respect to something such as equality itself appear to be quite uncommon. If they were common, few readers would grasp what Plato is trying to do with the sticks and stones argument. I am arguing that anyone who can come to see the point of the sticks and stones argument and the arguments against the lovers of sights and sounds at *Rep.* 479–480 only appears to be mistaking perceptibles for equality itself (even if they themselves thought they were saying that equal perceptibles = equality itself). Of course, one *might* make this mistake in the wax museum (mistaking one *perceptible* for another), but no one thinks to themselves these sticks and stones *are* the *abstract object* equality itself.

The theory of recollection solves the beginning problem by explaining why and how we can inquire. It explains this by asserting that we have unwitting cognitive contact with things that are beyond the limits of our sense experience—the kind of cognitive contact that must be made by the person who mistakenly identifies equal sticks and stones with equality itself. This is what we have now identified as E2.

The evidence for the claim that there is a cognitive connection between ordinary people and the Forms in the *Phaedo* depends, in part, on who the audience of the sticks and stones argument (74b7–c5) is supposed to be. Scott argues that the audience must be people who are already philosophers (who are in E3 or beyond). He does this by focusing on the reference of the pronoun *we* throughout the passage. Scott argues that the *we* of the *Phaedo*'s recollection passage (75d7–76d6) does not refer "predominantly" to ordinary people.[19] He finds places where it uncontroversially refers only to Socrates's inner circle. He then asserts that maintaining that in some cases the *we* refers only to philosophers, while allowing it to refer to ordinary people in all other cases, forces the reference of the pronoun to veer back and forth randomly.[20]

However, there is a cue in the text that switches the focus of the sticks and stones argument away from its actual interlocutor (Simmias). I speculate that it is Plato's intention to get his readers to insert themselves as interlocutors here. Socrates begins by securing Simmias's agreement that there is something that is equal that is not stick equal to stick or stone equal to stone (74a11–12). He asks Simmias if we have knowledge of it, and Simmias answers positively (74b3). He then asks if it is from sticks and stones that we acquired knowledge of this equal itself that is different from them (74b4–6) and without any interlocution on Simmias's part, immediately adds, "Or does it not seem other to you?" (74b6–7). It is at this point that Socrates launches into the three-line argument.

Why does Socrates ask, "Or does it not seem other to you?" when Simmias has, in essence, already agreed that it is "other"? I suggest that he does this in order to address an argument to those who are not inclined to agree with him and Simmias that equality is other than equal sticks and stones—those not in Socrates's inner circle (those in Socrates's inner circle are already philosophical and believe in the Forms). Socrates is only

---

19. Scott 1995, 65.

20. At 75c10–d3, Socrates refers to things over which "we" set the seal "what it is." Also, at 76d8–e1, Socrates says "we" are always talking about the beautiful and the good and referring all things to them.

rhetorically addressing this question to Simmias. Plato is turning Socrates's attention to the reader. He is going to try to persuade the ordinary people in his audience of something *despite* the fact that Simmias already believes it. The audience for this argument is people who occupy E2.[21] Plato also documents the ordinary person's unwitting cognitive contact with something other than perceptible objects in the *Meno*.

The *Meno*

We have already rehearsed Socrates's demonstration with the slave at *Meno* 82b–86c in chapter 1. Socrates provides Meno with a demonstration of how recollection works by having Meno call over a young slave who has never been formally educated. Drawing a square in the sand, Socrates first asks the slave how long the line upon which a square with twice the area of the original square must be. The slave answers Socrates's questions and eventually cites the wrong line as the answer to the question (83b7). When Socrates shows him that his answer is wrong, the slave admits to being in *aporia* (84a1). Socrates walks the slave through the steps of discovering that, in order to make a square twice as big as the first square, they will have to draw a square on the diagonal of the first square. Mostly Socrates asks the slave questions to which the answers are either yes, no, or a low number. Socrates emphasizes to Meno that he just asks questions and never tells the slave what to say. At 84e4–85a1, Socrates shows the slave the diagonal and by 85b2 the slave recognizes that it is the line for which they have been searching. The diagonal is a concept that he has not entertained before, but the slave seems to recognize it as the thing for which they were looking: the base upon which they can draw a square with twice the area of the original square. This demonstrates what Meno's paradox denied could happen and they conclude that the slave must have found the knowledge within himself, so he has recollected (85c–d).[22]

---

21. Thus, the appearance of Forms at *Phdo.* 65–66 is not evidence against the claim that *Phdo.* 74b–c is an argument for their existence as the earlier conversation is directed toward Simmias in his own person and not beyond him to an audience of "philosophically naive readers" or ordinary people.

22. In defense of his D, Scott asserts that the young slave does not begin to recollect until Socrates starts to ask him questions in the proper order (82e); everything that

The text shows the useful inconsistency contained in the beliefs and commitments the slave has brought to the exercise and gives evidence that he is already in E2 and in touch with Forms such as the square itself and the diagonal itself at the beginning of the encounter with Socrates. As I will now show, it does this by having the slave give voice to beliefs that could not ever be about mere particulars and cannot have come from an empirical source.[23] Plato appears to take pains to show that the slave refers to something other than the drawing in the sand even before 82e where Socrates first has Meno observe him recollecting. This shows that the slave is in touch with the Forms. The structure of these beliefs harbors the inconsistencies that Socrates exploits. The relief of these inconsistencies allows for the eureka moments that occur when the slave separates the abstract geometrical objects from their perceptible instantiations. This draws the slave toward E3.

Socrates begins his discussion with the slave at 82b9 by drawing a square in the sand and checking that the young slave knows "that a square figure is such as this" (*tetragônon chôrion hoti toiouton estin*). Note that Socrates does not simply call the figure in the sand "a square figure"; Socrates does not take himself to be speaking about the perceptible figure drawn in the sand. What does the slave take Socrates to be talking about? If he is in E1, it must be the figure in the sand; the young slave is exercising his ordinary knowledge, which, according to Scott, is purely empirical. If he is in E1, then prior to 82e, he will say nothing that he did not learn through his senses and will not refer to any objects to which his soul was connected from before birth.

However, the text tells otherwise, after the slave agrees that the square is such a figure and that it has all four sides equal and lines through the middle that are equal, Socrates poses the question, "Isn't it the case that

---

he brings with him to that moment is purely empirical and was learned in Meno's household, not through recollection. This, Scott concludes, is more consistent with his interpretation than with the traditional one because, in the traditional view, recollection is involved with even the mundane concepts that the slave brings to the exercise with Socrates. Scott is in essence claiming that the slave was in E1 prior to the moment when Socrates helps him to recollect "in the proper order" (1995, 35).

23. Perhaps the beliefs are acquired at the moment of recollection, but the objects to which they refer were already (and always were) available to the slave to have beliefs about.

such a figure can be larger and smaller?" (82c4).[24] Assuming that Socrates drew the square freehand in the sand it is hard to believe that the four sides even *appeared* equal to one another. The slave's agreement to the statement that they are equal is a clue that he does not understand Socrates's question to be about the perceptible square in the sand *alone*. But, even leaving that aside, why does Plato bother to have Socrates ask the question about the figure being both larger and smaller? The person who is really in E1 would find this a very strange question indeed. The person in E1 cannot automatically understand "such a figure" (understood as "a figure like this one") as "a figure that has this shape (is a square) but is different in *other* properties (properties that are irrelevant to its identity as a square)." It is only if one already understands that there something like "being a square," that is independent of all physical properties that this particular instance of a square has, that one can see that Socrates hereby intends to be speaking of *anything* with this *same* shape no matter what other (irrelevant to being a square) properties it has.[25] Socrates is using this phrase to communicate to the slave that he is *not* talking about the particular square in the sand. Moreover, the slave's answer—if it can be taken at face value[26]—indicates that the slave also—whether he realizes it or not—is not talking about the figure in the sand or even the collection of all of the perceptible squares that he has seen in his life. No individual perceptible square can be larger and smaller than it is.

The claim that the square can be bigger and smaller is not about the particular square in the sand. It is not about (or true of) any particular square. The slave's lack of confusion when asked the question, let alone his assent to the claim, shows the slave is thinking about something other than the particular square in the sand or particular squares in the sand in general. Plato takes the slave to have access to an abstract square; even if the slave himself does not recognize or understand it and even if he has not yet fully recollected it. In understanding the question, and in answering it correctly, we might say that the slave has formed beliefs *about*

---

24. οὐκοῦν εἴη ἂν τοιοῦτον χωρίον καὶ μεῖζον καὶ ἔλαττον;

25. That is, unless one already understands what a square is and that it cannot be reduced to all of the individual particular squares, one cannot know what a "figure like this," namely, one that has these (square-identifying) features but not others, is.

26. So, leaving aside the question of whether the young slave is too intimidated to say what he actually thinks or follows nonverbal cues to say what he does say.

the square *itself,* but these beliefs are triggered by the visible figure. The young slave—unconcerned that the particular square does not exhibit the property that has been attributed to it—seems to readily think "beyond" the square in the sand and this shows that he is not in E1.[27]

There is no need to pinpoint when recollection began but, clearly, the slave is in touch with the square itself from before Socrates tells Meno to watch the slave recollect. Plato could simply understand our having recollected as our having a connection to the Form in our soul that allows us to be in E2.[28] There is insufficient textual evidence to conclude that the slave does not recollect before the moment when Socrates directs Meno to attend to his doing so.[29] The text does not say that the slave is only now beginning to recollect. It says that he will now "recollect things in order as it is necessary to recollect" (82e12–13). If things have to be discovered in a certain order, then having an interrogator (especially one who knows the answer) will facilitate and accelerate recollection. So, Socrates could simply be making recollection overt enough for Meno to observe it rather than affording the young slave the first recollection experience of his lifetime.[30]

---

27. The Pythagorean Theorem, used in the demonstration, also discloses a truth that cannot be demonstrated empirically—that the hypotenuse of the right triangle is incommensurable with its leg. This is a feature of the square (that the side is incommensurate with the diagonal) that is now becoming part of the young slave's overt understanding. It is something that he could not have learned empirically. Scott could argue that the Slave is already recollecting at this point in the demonstration and is aware of the Form through Socrates's overt efforts to aid his recovery of this truth from within himself. But, what of Pythagoras who managed to uncover this truth without a teacher guiding him to recollect "in proper order" and without the aid of a trained dialectician? Throughout his struggle to unearth the proof, Pythagoras was in touch with the square (or right triangle or diagonal) *itself.* Williams (2002, 140) makes the point that Pythagoras must have recollected. Scott thinks it plausible to understand Pythagoras's beliefs as different in kind from the slave's (1995, 43).

28. It could be this innate connection that is a prerequisite for {B} that is doing the work. If this is the case, the argument in the *Phdo.* would demonstrate that there is this thing to which we have access and would be an argument for the existence of the Forms, something that Scott has to deny (1995, 58–59).

29. Scott regards it as obvious that the slave is not recollecting before that moment (1995, 35).

30. Socrates's statement that all seeking and learning are recollection (81d4–5) would seem to underwrite this as well.

An Unwitting Cognitive Connection

Plato shows us that ordinary people start by thinking that their concepts and beliefs are about perceptible particulars and are drawn by philosophy to break away from that presupposition:[31] the ordinary person's beliefs must be about the same things as the philosopher's; otherwise, we could not think of the ordinary person's beliefs as *deceptive*. Therefore, the ordinary person's thought is constrained by—and is about—the same objects as the philosopher's. Scott acknowledges that there must be a link between ordinary concepts and the Forms. But, he claims that it is purely ontological and not cognitive (Scott 1995, 68–69).

Scott illustrates this point with an analogy:

> One person sees the original of a painting in a museum; another sees a forgery. They have similar representations in their minds not because they have communicated with each other, but because there is a similarity between the objects themselves. (1995, 69)

Certainly, there is a strong ontological connection between the Form and the particular. However, Plato shows something beyond that. He shows us that a young slave prior to recollection is *thinking about* Forms despite the fact that he would not characterize himself that way, just as the slave was thinking about diagonals before he could characterize himself that way. His coming to have the ability to characterize himself that way comes from his recognition that his beliefs cannot be about perceptible particulars on pain of being false.[32] Prior to becoming aware of the inconsistency in his beliefs, he does not recognize that his beliefs are about the Form and does not have beliefs that can count as knowledge even if they are true. If he has true beliefs about the Form, he does not understand what they are about or discern that it is possible for some beliefs to be truer of that same Form than others are. But, he is in touch with it. He is working, *cognitively*, with something beyond sense experience and with something that was not given to him through sense experience. This is certainly more

---

31. Scott treats this as an impossibility (1995, 5–7).
32. He might also have to learn some vocabulary, such as "diagonal."

than an ontological relationship. I call it cognitive because it is *activated* by the slave's *thoughts* and *intentions*. To return to Scott's analogy: if Julie unwittingly looks at an accurate forgery of a Van Gogh—knowing neither that it is a forgery, nor that it is a forgery of a Van Gogh—and says, "That painting's creator has a great sense of motion and color," Julie intends to speak about whoever the painter of the original painting (not the forgery) actually was and succeeds in doing so. In this case, she, without realizing it, speaks about Van Gogh and says something true or false about him. Still, Julie is tremendously mixed up about what she is attributing to whom. Julie is unwittingly looking past the forgery and speaking about the original painting and the original artist, because that is her intention. Yet, she does so in a challenging situation that makes it very hard to analyze the veridicality of her statement. This is again an illustration of E2. Julie manages to come in contact with the original's painter without properly distinguishing the original from the copy.[33] Further, Julie's contact with the original goes beyond an ontological relationship. She intends to comment about the artist of the original (Van Gogh) and she succeeds in doing so by intending for her comment to be about that artist without realizing that she is not talking about the creator of the painting at which she gazes.

Conclusion

There is evidence to suggest that Plato assumes and relies upon an ordinary person's unwitting cognitive contact with Forms in order to make plausible

---

33. At *Phdo.* 74a5–7, Socrates notes that when recollecting from similar things we are also compelled to consider whether the trigger that prompted our recollection falls short of the Form or whether its resemblance to the Form is complete. Even here, this must certainly be done through having some contact with the Form, and not only by those who know the Form. We can see that it is done by ordinary people who (according to Scott's—and my own—criteria) don't know the Form. We introduce the sticks and stones argument to undergraduate students with little philosophical exposure every day in our classes and we assume that they see its point. They understand that the equality of sticks and stones is being shown to be "other than" equality itself, even if they—by many other measures—are often wrong about equality itself. They couldn't comprehend the way the argument works if they themselves did not have in mind something other than sticks and stones to which they could come to understand "equality itself" to refer. That is, they could not do this if they were not in E2.

his examples of recollection. There are even moments when Plato appears to take pains to make his presupposition that everyone begins inquiry with unwitting contact with the Forms overt. Perhaps Plato believes he should hint at this presupposition to force his readers to struggle with the same question that he is struggling to answer: How are we able to grasp our object of inquiry sufficiently in a way that allows our inquiry to be about a particular object, let alone *that* particular object? Plato wants this presupposition to occur to his readers so that they are equally able to struggle with the only answer that he himself can find to give: we are *all*—slaves, ordinary people, nonphilosophers and philosophers alike—endowed, somehow, with an unwitting, but cognitive, relationship with objects that are beyond our sense experience and that, nevertheless, regulate our sense experience.

Chapter 4

Nonphilosophers and Beauty Itself in *Republic* V

Nowhere outside of the *Meno*, *Phaedo*, and *Phaedrus* does Plato explicitly commit himself to recollection, nor is there any dialogue in which he rejects it explicitly. Still, as I suggested in the introduction (15–17), even though Plato appears to give up on uncovering and accounting for why we can have unwitting cognitive contact with things such as the diagonal itself via recollection, he appears to rely on the fact that we do have this type of contact with what come to be known as his Forms even after he ceases to advocate for recollection. In the introduction, I compared Plato's way of handling recollection to what Nathan (2021) calls "black boxing" in science. Theorists can choose to isolate a phenomenon and label it and then use that label as a placeholder for whatever would account for it even though they are either not equipped to, or not interested in, filling out an account of the phenomenon at the time. This allows them to move on and continue to make use of the theory. Later, they, or someone else, might try to give an account of what is in the black box. Meanwhile, the theory has been able to go on and serve as the basis for further scientific discovery. Both Mendel and Darwin can be understood as having embraced this kind of strategy.

In the *Meno* and *Phaedo*, Plato isolates the phenomenon that people manage to refer to things that they neither possess true beliefs about nor know. They do this when they launch inquiries concerning them. They even seem to understand when someone proposes an inquiry that is about something that they have never experienced. Since it is necessary to solve the beginning problem before he can go on to talk about belief and knowledge, this is a phenomenon for which Plato must either account or make a placeholder before he can continue to explore epistemology. However, in these two dialogues, he is also interested in the immortality of the soul. As a result, he fills in the explanation for the phenomenon that he has framed in a way that overshoots the beginning problem. The phenomenon that he wished to account for is our ability to refer to something with which we are unacquainted. He demonstrates our ability to do something that relies on this reference, but only really addresses the claim that, *given that we can make this kind of reference*, we must have immortal souls.

I propose that Plato stops talking about "recollection" as an explanation for why we can make this kind of reference once he ceases to argue for the immortality of the soul. However, after he moves on and leaves any overt commitment to recollection behind, Plato continues to assume that *something* solves the beginning problem. He assumes that all people have an unexplained capacity for this unwitting cognitive contact with things like his Forms—the kinds of things that Plato thinks will be the object of any knowledge we might ever be able to acquire.

In this chapter, I show Plato assuming (without trying to explain) the kind of reference that resolved {B} (by solving {R}) in the dialogues that focused on recollection. There is evidence in the *Republic* that Plato believes that all people have an unwitting cognitive relationship with abstract objects like equality itself. This same evidence shows that here, too, Plato holds that this contact is what allows our beliefs to be *about* whatever determines their truth-values. This contact allows our beliefs to be about things such as beauty itself. In other words, outside of the dialogues that discuss recollection, Plato frequently shows nonphilosophers in possession of some kind of unwitting ability to refer to things like equality itself and beauty itself. He shows them in possession of this ability because otherwise they would not be able to do what he describes them as doing. Sometimes it is under the guise of beginning an inquiry, as in {B}, and sometimes it is not. I now proceed to call attention to Plato's assumption that we are all able to have this unwitting cognitive contact with abstract objects (like his Forms) even in the absence of any attempt to 'explain' why we have it through the theory of recollection.[1]

---

1. I am not sure that we should ever have counted the theory of recollection as an explanation. Even in Plato's mind, it could simply be the concession that there is a mysterious phenomenon that he has chosen to black box so that he can move on.

Evidence from *Republic* V shows that those Plato refers to as "lovers of opinion" or "lovers of sights and sounds" (*philotheamones*) also have unwitting contact with the Forms. In *Republic* VI, Plato claims that everyone refers to and thinks about the Form of the Good. In *Republic* VII, even the prisoners at the very bottom of the famous cave refer to and make use of the Forms unwittingly. Farther into *Republic* VII, an exercise designed to train philosophers can also provoke ordinary people to turn their attention to abstract ideas.

Republic 475e4–479d5: The Lovers of Sights and Sounds

After declaring at *Republic* 473c11–d3 that cities will have no respite from evil until philosophers rule as kings or kings become philosophers, Socrates and Glaucon try to figure out who the philosophers are. When Socrates asserts that they are insatiable for every kind of knowledge, Glaucon assumes that he is referring to lovers of sights and sounds. Then at 475e4–479d5, Socrates explains to Glaucon how to distinguish lovers of sights and sounds from philosophers.

While lovers of sights and sounds are perhaps more voracious in pursuit of sights and sounds than are those in the general population, textual evidence shows that Plato finds their self-described ontologies to be like those of the ordinary person. The lover of sights and sounds is presented by Plato as someone who, when asked outright, rejects the notion that there are abstract objects. He rejects the existence of some, single, beauty itself that exists in addition to the many beautiful particulars.[2] A close look at the text surrounding this passage makes this clear: the lovers of sights would deny the existence of beauty itself, thus, in

---

2. Penner (1987, 20–25, 57–140) is noteworthy for his identification of the lovers of sights and sounds with nominalists. Penner's point is to identify them with people who believe that all there is to beauty itself is beautiful sights and sounds. They are ordinary people who take the naive stance that perceptibles are all that exists. They are not metaphysicians who walk around reciting to themselves the considered philosophical view, "I am a nominalist." Scott (1995, 78) uses the lovers of sights and sounds as examples of ordinary people. He points out that at 476b, it is stated that lovers of sights and sounds love beautiful sounds, but their thought is unable to "go to the beautiful itself" and that those who can go to the beautiful itself would be few and those few would be philosophers. This sets up Scott's extension of his own interpretation of recollection-type reasoning into these middle books of the *Rep.* even though he, no doubt, concurs that Plato does not commit himself to recollection there.

essence, describing themselves as in what we, in the last chapter, called E1 (476c2–3, 478d10–e1). Nevertheless, their beliefs about beautiful sights and sounds, and their behavior with respect to them, would allow us to assign them to E2.[3] *Republic* 475e4–479d5 describes the strategy by which Socrates makes the dissonance in their beliefs become apparent, at least to us, if not to them. Plato appears to think that this inconsistency is part of what allows the ordinary person to be a potential philosopher: Every ordinary person has latent beliefs that demonstrate their disposition to manifest particular beliefs about things such as beauty and equality. When these latent beliefs themselves become occurent (perhaps under Socrates's questioning) they compel that person to acknowledge the need for abstract objects—such as the Forms—in their ontology.

As we have already noted, the discussion of the lover of sights and sounds grows out of Glaucon's inability to distinguish them from lovers of truth based on Socrates's explanation of the philosopher at 475b8–9 and 475c6–8. Glaucon is concerned that those described will include lovers of sights and sounds, and so he and Socrates set out to distinguish lovers of sights and sounds from lovers of truth. Socrates surprises Glaucon by asserting that the lovers of sights and sounds resemble philosophers (475e2). In response to Glaucon's incredulity, Socrates initiates what will become a lengthy argument that is interspersed throughout the text from 475e6 to 479c5. In this argument, he is ostensibly showing the difference between the lover of sights and sounds and the philosopher. As Socrates

---

3. The application of E1–3 to the lovers of sights and sounds would work as follows:

> E1 This person thinks that there is no, one, beauty itself in addition to the many beautiful things and behaves accordingly, professing belief only in the many beautiful things.

> E2 This person believes that beauty itself is the many beautiful things (believes the statue is Simmias the person) and goes on to treat beauty itself as if it is the one thing that the many beautiful things have in common (tries to shake the statue's hand). This person can come to realize that she holds inconsistent beliefs. [My parentheses here show the relevant moment of the analogy, see chapter 3, 72, above.]

> E3 This person at least realizes that her behavior commits her to the existence of one beauty itself that exists in addition to the many beautiful things. Ultimately, such a person can come to know that there is one beauty itself and to understand the many beautiful things in virtue of it.

compares the lover of sights and sounds to the philosopher, he is also consoling the lover of sights and sounds, saying that while they compare unfavorably to philosophers, they are better off than those who are ignorant. As I interpret this consolation of the lovers of sights and sounds in the text, it is concurrent with, but separable from, a further important argument, made neither to Glaucon nor to the lover of sights and sounds, but to Plato's audience. This argument concerns such things as beauty itself and whether anyone's beliefs (especially those of the lovers of sights and sounds, but also, our own) are actually about abstract objects such as beauty itself. I now focus upon this concurrent argument. In chapter 7, I will look at some features of the overt argument that attempts to console the lovers of sights and sounds in my discussion of *doxa*.

Socrates prefaces the concurrent argument with the tacit claim that Glaucon might have exceptional views about beauty and ugliness: "It would not be easy to explain this to another, I said, but I believe that you will grant me this" (475e6–7). There is no evidence that any lovers of sights and sounds hear, or are convinced by, this concurrent argument. None are present, but they are interlocutors here, to the extent that Glaucon, on occasion, plays their role at Socrates's behest. I contend that Plato directs this argument to any readers who might be sympathetic to the position of the lovers of sights and sounds, and that he believes that there will be many. Plato creates the lovers of sights and sounds as a caricature of ordinary people and their underexplored appreciation of their own beliefs and ontological commitments. Thus, as I rehearse this concurrent argument, I use "lovers of sights and sounds" to refer to Plato's own characterization of his readers as caricatured by the lovers of sights and sounds. I am not limiting myself to making claims about what is overtly stated by a character called the lover of sights and sounds in the text. Plato is using the fictional lover of sights and sounds to draw his reader into the argument and to change his reader's mind.

The Concurrent Argument in Summary

Before extracting the argument for which Socrates's (above) comment to Glaucon sets the stage from the text, I offer the following outline of it:

> P1: since beauty and ugliness are opposites, they are two and each is one (475e9–476a2)

P2: (NI) beauty ≠ ugliness [from P1]

P3: (NM) beauty is not many and ugliness is not many [from P1]

But, the lover of sights and sounds believes that,

P4: (LSS1) beauty itself = beautiful sights and sounds (476b4–c8)

P5: (LSS2) ugliness itself = ugly sights and sounds (from P4)

P6: (LSS3) beautiful sights and sounds = ugly sights and sounds (478e7–479b2)

P7: P2 is inconsistent with P4–6

P8: P4–6 are inconsistent with P1–3

So,

C1: the lover of sights and sounds has inconsistent beliefs

P9: (implied) the lover of sights and sounds is unlikely to be willing to give up P1

C2: (implied) a reasonable lover of sights and sounds (or ordinary person reading the *Republic*) will forsake P4 in order to maintain P1 and will, as a result, no longer be a lover of sights of sounds (that is, he will move into the early stages of E3, which is the prerequisite for becoming a philosopher).

The Argument in Steps: *Socrates Singles out Glaucon*

As already stated, at 475e6–7, Socrates declares that he thinks Glaucon is special in his ability to grant that, since the beautiful is the opposite of the ugly, they are two, and so each is one. I assume that Plato intends for this to generalize to all opposites (and in fact we will see him make such a generalization at 479b3–10). From this statement, it follows that Socrates has also tacitly asserted (and Glaucon has already tacitly agreed to) the nonidentity of beauty and ugliness:

P2 (NI) beauty ≠ ugliness

Because he says that beauty and ugliness are each one, we can infer that Glaucon also thinks that:

P3 (NM) beauty is not many, and ugliness is not many.

The Lovers of Sights and Sounds hold Inconsistent Commitments

Socrates's point is brought into the sharpest relief when we focus upon (NM) as that which Glaucon is exceptional in his ability to accept. After all, the lovers of sights and sounds are unable to agree that there is only one beauty itself; lovers of sights and sounds think that beauty is a multiplicity. In contrast, everyone (Glaucon, the lovers of sights and sounds, and we the readers) seems to agree that beauty and ugliness are distinct. Plato's project is to show us that lovers of sights and sounds in particular—even though they might *want* to—cannot agree that beauty and ugliness are distinct. In fact, the argument is clearest when we see that Socrates is demonstrating that these two implied premises, (NI) and (NM), stand or fall together. These are two metaphysical claims, one of which the lover of sights and sounds (at least tacitly) accepts, namely (NI), and the other of which he (overtly) denies, namely (NM). However, they are intimately related in a way that is not apparent to the lover of sights and sounds. The fact that the lover of sights and sounds commits himself to one and not the other is a further symptom of the lack of consistency in his thoughts about his sense experience. It is by revealing that it is inconsistent to agree to (NI) and not (NM) that Socrates will move us, his audience, away from sympathizing with the lovers of sights and sounds toward embracing (NM). Let us look at how he does this.

Diagnosing the Supposed Ontology of the Lover of Sights and Sounds

At 476b4–c8, Socrates establishes the ontology of the lover of sights and sounds in a manner that appears to conform to E1:

> What about someone who believes in beautiful things, but doesn't believe in beauty itself and isn't able to follow anyone who could lead him to the knowledge of it? Don't you think

> he is living in a dream rather than a wakened state? Isn't this what it is to dream: if someone—whether asleep or awake—thinks a likeness is not a likeness but that which it resembles? (476c2–7, following Grube's translation)[4]

The lover of sights and sounds believes in beautiful things but not beauty itself and is unable to follow one who leads him to the knowledge of beauty itself. Thus, Socrates describes the lover of sights and sounds as living in a dream state even while awake. In a dream, I will see an elephant and, rather than thinking that I am having a phantasm that seems a lot like an elephant, I mistakenly believe that I am seeing an actual elephant. Likewise, the lover of sights and sounds sees individual beautiful perceptibles—a particular sunset, the Mona Lisa—and, mistakenly, believes he is seeing beauty itself. Thus, the lover of sights and sounds lives in a dream because he mistakes beautiful things for beauty itself, thinking that they are the referent of the term *beauty itself*, but still thinking other things about beauty itself (such as that it is distinct from ugliness itself) that are inconsistent with this belief. This description has the marks of E2.

The Relationship between the Lover of Sights and Sounds and Beauty Itself

An explanation is in order of why lovers of sights and sounds can think they reject the notion that beauty is one even while they occupy E2. The lover of sights and sounds thinks that beauty itself *is* the beautiful perceptibles in the world, just as the opponent in the sticks and stones argument thinks that equal sticks and stones are equality. Now, why is this analogous to the person in E2 who thinks that the wax statue is Simmias? After all, the person in E2 *already acknowledges* that Simmias exists and is a person, whereas the lover of sights and sounds does no such thing with equality itself and beauty itself. The point is that—even though they do not acknowledge it—Socrates is pointing out to the lovers of sights and sounds that, when it comes to beauty and beautiful perceptibles, they are behaving just like someone who believes the following:

---

4. ὁ οὖν καλὰ μὲν πράγματα νομίζων, αὐτὸ δὲ κάλλος μήτε νομίζων μήτε, ἄν τις ἡγῆται ἐπὶ τὴν γνῶσιν αὐτοῦ, δυνάμενος ἕπεσθαι, ὄναρ ἢ ὕπαρ δοκεῖ σοι ζῆν; σκόπει δέ. τὸ ὀνειρώττειν ἆρα οὐ τόδε ἐστίν, ἐάντε ἐν ὕπνῳ τις ἐάντ' ἐγρηγορὼς τὸ ὅμοιόν τῳ μὴ ὅμοιον ἀλλ' αὐτὸ ἡγῆται εἶναι ᾧ ἔοικεν;

[E2S] This wax statue is a person, and I can shake its hand just as I would a person's hand.

Clearly, that is something neither E2 nor the lover of sights and sounds would ever take themselves to believe—it is absurd. Clearly, with the statue, they immediately see for themselves that they mistook something that represents Simmias for Simmias himself. No one had to point out a problem with their beliefs. They never took themselves to believe, nor did they unbeknownst to themselves believe [E2S]. However, with beauty itself, Socrates does need to point out the absurdity of the lover of sights and sounds' beliefs in their relevantly similar situation. He points out that they behave just like someone who thinks:

[E2L]: The many beautifuls are beauty itself *and* they are also the many uglies, but *beauty itself is not ugliness itself.*

In this case, the behavior of the lover of sights and sounds is a clue to us and to them that they must unpack their own absurd, but unarticulated, belief. Socrates's goal is to point out to the lover of sights and sounds that they behave as if they hold this absurd belief. Once the lovers of sights and sounds see the absurdity of their belief, they (Plato assumes) are likely to change their belief and acknowledge that they mistook a representation of beauty for beauty itself.

[E2S] takes Simmias to be something than can be represented and [E2L] takes beauty itself to be something of which there could be representations. People with these absurd and unarticulated beliefs grant that there might be things that make us *think of* Simmias the person or beauty itself that are *other than* Simmias or beauty itself. However, in the case of each of these perceptible objects the person in E2 (the lover of sights and sounds) takes those representations to *be* beauty itself or Simmias the person rather than a representation of it. So each has, so to speak, two "blanks" in their thoughts: one for the thing itself (beauty itself, whatever it turns out to be, in the case of the lover of sights and sounds) and another for anything that might represent it. Their mistake is to think that these things they encounter *are* the things that they only *represent*. Thus, they also make the mistake of thinking that what they encounter *can do* what the actual things themselves can do (the person in E2 tries to shake hands with the wax representation of Simmias, the lover of sights and sounds thinks beautiful sights and sounds can be nonidentical with ugly sights and sounds). So, while the lovers of sights and sounds might take themselves to be in E1, they are actually in E2.[5]

Despite his occupation of E2, it makes sense to understand the lover of sights and sounds as believing that the perceptible world exhausts what-is.[6] His assumption that everything he talks about—including beauty itself—is a perceptible object is inconsistent with his latent belief that beauty itself ≠ ugliness itself. He thinks beauty is a (bunch of) perceptible object(s) at the same time as he thinks it is something like a criterion that allows him to distinguish beautiful things from ugly things. He can't have it both ways: either it is collection of beautiful things or it is the criterion by which we establish which things belong in that collection.

The lover of sights and sounds' view can be stated as an identity:

---

5. See Harte (2006, 26–27) for further textual arguments for understanding the lover of sights and sounds to be in E2 (i.e., making the same mistake as the person who thinks the wax statue is Simmias the person). Of course, the lover of sights and sounds never thinks to himself about either E1 or E2.

6. Fine (2003, 81) seems to get this wrong. She has the lovers of sights and sounds identify beauty with a particular adjective that they deem a cognate for beautiful: "The beautiful is the brightly colored." This cannot be how Plato was thinking. First, "brightly colored" is another abstract predicate and the lovers of sights and sounds will deny the existence of an abstract object that corresponds to it. Second, when we look at 479b, we see that the same will go for doubles/halves, bigs/smalls, lights/heavies. The argument would have Socrates elicit from the lover of sights and sounds that all brightly colored things are both brightly colored and dully colored. Thus, the lovers of sights and sounds are not simply making the mistake of using the wrong predicate to describe beauty itself. They are making the mistake of identifying beauty itself with the *extension* of the predicate beautiful. This is the same mistake we see interlocutors make at *Euph.* 5d, *Men.* 71e, and *Theaet.* 146d; when asked to identify an abstract noun, they give a list of perceptible particulars. The view that this is the mistake that Socrates finds these interlocutors making has been challenged by Nehamas (1999, 159–75) and Benson (2000, 100–108). They point out that a question like, "What is piety?" is not only ambiguous between universals and particulars (such as beauty and beautiful sights and sounds), but also between more general universals and more particular universals (such as "beauty" and "harmonious sounds"). Additionally, they claim that there is textual evidence that Socrates's interlocutors are offering universals as answers to the "What is F?" question. I would argue that the ambiguity between particular and universal carries over into these very "proof texts," which Nehamas and Benson must think are literally unambiguous. It seems to me a better understanding of what Plato is asserting the lovers of sights and sounds believe is the kind of thing we need *before* we attempt to disambiguate these texts.

(LSS1) beauty itself = beautiful sights and sounds.

Revealing the Inconsistency in the Lover of Sights and Sounds' Ontology

Stated as (LSS1), the lover of sights and sounds' ontology can be used to construct an argument the conclusion of which is also an identity. Although, Socrates does not articulate this argument to Glaucon or to the lover of sights and sounds, this is the concurrent argument that I contend Plato is making to his readers. We, Plato's readers—ordinary people—are being forced to feel the tension between our sympathy with Glaucon's agreement that beauty and ugliness are distinct and any instinct that might have drawn us toward the lovers of sights and sounds' identification of beauty with beautiful sights and sounds. We ordinary people who read Plato's texts are being shown that, whether we like it or not, our considered opinion should not be that when we say "beauty-itself" we are simply referring to all the beautiful sights and sounds.

The argument proceeds:

If (LSS1) beauty itself = beautiful sights and sounds

And (LSS2) ugliness itself = ugly sights and sounds

Then, (LSS3) [from 478e7–479b2] beautiful sights and sounds = ugly sights and sounds

Then, substituting for identicals, we get, (~NI) beauty itself = ugliness itself.

This conclusion can now be compared to the identity claim that has been attributed to Glaucon [(NI), beauty itself ≠ ugliness itself]. The lovers of sights and sounds cannot agree with Glaucon concerning (NI) due to their belief that,

(LSS1) beauty itself = beautiful sights and sounds.

It contradicts Glaucon's (NI).

Plato is not claiming that NI *logically* entails NM in some unqualified way, and neither am I. However, we must consider this in the context of the *professed* ontology of the lover of sights and sounds. The lovers of sights and sounds have argued that beauty itself is just another way of referring to the many beautiful sights and sounds and that ugliness itself works in a parallel manner. They have also agreed that the many beautiful sights and sounds are identical to the many ugly ones. So, if the fact that this would force beauty itself to *be* ugliness itself makes them want to reconsider that identity, they will need to reconsider the identity that led to it; namely, the claim that *all there is* to beauty itself (ugliness itself) is the many beautiful sights and sounds (ugly sights and sounds).[7]

An interlude (476e–478e) then follows during which Socrates tries to appease the lovers of sights and sounds. He tries to console them by saying that, while the lovers of sights and sounds do not have knowledge, they do have opinion rather than ignorance. Opinion, while it is worse than knowledge, is better than ignorance. As previously indicated, I consider this more overt argument in chapters 7 and 8.

Exploiting the Inconsistent Commitments of the Lover of Sights and Sounds

Let us further examine how Plato endeavors to have Socrates persuade any of his readers who might identify with the lovers of sights and sounds to embrace an ontology that extends beyond the perceptibles.[8] Socrates

---

7. The lovers of sights and sounds are presented at 476c2–7 as reductive eliminativists about beauty itself. Thus, if they give up on the identity of beauty itself with sights and sounds they will give up this eliminativist theory of beauty itself and will be forced to introduce some one beauty itself that exists in addition to beautiful things. (Of course, they could introduce a bunch of abstract beauties itself, but that would needlessly bloat their ontologies. Or, they might have believed only one thing was beautiful and not embraced NM as a contingent fact.) The point is that they must identify beauty with at least one abstract object and not with the many beautiful perceptibles. For them, that is giving up the claim that beauty itself is many, because the implication of their original claim is that beauty itself is many beautiful *sights and sounds*.

8. My interpretation parts ways with Fine's (2003, 66–84) early on. She rejects an existential reading of *esti* on the basis that it leads to a two-world theory. I also reject the two-world theory, but I believe that we can understand Plato to be using an existential *esti* without committing him to the two-world theory. See Penner 1987, 106–12, 206–31. I also disagree with Fine's claim that only a veridical *esti* can meet the "dialectical requirement" for the argument that begins at 476e (See Fine [2014, 48–55] for an extended description of the dialectical requirement, which she attributes to Irwin

begins his (imaginary—Glaucon is playing the lover of sights and sounds) cross-examination of the lover of sights and sounds at 478e7–479a1.[9] The argument that Socrates goes on to make is concise and thus requires elaboration. He elicits agreement from the lover of sights and sounds that every one of the beautiful things is also an ugly thing [P6 (LSS3)]. The argument is most easily appreciated when stated in terms of identities and nonidentities.

Recall that the lovers of sights and sounds believe:

P4 (LSS1) beauty itself = beautiful sights and sounds.

Thus, we should assume that they also believe:

P5 (LSS2) ugliness itself = ugly sights and sounds.

However, at 478e7–479b2 it is agreed that that every sight and sound that is beautiful is also ugly. In other words, the lovers of sights and sounds have agreed that:

(LSS3) beautiful sights and sounds = ugly sights and sounds.[10]

But what happens when we put (LSS1), (LSS2) and (LSS3) together?

[1977, 136–138]). The lovers of sights and sounds need only grant that what is known must exist and that what does not exist cannot be known (476e6–477a4) in order for the rest of the argument to proceed (well or poorly) by pushing these two premises plus the claim [knowledge ≠ belief ≠ ignorance] (477b5–6) to their logical conclusion. All of this is common sense. Socrates makes it clear that even he doesn't understand the conclusion to which they have been compelled by these assumptions (478e1–5): they still need to find out what can participate in both being and not being—*if there is such a thing*. This indicates that Plato himself does not think he has fully explained the realm of belief—of that which has both being and not being—at this point.

9. "These things having been laid down, let him speak to me, I will say, and let him answer me, that good man who does not believe in beauty itself or in any idea of it." The "good man" addressed here is the lover of sights and sounds (someone who does not believe in beauty itself or any idea of it).

10. Socrates continues by pointing out that this (P2) is the same for all opposites. By going through a somewhat random list of opposites (double/half, big/small, light/heavy). Because the list is random, he appears to be arguing that it is true of all opposites, not just those on the list.

(LSS1) beauty itself = beautiful sights and sounds

(LSS2) ugliness itself = ugly sights and sounds

(LSS3) beautiful sights and sounds = ugly sights and sounds[11]

When we take the transitivity of identity into account, we see that anyone who has come along this far is committed to a further identity:

(LSS4) beauty itself = ugliness itself.

Now we see why Socrates singled out Glaucon for his ability to believe:

(NI) beauty itself ≠ ugliness itself

even though it seemed completely uncontroversial to us at the beginning of the passage (475c6–8).

The Conversion of the Lover of Sights and Sounds

Plato has Socrates attempt to convert any of his readers who are sympathetic to the lovers of sights and sounds by showing us that they cannot maintain their views while distinguishing beauty from ugliness. If they think that "beauty" and "ugliness" refer to the same things, and they think that all there is for them to refer to are perceptible objects, then they must think that to say that something is beautiful is no different from saying that the thing in question is ugly. In other words, Socrates is making lovers of sights and sounds choose between two of their own conflicting convictions. Unless they are willing to reject (LSS3), they must choose between (LSS1) and (NI). Since the double itself and the half itself operate the same way as beauty itself and ugliness itself (479b3-4), rejecting (LSS3) would be tantamount to rejecting their belief that two drachmas are both double one drachma and half of four. The fact that they have—so

---

11. Perhaps some will find it unpersuasive that every beautiful thing is also ugly. If so, it is important to remember that Plato is eager to have you substitute any other pair of opposites for beauty and ugliness. Every large thing is also small, every double is also half, and every thick thing is also thin (*Rep.* 479ab).

far—tried to maintain both (LSS1) and (N1) is what demonstrates that they are in E2. I think that Plato assumes this is true of those among his readers who sympathize with the lovers of sights and sounds as well. To maintain (NI) is to commit to beauty itself and ugliness itself, each being one thing that is *other than* a perceptible.

Is showing that the lovers of sights and sounds will ultimately reject (LSS1) and (LSS2) tantamount to showing that they have an unwitting cognitive connection with an abstract object such as beauty itself? The tension between (LSS1), (LSS2) and the (Plato appears to believe) even stronger conviction in (LSS4) compels them to change their minds. This makes it apparent that they were already embracing (NI) and in so doing were wanting to refer to a beauty itself that was not just a bunch of perceptibles. In fact, whenever they (in the past) looked to a criterion by which to distinguish a beautiful perceptible from an ugly one, they did have cognitive contact with this sort of criterion even if they didn't realize that they were in contact with an abstract unity. They intended to look to a criterion that differentiated beautiful perceptibles from ugly ones and so intended to—and did—think about the kind of beauty itself that cannot have the nature of the one assumed in (LSS1). They had unwitting cognitive contact with an abstract beauty itself.

Thus, to commit to NI is to have that beauty itself, which is other than beautiful sights and sounds, featured in one's mind. It must be featured in one's mind in the same way that the person who mistakes a wax statue for Simmias himself has Simmias himself featured in his mind (see chapter 3, 71–75, above). Since the lover of sights and sounds is in E2, he is now able see and adjust his beliefs. This results from his recognition of the inconsistency between (NI) and (LSS1). He is able to note this inconsistency in his own prior beliefs because his beliefs about beauty itself have always been, and continue to be, about the same thing: a beauty itself that is not identical to, and exists in addition to, beautiful perceptibles.[12]

---

12. This interpretation meets Fine's "condition of non-controversiality" and "dialectical requirement" (2003, 68, 87). The lover of sights and sounds has conflicting convictions. It is the fact that they do not add up that forces him to introduce abstract objects into his ontology.

Can the Lovers of Sights and Sounds Resist?

Plato must also believe that everyone, even those who profess to be lovers of sights and sounds, has some inclination toward (NI) over (LSS1) and (LSS2), enough of an inclination that they will be willing to exchange these latter two for their negations:

(~LSS1) beauty itself ≠ beautiful sights and sounds

(~LSS2) ugliness itself ≠ ugly sights and sounds.

There is at least one good reason why everyone should be motivated to change their minds and accept (NI), (~LSS1), and (~LSS2) over their original convictions: they use the words *beauty* and *ugliness* to convey opposites.

Someone might object that the lovers of sights and sounds have an option that Plato has not considered: can't they agree that "beauty itself" and "ugliness itself" *refer* to the same things while maintaining that they *mean* different things? However, Plato can respond that no one has this option. Someone who believes only in the perceptible world must maintain that beauty and ugliness are reducible to perceptibles in a way that eliminates anything additional that might be a "meaning"; they have nothing like what Frege called a "sense" in their ontology. If all that exists are perceptibles, then "meaning" cannot refer to something other than perceptibles. If meaning exists and is distinct from reference, then both meaning and reference will have to reduce to perceptibles. So, someone with the professed ontology of the lovers of sights and sounds cannot say that, while "beauty itself" *refers* to sights and sounds, it *means* something other than sights and sounds. This use of *meaning* is an effort to refer to at least one abstract object. Anyone who speaks this way has, thereby, posited something (the meaning of the word *beauty*) that exists as an abstract object that is not identical to the abstract object that is the meaning of the word *ugliness*. That is, if meaning ≠ reference, then meanings must be something other than individual (or groups of) perceptible objects. If the lovers of sights and sounds want to say that "beauty itself" refers to the *meaning* of "beauty itself," then they are giving up (LSS1) in favor of (~LSS1) and no longer believe that the world contains only perceptibles and no abstract objects. They are admitting something that is not a perceptible—the meaning of a word—into their ontologies. So, the lovers of sights and sounds have E2 commitments. In fact, Glaucon's lauded (NI) could simply be the conviction that "beauty itself" and "ugliness itself" have different meanings.[13]

It is not that Plato assumes that the lovers of sights and sounds *want* to use the terms *beautiful* and *ugly* in distinct and opposite ways. Plato sees that the lovers of sights and sounds *do* use these terms as opposites. Plato sees that this is inconsistent with the lovers of sights and sounds' commitment to the lone existence of perceptible objects. Therefore, even if lovers of sights and sounds profess to be in E1, they behave as if they were in E2. Even without being drawn into a metaphysical discussion, the behavior of the lovers of sights and sounds already betrays the inconsistency in their beliefs. This shows that they are thinking about something other than perceptible objects.

As I pointed out at the beginning of this chapter, the argument that I have just rehearsed is a more tacit argument that is concurrent in the text with an overt argument that the lover of sights and sounds is better off than the ignorant person even if they are worse off than those who have knowledge. That argument is also important to this project, but it requires that we first look at the structure of *doxa* for Plato in a way that goes beyond the unwitting cognitive connection that *doxa* must have to its object. Thus, I defer it until chapters 7 and 8. I will conclude this chapter by looking at a few other passages in the middle books of the *Republic* where we see evidence that Plato thought that ordinary people can have an unwitting cognitive connection with the Forms.

Doxa and the Good

At *Republic* 505d, Plato has Socrates say some remarkable things about the manner in which every person (every soul of every person) pursues the good. First, Socrates asserts that *all* people *want* what is *actually* good. Further, if anyone has false beliefs about what is actually good, they do not want their false beliefs to misdirect them to what only *appears* to be good:

---

13. This underlines what was said previously about how much more we need to understand about Plato's epistemology than is given to us in the *Men.* and *Phdo.* before we can even approach the question of whether Plato thinks recollection or anything else resolves {E}. Clearly, the lover of sights and sounds has come to recognize that what he seeks is something other than perceptibles, but is that sufficient for coming to recognize beauty itself or is that just a step in the right direction?

> Nobody is content to acquire things merely believed to be good, however, but everyone wants the things that really are good and disdains mere belief here. (505d7–9, Grube's translation)[14]

That is, everyone, when they want something, wants *whatever* is actually good. Furthermore, they want the actual good even if the content of their beliefs about it have mischaracterized it. Socrates takes them to *intend* to be thinking *about*—and directing their desire toward, what is actually good even if they have neither true beliefs about it nor a satisfied description of it.[15] Socrates then goes on to say:

> Every soul pursues the good . . . it divines that the good is something but it is perplexed and cannot adequately grasp what it is or acquire the sort of stable beliefs about it that it has about other things. (505d11–e3, Grube's translation)[16]

Thus, Socrates confirms not only that there might be some who intend their desires to be about something (the actual good) concerning which they are ignorant. He also shows us that he suspects that this is true of *every soul*. Certainly, some of the people who are mistaken about, or ignorant of, the actual good are going to be slaves, lovers of sights and sounds, and many other ordinary people.

Moreover, Socrates declares this after making it clear elsewhere in the *Republic* that Thrasymachus thinks the good (or at least justice) is power (338c) and the lover of sights and sounds thinks that the good (or beauty) is beautiful perceptibles (476c). In other dialogues, it appears that other interlocutors have confused the good (or piety) with the god-beloved (*Euph.*, 7a) and the ability to do whatever one is momentarily inclined to do (*Gorg.*, 466b). So, Plato seems to be quite clear in this instance that when people pursue the good they are intending to pursue and are cog-

---

14. ἀγαθὰ δὲ οὐδενὶ ἔτι ἀρκεῖ τὰ δοκοῦντα κτᾶσθαι, ἀλλὰ τὰ ὄντα ζητοῦσιν, τὴν δὲ δόξαν ἐνταῦθα ἤδη πᾶς ἀτιμάζει;

15. This may well be, for many people, a case where the intention and the contact are not unwitting. As I said in the introduction, I do not clam that the contact is always unwitting, I only emphasize that it *can* be unwitting, because the unwitting cases are those for which it is more controversial to claim that there is contact.

16. ὃ δὴ διώκει μὲν ἅπασα ψυχὴ . . . ἀπομαντευομένη τι εἶναι, ἀποροῦσα δὲ καὶ οὐκ ἔχουσα λαβεῖν ἱκανῶς τί ποτ' ἐστὶν οὐδὲ πίστει χρήσασθαι μονίμῳ οἵᾳ καὶ περὶ τἆλλα.

nitively connected to the actual good but are so unwittingly. That is, they somehow think they want something that happens to be neither identical with, nor a means to, their actual good, while it is also clear—at least to Plato—that they want and are connected to what is actually good.[17]

The Prisoners in Plato's Cave

There is a moment in the allegory of the cave that also alludes to the ordinary person's unwitting cognitive contact with the Forms. At *Republic* 514a1–517a7, Plato has the prisoners in the cave unwittingly contemplate the analogues of things-in-themselves or Forms. Thus, Plato here shows the prisoners to be in unwitting cognitive contact with those stand-ins for abstract objects, even while thinking they are talking about shadows. He shows that the prisoners are in E2. This occurs when Socrates describes a hypothetical contest that takes place in the cave:

> If the men below had praise and honor from each other, and prizes for the man who saw most clearly the shadows that passed before them, and who could remember best what usually came before and which after, and which at the same time, and thus could most ably predict the future . . . (516c7–d2, Grube's translation)[18]

It looks as if all, or most, of the prisoners honor and praise whoever among them is able to discern something in their present sense experience that alludes to (and puts them in touch with) something beyond that sense experience. They treat that which is beyond their sense experience as something that is common to all their own, subjective, and their communal, intersubjective, sense experiences. The prisoners treat their hypotheses

---

17. Whether it is goodness itself, what is actually good for them and, therefore, partakes in the Form of the Good, or for they themselves to partake in the Form of the Good is too big an issue for me to clarify here. For more on interpreting desire and desire for the Good in Plato, see Penner 1991; 2003; and 2007 and Reshotko 2006; 2011; and 2013.

18. τιμαὶ δὲ καὶ ἔπαινοι εἴ τινες αὐτοῖς ἦσαν τότε παρ' ἀλλήλων καὶ γέρα τῷ ὀξύτατα καθορῶντι τὰ παριόντα, καὶ μνημονεύοντι μάλιστα ὅσα τε πρότερα αὐτῶν καὶ ὕστερα εἰώθει καὶ ἅμα πορεύεσθαι, καὶ ἐκ τούτων δὴ δυνατώτατα ἀπομαντευομένῳ τὸ μέλλον ἥξειν. . . .

about the shadows as something that hits or misses some truth that is over and above those shadows and governs them. They cannot discern the nature of these governing principles, and nothing in the image that Plato paints suggests that they are anything other than confused about them. Still, both Plato and the prisoners themselves treat the shadows as an experience about which the prisoners can be right or wrong. They treat their experience as something that is governed by principles about which one can be more and less correct. Socrates does not chide the prisoners for imagining that there is something ordering their experience other than the random whim of the puppeteers. The prisoners applaud those among themselves who come to better conclusions about the regularities of the shadows. Plato, Socrates, and the prisoners themselves all seem to assume that those who are more correct are more correct *about* something other than the shadows of the puppets. They are correct about some common features that the shadows have and about the predispositions of the shadows to come in a certain order due to the relationships among those properties. The prisoners, despite being utterly misled about what reality consists in, are shown to make predictions that arise from possessing some cognitive relationship to abstract properties. They refer to these abstract objects, make use of them even while not recognizing their existence or what their activities entail, and perhaps even while claiming that nothing other than the shadows exists.

From the point of view of Plato, Socrates, and the reader, despite the possibility that the shadows radically misrepresent something about the nature of reality, the prisoners are, in some way, managing to "look through" this elaborate misrepresentation and they are *trying* to look through it. They acknowledge that they *should* try to look through it by giving prizes to those who appear to be successful. Some of the prisoners do it to the point of getting something about it right. In fact, they are getting something right without realizing exactly what it is about which they are right. Further, the prisoners are referring to and being right about something about which each remains largely (or even entirely) ignorant.[19]

---

19. Harte points out that "the prisoners combine reference with ignorance of the (essential, identifying) nature of that to which they refer," and, "Plato's prisoners talk about things of which they are (in their case, apparently quite radically) ignorant" (2007, 205). She adds that "Plato's prisoners are not only ignorant about the nature of that to which they refer, they are also subject to confusion as to which item in their environment is the item to which they refer" (2007, 206). She concludes, "The

Republic 523e3–524a4: Provoking the Ordinary Person

At 523a, Socrates introduces Glaucon to a principle that distinguishes studies that lead prospective philosopher rulers in the direction of reality from those that do not. He does this by noting that only some sense impressions provoke reflection. Holding up his fingers, he declares that if we view fingers as fingers, they do not provoke us to reflect because we do not take the same sense impression to represent both finger and not-finger equally. Fingers represent "fingerhood" adequately; the intelligence is not provoked to help us figure out whether a finger is a finger (523c11–e2). However, if we look to fingers to teach us what is big or what is small, then we do provoke the intelligence because the same finger is equally a big thing and small thing—a finger is not an adequate representation of smallness or bigness (523e3–524a4). Philosophers in training will need to study the sorts of subjects that provoke reflection; they need to study those things that are least adequately represented by perceptibles. This is because, when one mistakes perceptibles for the things that are not adequately represented by those perceptibles, the inconsistency of the beliefs in one's original E2 mindset are most likely to be revealed.

The earlier argument against the lovers of sights and sounds has shown the steps to making an argument that will awaken the lovers of sights and sounds from their dream states and force them to acknowledge the existence of those things against which they must measure their dreams. The first step is to point out that every example of a beautiful sensible particular is also an example of an ugly sensible particular.[20] You then compel the lovers of sights and sounds to struggle and to choose between their conviction that "beauty itself" and "ugliness itself" refer to some list of particular perceptible objects and their conviction that beauty itself and ugliness itself are not one and the same thing but are two distinct and opposite things.

The finger passage at *Republic* 523a repeats the same principles and adds nothing other than a piece of advice for ensuring that the argument is

---

prisoners are still referring, strictly and properly speaking, to real Fs, while being ignorant of them" (2007, 207).

20. Notice this does not entail the supposition that sensible particulars are "imperfect" examples of predicated qualitative opposites while the Form is a "perfect" example. For more on this see Penner 2003.

as effective as possible.[21] The finger passage contains echoes of the argument against the lover of sights and sounds. It comes shortly after the famous parable of the cave (514a–517b). Furthermore, it is part of the answer to the question concerning how philosopher rulers are to be educated so that they "see the Good and follow that upward journey" (519c10–11) and can govern the city as "a waking reality and not as in a dream" (520c6–7). It is the lovers of sights and sounds who live their lives in a dream state (*Rep.* 476c2–4). Thus, the statement that philosophers will not govern the city as if in a dream is being connected to the fact that, even if they began as lovers of sights and sounds, they have been converted by being educated through the methods dictated by the finger passage.

It is granted that even the small group of natively capable students who will be selected to become philosophers will begin as lovers of sights and sounds (that is, they will be in E2) and will then be awakened to awareness of the Forms with which they are already in contact. While beliefs might change radically once a person has turned around and focused upon each item in the upward path that ascends from perceptible particulars to things-in-themselves, Plato is showing that being a lover of sights and sounds is an earlier developmental stage in the process of becoming a philosopher. He shows that philosophers come to have whatever knowledge they do have through a radical rethinking of beliefs that were already about, and constrained by, the Forms.

The finger passage reveals that the manner in which we focus upon our sense perceptions determines whether our souls are awakened and drawn toward reality. If we focus on one aspect of our perception, we will deem it adequate. It will not arouse confusion or controversy because it does a good job of indicating one thing without indicating that particular thing's opposite. In this case, it will not force us to look beyond that sense perception. It will be adequate.

If Socrates holds up his fingers in front of a bunch of lovers of sights and sounds (or an Introduction to Philosophy class) and asks, "Are these fingers?" he will not generate much discussion. His pupils will say, "Yes." If he holds up his fingers and asks, "Are these large?" he is likely to generate some controversy. Some will say "Yes," some "No." They are likely to try to clarify their thoughts about largeness in order to persuade one another or to be sure in their own minds that they are answering correctly. And they

---

21. Kamtekar (2009, 143) also uses this passage to argue that conflicting sense experiences can give those with *doxa* access to what-is.

will come to notice that they don't clarify what largeness is by looking to, and further analyzing, fingers—or by looking to, and further analyzing, other perceptible objects. Rather, they go to some preconceived criterion that they have that governs what is large and bring it to bear on how they might best sort out what is presented to them by their sense experience. By giving them an inadequate sense experience—a controversial perceptible example of something for which *no unambiguous perceptible example can be found*—Socrates compels them to go to something other than a sense impression to adjudicate how the example should be characterized. To what are they compelled to go? To some understanding of largeness that they did not get through sense experience; one that is provided by their intelligence and one to which someone who believes only in the perceptible world could not be committed. When they reflect on the exercise they have just performed, they have the opportunity to cease to be enamored of the sights and sounds and be drawn to study that which they have used to sort out the confusion engendered by experience. Perhaps this constitutes a step on the journey from E2 to E3.

The finger passage is saying, "When you want to make this argument, choose your opposites carefully, you will be more immediately successful if you choose opposites such as beautiful/ugly or thick/thin instead of opposites such as finger/not-finger or chair/not-chair." The finger passage describes what facilitates one's awareness of the incoherence of one's own beliefs. This awareness is one that natively capable and well-prepared youth *must* achieve in order to *become* philosophers. Plato realizes that the ordinary person doesn't attribute his indecision about whether to label a particular finger "big" or "small" to confusion between the references of "big" and "small." In fact, Plato even refers to members of the *hoi polloi*— to "the many" or "the common person"—as the targets of this exercise:

> For in none of these cases is the soul of *most* [or *ordinary*] people compelled to question its judgment [asking] "what is a finger?" (523d3–5)[22]

The implication is that while the souls of most people—ordinary people—are not compelled to ask themselves, "What is a finger?" as a result of being asked if a particular finger is a finger, the souls of ordinary people *are* com-

---

22. ἐν πᾶσι γὰρ τούτοις οὐκ ἀναγκάζεται τῶν πολλῶν ἡ ψυχὴ τὴν νόησιν ἐπερέσθαι τί ποτ' ἐστὶ δάκτυλος. . . .

pelled to ask, "What is largeness?" upon being asked if a particular finger is large. So, Plato's point is that the finger exercise succeeds with ordinary people if they are asked about opposites.[23] It is the ordinary people who will have their awareness stimulated by being asked about the size of the finger rather than the "fingerness" of it. Plato, in the finger passage, shows us that some of the most mundane exercises that we do—noticing that the same finger is bigger than one and smaller than another—could not be done unless we tried to think about things that we cannot experience empirically—bigness to the exclusion of smallness—unless we were in E2.

Conclusion

In chapters 1–3, we concluded that, whatever else Plato was trying to accomplish with his theory of recollection, the texts that describe it include textual evidence for the thesis that inquiry requires an unwitting cognitive connection to its object where that connection is independent of any content that its cognizer is cognizing. We also surmised from this evidence that if Plato is using recollection to resolve {B}, then it is because he recognizes inquiry's need for this unwitting cognitive connection. I concluded that, in order for this connection to fulfill its role, it must result from the intentions of the human subject of the inquiry.

In this chapter, we have surveyed the places where Plato shows that inquiry and learning must be connected to the way things are by the intentions of the human subjects of those inquiries and learning experiences. These provide evidence that Plato assumes that this is the case

---

23. For the philosophically astute, it would seem to work just as well with substantives. I can arouse controversy even among the uninitiated by asking if my finger is a finger if I happen to have a digit that is damaged or deformed—or even if I simply hold up my thumb—and ask if it is a finger. This works with any substantive. While qualitative opposites are unique in that there are no unambiguous examples of them, they are not unique in having ambiguous examples—every substantive admits of ambiguous examples. It would be absurd to think that Plato was somehow unaware of this asymmetry with respect to the uniqueness of qualitative opposites as compared to substantive opposites. It is, therefore, equally absurd to think that in pointing out that examples of qualitative opposites are more effective for performing this pedagogical exercise Plato took himself to be saying anything about the range of Forms. It is thus implausible to think that this passage is evidence that there are no Forms of substantives.

and that it resolves {B} even if there is no such thing as recollection. We have looked at examples of ordinary people who have an unwitting connection to the objects of their inquiries and to the truth-makers for their true and false beliefs. We see that this unwitting connection is a result of their intentions to refer to beauty itself, the horse itself, and thickness itself. Their inconsistent beliefs show that they are trying to refer to these abstract objects even if they don't realize that they are abstract. Even if they are confused about whether they are referring to an abstract unity or a perceptual multiplicity.

In these dialogues, these ordinary people are Meno's slave, the readers of the *Phaedo*, lovers of sights and sounds who live in a "dream state" because they mistake perceptible beautiful things for beauty itself, prisoners in Plato's cave, and the common person who might become educated in the hopes of being trained to be a philosopher ruler. Plato takes these ordinary people to be connected to the way things are by being connected to such things as equality itself, and beauty itself, and all the other abstract objects that come to be referred to as "Forms."

Before we move on to look at how this contact works together with *doxa* in the middle books of the *Republic*, it will help us to take a careful look at some evidence concerning the structure of *doxa* according to Plato. This evidence comes from an unlikely place: the Diotima speech in the *Symposium*. While that dialogue, and her speech, are about *erôs*, in chapter 5 I will show that it contains some hints about Plato's assumptions regarding the structure of *doxa*. In chapter 6 we will confirm these elements regarding the structure of *doxa* in passages that discuss it more overtly in the *Phaedrus* and *Theaetetus*. We will also see that those dialogues offer further evidence of Plato's commitment to unwitting cognitive contact in order to underwrite his view on *doxa* and its structure.

Chapter 5

Doxastic Structure at *Symposium* 201d1–212c3

In the upcoming chapters (7–9), we will go on to observe that Plato's assumption of unwitting cognitive contact between those who entertain *doxa* and objects such as beauty itself in the *Republic* allows for *doxa* of what-is—*doxa* of Plato's Forms. This will allow us to see that Plato thinks *doxa* is about the same objects that knowledge is about. I argue that, despite what some think are appearances to the contrary, Plato thinks that everybody opines beauty itself. However, in this chapter, we pause to take a look at some places in the dialogues where Plato gives us a peek at how he thinks *doxa* is structured, how that structure underlies better and worse *doxa*, and any connection there might be between doxastic structure and ignorance or knowledge.

In chapters 1–3, I joined other scholars in thinking of *doxa* as laid out on a spectrum that has the worst kind of *doxa* at one extreme and the best kind of *doxa* at the other. It is my eventual goal to argue that Plato identifies the worst kind of *doxa* with ignorance. In this book, I am not discussing the nature of knowledge, so I will only make a soft suggestion that the best kind of *doxa* is the most like—or the closest in function to—knowledge. In all the chapters so far, I have argued that the cognitive states in this doxastic spectrum cannot rely on their content to enable them to be about the object that they must be about in order to be true or false, or more accurate rather than less accurate. Thus, in chapters 1–4, I have concluded that there is evidence for what I call "unwitting cognitive contact" that solves what we set out (in the *Men.*)

as the "beginning problem" {B} by allowing a subject's *doxa* to be about the object she (confusedly) intends for her *doxa* to be about, and I have elaborated upon that evidence. It is time to now turn our attention to the *doxa* to which we are connected by this contact.

In this chapter, I pause to say more about what this supposed doxastic spectrum, which does not include, but relies upon, unwitting cognitive contact, must be like, given other assumptions that Plato makes about *doxa* in some revealing moments in the *Symposium*. This is an unusual moment for looking at *doxa* or anything related to Plato's epistemology. I will extract some views Plato seems to hold about doxastic structure from Diotima's speech at *Symposium* 201d1–212c3. In the next chapter, I will corroborate these observations with some more likely passages about *doxa* from the *Phaedrus* and the *Theaetetus*.

This analysis of Diotima's speech in the *Symposium* yields a picture of *doxa* that is importantly different from the way belief, true belief, and justified true belief are deployed in contemporary epistemology. Diotima appears to begin to construct a hierarchy of epistemic states. While there are other places in the dialogues where similar hierarchies also appear to loom, the Diotima speech shows that Plato does not give us a way to make sense of a hierarchy of epistemic states that goes from ignorance to knowledge, where those states are to be identified with *individual* false, true, and both reasoned and true propositional beliefs. I argue that only entire doxastic structures can be evaluated as better or worse than one another. Further, it is not clear that even these sorts of individual beliefs can be placed into a unidimensional hierarchy. This fits with other recent interpretations that claim that Plato's *doxa* cannot be correlated with the notion of "belief" used in contemporary epistemological discussions that assess whether knowledge can be justified true belief. In looking to this passage in the *Symposium*, I by no means assert that the structure of *doxa* is the issue that is at the forefront of Plato's concerns therein. However, the beauty of the dialogues and their richness is that Plato often—masterfully and intentionally—takes care of more than one philosophical concern at once. This is what he did in making the concurrent argument in *Republic* V that I discussed in chapter 4. It appears to me that Plato, in having Diotima make an overt argument for the benefit of Socrates (and the reader), is again making a concurrent argument for his reader. However, I cannot be sure of that and can give no evidence to "prove" it. It might be that we are merely seeing Plato's more subliminal assumptions concerning *doxa*. Still, I believe there is good reason to treat this as evidence regarding his assumptions about *doxa* throughout the group of dialogues that I am discussing in this book.[1]

In discussing the *Meno*, I have taken pains to present the unwitting cognitive grasp that Plato relies upon in order to make inquiry and belief possible as something *other than* knowledge or ignorance that is also *not in between* knowledge and ignorance. There is a spectrum of epistemic states that goes from the best kind (presumably closest to knowledge) to the worst kind (presumably ignorance), but this unwitting cognitive connection is not on that spectrum. It is other than anything on that spectrum because it is a prerequisite to anything that lies anywhere along that spectrum. Plato does not say anything about any state being in between knowledge and ignorance in any of the dialogues that we have already discussed. There are statements made in the *Meno* that it might *seem* harmless to paraphrase as introducing a search for something that is in between knowing and not knowing. However, Plato never says that anything found through recollection lies *in between* knowing and not knowing. Rather, in the *Meno*, we see Plato reduce the claim that every candidate for an object of knowledge is either known or not known to absurdity.[2] Plato has the *relationship* between a cognizer and that *about* which she cognizes be something other than anything on the spectrum of epistemic states that goes from knowledge to ignorance.

I emphasize this because I now want to distinguish this unwitting cognitive contact from places where Plato *does* have his characters say that there are kinds of *doxa* that are *in between* knowledge and ignorance, specifically at *Symposium* 202a2–212a7 (in this chapter) and *Republic* 475e4–479d5 (in chapter 7).

Doxa in Plato

As I already noted in the introduction to this book, questions concerning Plato's deployment of the Greek word *doxa* have become a bit more pointed in recent years than they were in the prior few decades. In Plato's works, *doxa* is translated by the English *belief, opinion,* or *judgment*. Some scholars

---

1. See my discussion of chronology in the introduction, 18.
2. Where known or not-known can be understood as either all or nothing or as just adhering to the law of excluded middle, see chapter 1 (32–36). I will clarify these as (S1M) or (S1S) in chapter 6 (148–150).

have voiced concerns that contemporary accounts of *doxa* in Plato make it out to be propositional and a component of knowledge.[3] None of these scholars disputes that there are at least two moments in the dialogues that suggest that true belief is a prerequisite for knowledge and also that it gets transformed into knowledge by some sort of reasoning process.[4] However, these same interpreters argue that we find many uses of the term *doxa* in the dialogues that make it hard to render it consistent with contemporary analytic epistemology's use of the term *belief* where a belief is the taking of an individual piece of propositional content to be true.[5]

I will now look at what appear to be Diotima's assumptions in her speech at *Symposium* 201d1–212c3 to show that what Plato represents as *her* understanding of *doxa* inspires a similar critique of any assimilation of her use of *doxa* to this contemporary analytic use of "belief." While Diotima initially seduces us toward the assimilation that interpreters have made between *doxa* and contemporary notions of belief, she does this only to dash any hopes we have of establishing a resonance between the two. Despite her use of the terms *true* and *false* and *reasoned* in her descriptions of *doxa*, Diotima's speech seems designed by Plato to make us despair of treating *doxa* as something that can be individuated into discrete entities that represent propositions. It also flies in the face of any claim that these sorts of propositions might be closer to knowledge than any others, much less that one of them can be (or can become an individual piece of) knowledge.

In Between Knowledge and Ignorance

At *Symposium* 202a9, Plato's Diotima makes an epistemologically significant claim and tries to persuade Socrates to agree with it: true *doxa* that is not reasoned is in between knowledge and ignorance.

---

3. See Vogt 2012; Moss and Schwab 2019, 8.

4. *Men.* 97a–98b and *Theaet.* 201c7–d3. Of course, neither of these incontrovertibly implies the thesis that knowledge is identical to true beliefs that have been justified. Whatever reasoning is required on top of true belief might transform it (in Plato's view) into a knowledge that is not also belief.

5. Moss and Schwab 2019, 1.

"Don't you recognize," she said, "that having correct beliefs, even without being able to give a rational account of them, is neither a matter of knowing (since how could something irrational be knowledge?), nor of ignorance (how could something that hits on what is the case be ignorance?)? Correct belief is, I imagine, something of the sort in question, between wisdom and ignorance?" (202a5–9, Rowe's translation)[6]

This is reminiscent of the claim made at *Meno* 97a–98b, that true belief, all by itself, can disappear in the night, but when it is tied down with "causal reasoning" (98a3–4) it comes even closer to—or is—knowledge. This also seems to resonate with the contemporary claim—familiar from justified true belief [JTB] theories of knowledge—that knowledge is true belief that has been appropriately justified. A closer look at Diotima's contribution to the *Symposium*, however, shows that she is making some controversial assumptions about *doxa*. Further, these assumptions fail to accommodate contemporary notions about true belief and justified true belief.

Why does Plato have Diotima make these controversial suggestions? Might these claims about *doxa* in the *Symposium* be evidence that Plato's use of *doxa* in his dialogues is inconsistent with our contemporary notion that knowledge is justified true belief?[7] Our contemporary JTB theories may have infected twentieth and twenty-first-century commentators' readings of this passage and of *Meno* 97a–b. Our JTB theories encourage us to think of beliefs as mental states that have individual propositions as their objects. These contemporary theories further encourage us to think that these individual beliefs can be true and then become justified. When

---

6. τὸ ὀρθὰ δοξάζειν καὶ ἄνευ τοῦ ἔχειν λόγον δοῦναι οὐκ οἶσθ', ἔφη, ὅτι οὔτε ἐπίστασθαί ἐστιν—ἄλογον γὰρ πρᾶγμα πῶς ἂν εἴη ἐπιστήμη;—οὔτε ἀμαθία—τὸ γὰρ τοῦ ὄντος τυγχάνον πῶς ἂν εἴη ἀμαθία;—ἔστι δὲ δήπου τοιοῦτον ἡ ὀρθὴ δόξα, μεταξὺ φρονήσεως καὶ ἀμαθίας.

7. Epistemologists point to Plato's *Theaet.* 201cd as the origin of this theoretical standpoint. "Justified true belief" is the most common moniker for reasoned true belief in contemporary analytic philosophy (already very much in parlance prior to Gettier's famous counterexamples [1963] that became a touchstone for all discussion of this sort in analytic philosophy). Unfortunately, this seems to have resulted in the misreading of some contemporary notions concerning belief and knowledge back into Plato's dialogues.

this happens, these theories decree them discrete, individual, propositional units of knowledge. However, a careful analysis of Diotima's speech shows Plato inviting us to understand the content of *doxa* as something more amorphous and less easily individuated than propositions can be. It is something more like a "cloud" of *doxa*.[8] Further, it hints at the idea that knowledge will not result from the justification of an individual propositional belief.

Perhaps we, who have been primed in such a way as to find it hard to think about beliefs in any way other than as discrete individual entities, might think of these clouds as formations of interconnected beliefs. Still, it is not at all clear that Plato would understand *doxa* as a composite of individual entities. If there are such things as individual true beliefs that are accounted for by reason, then Plato, in the guise of Diotima, shows us that even those individual true and justified beliefs can be part of a larger cloud of *doxa* that itself constitutes what we might find it fit to call "ignorance." This picture seems important to the development of some idea of what knowledge is like for Plato. Plato's text in this part of the *Symposium* implies that false, true, and even reasoned *doxa* is compatible with ignorance, or at least with lack of knowledge. This is a place where it is hard to reconcile a Platonic understanding of knowledge with the more recent notion of justified true belief.

A Hierarchy of *Doxa*?

While indicating that there is something in between knowledge and ignorance, *Symposium* 202a5–9 could seduce us into also assuming that there is an array of epistemic conditions that form a hierarchy.[9] This is the case especially when we look at how Diotima follows up her claim concerning knowledge, ignorance, and what lies in between:

---

8. In these contexts, I would suggest that Plato uses *doxa* more in the manner of a mass noun than a count noun. Still, I do not contend that Plato and his interlocutors never use it as a count noun nor that this is vastly different from ordinary (nonphilosophical) English usage of *belief* and *knowledge* and other similar terms (as we will see shortly). It is true that both *doxa* and *belief* are used in the plural in ordinary language (and in Plato's dialogues).

9. This is not so different from the way in which I have already been sympathizing with others who conceive of a doxastic spectrum up until this point.

Don't you recognize . . . that having correct beliefs, even without being able to give a rational account of them, is neither a matter of knowing (since how could something irrational be knowledge?), nor of ignorance (how could something that hits on what is the case be ignorance?). (202a5-9, Rowe's translation)[10]

It looks like we might construct a hierarchy where knowledge is the best epistemological state and ignorance is the worst. True *doxa* would then be somewhere in the middle in value, but less valuable than reasoned true *doxa*. Reasoned true *doxa* has looked to the JTB theorists like a candidate for knowledge. We might suppose that reasoned true *doxa* is the kind of *doxa* that is closest to the knowledge end of the hierarchy.

The fact that Plato refers to more than one kind of ignorance in other dialogues might bolster the case for a hierarchy of epistemological states. Plato has Socrates distinguish the condition in which a person is ignorant but thinks that she knows what she does not know (let us call this "double ignorance") from the one in which a person realizes that she is ignorant (let us call this "Socratic ignorance" since it is the condition in which Socrates finds himself at *Apology* 23b). It could be that, for completeness, we should isolate a third condition, an innocent or unreflective ignorance, where a person does not know something but also has not reflected upon her ignorance. However, while it makes sense to assume that Plato would have recognized that kind of ignorance, he never makes a point of singling it out in the dialogues. These conditions would fall under the generic category of ignorance, but they appear to form a hierarchy of kinds of ignorance: Socratic ignorance is a better kind of ignorance than double ignorance, but it is worse than knowledge. The person who recognizes that she does not know what she does not know has made progress. Many texts testify to this: at *Apology* 22d3-e1, when Socrates describes his encounter with the craftsmen, he allows that human beings have some knowledge of some particular craft, but he says that this "human wisdom" is worth "little or nothing." The poets and craftsmen do not possess a "knowledge greater than human," because their confidence in their human knowledge of their craft is keeping them from appreciat-

---

10. τὸ ὀρθὰ δοξάζειν καὶ ἄνευ τοῦ ἔχειν λόγον δοῦναι οὐκ οἶσθ᾽, ἔφη, ὅτι οὔτε ἐπίστασθαί ἐστιν—ἄλογον γὰρ πρᾶγμα πῶς ἂν εἴη ἐπιστήμη;—οὔτε ἀμαθία—τὸ γὰρ τοῦ ὄντος τυγχάνον πῶς ἂν εἴη ἀμαθία;

ing how little they know; it somehow makes them think that they know things that they don't. This is the worst possible situation to inhabit. We see this because Socrates, who is said to be in a better situation, differs from them both in not knowing what they know, but—and this is what is emphasized—in not thinking that he knows what he does not know (Socratic ignorance).

Plato has Socrates put this same sentiment more plainly and succinctly at *Meno* 84a2–b1. After bringing the slave to *aporia*, Socrates alludes to the metaphor of the torpedo fish that Meno used earlier (80a6, c6) so that we can see that Meno also made the mistake of thinking he knew what virtue was when he did not. Socrates observes that neither Meno nor the slave were harmed by being made numb—in fact, they benefited from it. Whereas before they did not realize that they were making faulty assumptions about virtue and the length of the side of a square (double ignorance), now they do realize it (Socratic ignorance), so they can put these assumptions aside and seek the truth.

These passages demonstrate that Plato holds double ignorance to be the worst epistemological state and Socratic ignorance—where one does not know, but also realizes that one does not know (sometimes indicated by *aporia*)—to be a better epistemological position than double ignorance. Thus, it seems that a hierarchy that has ignorance at the bottom and knowledge at the top would move straightforwardly from double ignorance, to Socratic ignorance, to false *doxa*, to true *doxa*, to reasoned true *doxa*, and then to knowledge (if knowledge is different from justified true *doxa*). Nevertheless, Diotima also conveys the impression that true, but unreasoned, belief is in between knowledge and ignorance and that true, but unreasoned, belief is distinct from both knowledge and ignorance. In the end, what we will learn from the *Symposium* is that the *doxa* part of this progression is complex and defies simple, unidimensional, hierarchical classification. It might be best to say that Diotima shows us how we should not construe *doxa*.

Let us look at some examples that betray this lack of hierarchical structure. Some beliefs—especially some false beliefs—are going to be constitutive of double ignorance, while others are more likely to constitute Socratic ignorance. That is, persons who are experiencing ignorance are not necessarily experiencing total blanks when it comes to *doxa*, and it stretches credulity to suppose that they are.[11] Furthermore, Plato does not

---

11. Scott 2006, 76–77; Fine 2014, 23, 76–83.

portray ignorant people as devoid of beliefs. In the dialogues, those who appear to know less than Socrates appear so *because* of their beliefs. And even the state of *aporia* or Socrates's own particular kind of ignorance is composed of beliefs about one's own former and present beliefs. Socrates believes that any belief he has, no matter how convincing it seems at the moment, should be treated as provisional. Meno and the slave come to believe that their former beliefs were false and that they have no new ones with which to replace them. Beyond those considerations, in the *Symposium*, Diotima shows us that it is hard to construct a convincing hierarchy of *individual* false, true, and reasoned or unreasoned beliefs (or "pieces" of *doxa*). This is partly because it seems very hard to make a case for individuating *doxa* in any kind of principled manner.

When we look at the top of this supposed hierarchy, it might appear orderly, just as the bottom did at first blush. Perhaps *Meno* 96d shows us the upper part of the hierarchy: after illuminating what seems to be a strong connection between those who are virtuous (who bring benefit) and those who are wise, Socrates berates himself for not realizing that a person can benefit another with true belief. It seems that knowledge is not required. A guide to Larissa who has true belief will be no worse at getting a traveler to his destination than a guide who has knowledge of the road to Larissa. True belief is no less useful than knowledge (97cd). When Meno wonders why knowledge is more highly prized than true belief, Socrates brings up the legend of Daedalus's statues: they are so lifelike that if not tied down they escape in the night. He analogizes true belief to these lifelike statues. True beliefs are useful for as long as one has them, but they are not tied down and can, therefore, disappear. One turns true belief into knowledge by tying it down with a "reasoned account" (*aitios logismô*, 98a3–4). Thus, while we might take the *Apology* to have shown us the lower end of the epistemological hierarchy—it is anchored by double ignorance, with Socratic ignorance as the next step up—this passage appears to illustrate the upper end of the hierarchy: the ultimate state is knowledge, and reasoned true belief is either identical to knowledge or falls right below it.[12] However, will this neat picture find support from Diotima's assumptions?

---

12. Socrates says that "after they are tied down they become knowledge" (*Men*. 98a5–6). This leaves whether they remain *doxai* while becoming knowledge or are transformed into knowledge that is no longer a species of *doxa* undetermined.

Symposium 202a

We appear to be able to place double ignorance at the bottom of a hierarchy and knowledge at the top. Although, even here, it is hard to figure out how to rank some of the clouds of *doxa* that constitute something like double ignorance as they mix together more and less accurate, and more and less reasoned, beliefs. How orderly can we make what is in between these two extremes? The continuation of the exchange between Diotima and Socrates with which we began is illuminating with respect to this question. At *Symposium* 202a, Socrates rehearses, in flashback, Diotima's scolding of him for making a false dichotomy; responding to her claim that love is neither beautiful nor good (201e6–7), he asks, "Is love ugly then and bad?" Diotima responds: "Do you really think that if a thing is not ugly it has to be beautiful?" (201e10–11). When Socrates maintains his belief that the not beautiful is ugly, she prods him further:

> Do you also suppose that if something is not wise, it is ignorant? Don't you see that there is something between wisdom and ignorance? (202a2–3, Rowe's translation)[13]

So, if there is indeed a hierarchy, we now have further instruction about what falls in between knowledge and Socratic ignorance: what is reasoned is better than what is unreasoned, and what is true is better than what is not. Even better is for *doxa* to be both reasoned and true. But, what if we have just one or the other—*doxa* that is true but unreasoned, or *doxa* that is reasoned but not true—is one to be preferred? This question will not be answered. In fact, this question allows us to see how complicated *doxa* is and how untenable is the notion of a hierarchy of beliefs.

Doxa: a Rich, but Messy, Epistemic State

What happens next in the *Symposium* allows us to see that, if knowledge is to sit unambiguously at the top of a hierarchy that has double ignorance at the bottom, the possession of an individual belief that is reasoned and true will not suffice for knowledge. For when Diotima chides Socrates for thinking that Erôs must be ugly if he is not beautiful, Socrates gives a new reason for thinking Erôs is beautiful: everyone believes that Erôs is a god

---

13. ἦ καὶ ἂν μὴ σοφόν, ἀμαθές; ἢ οὐκ ᾔσθησαι ὅτι ἔστιν τι μεταξὺ σοφίας καὶ ἀμαθίας;

(202b6–7) and everyone believes that all gods are beautiful and happy. Socrates includes himself among those who believe that Erôs is a god (202c5).

Diotima responds to the assertion that everyone believes that Erôs is a god by asking if by "everyone" he refers only to those not-knowing or also to those knowing.[14] In what follows, we will note that, in Diotima's interrogation of Socrates, Plato has her describe Socrates's epistemic condition by combining seemingly individual beliefs that are unreasoned with those that are reasoned, and beliefs that are true with those that are not, somewhat indiscriminately. This makes it evident that Socrates has a rich interrelated *doxastic system*. Some of the components of this system conflict with others. Perhaps much of this cloud of *doxa* is reasoned, but not all of it is true. However, while Socrates does have some reasoned beliefs that are true, even these, it seems, should not be called "knowledge," as he assents to them even while he assents to further beliefs that contradict them. For example:

> "And yet," I said, "he is believed by everyone to be a great god."
> "Do you mean," she said, "by everyone who is ignorant or by everyone who is knowledgeable as well?"
> "By absolutely everyone."
> With a laugh she said, "And just how Socrates, could he be agreed to be a great god by people who say he's no god at all?" (202b6–202c1, Rowe's translation)[15]

Apparently, Diotima reasons that anyone who *knew* Erôs, would not even be able to entertain the belief that Erôs is a god, because this is a false belief. She seems to think that it is not possible to *know* Erôs—or to *know* anything about Erôs—if one also believes, falsely, that he is a god. We can *believe* what is true about something about which we also *believe* what is

---

14. It is unclear what the object of εἰδότων is supposed to be here: knowing that Erôs is beautiful? Knowing that Erôs is a god? Neither one really makes sense. My conjecture is that the object is Erôs itself. Those knowing Erôs cannot think that because he is a god he is beautiful; since they would have to realize that he is not a god. Diotima does not count Socrates among those who know Erôs. She realizes that he has to believe that Erôs is not beautiful and therefore is not a god, since he does believe (and reasonably so) that all gods are beautiful.

15. καὶ μήν, ἦν δ' ἐγώ, ὁμολογεῖταί γε παρὰ πάντων μέγας θεὸς εἶναι.—τῶν μὴ εἰδότων, ἔφη, πάντων λέγεις, ἢ καὶ τῶν εἰδότων; συμπάντων μὲν οὖν.—καὶ ἡ γελάσασα καὶ πῶς ἄν, ἔφη, ὦ Σώκρατες, ὁμολογοῖτο μέγας θεὸς εἶναι παρὰ τούτων, οἵ φασιν αὐτὸν οὐδὲ θεὸν εἶναι;

false. However, we cannot *know* anything about that concerning which we also *believe* what is false.

It will be hard to establish a hierarchy among Socrates's beliefs based on whether they are reasoned and true: Socrates believes that Erôs is a god. Does he have a reason? It is not clear from the text. If he does not, then this is an unreasoned false belief. Perhaps we could provide a rationale: Socrates believes that love is good and beautiful. Why does he believe that love is good and beautiful? Because everyone desires it, and what do people desire if not what is good and beautiful?[16] He also believes that all gods are good and beautiful. If this is his rationale, then Socrates has a belief that Erôs is good and beautiful, and this belief is reasoned but is not true: it is a reasoned false belief.

Socrates also believes that all gods are happy and beautiful (202c6–9). He believes that anyone who is happy possesses good and beautiful things (202c10–12). We are, perhaps, to understand this as a reasoned belief, as it is implied by an argument that Socrates makes at *Lysis* 218b.[17] If Socrates believes that Erôs is a god, then he must believe that Erôs is happy, and so he must believe that Erôs possesses beautiful things. This would also seem to be a reasoned belief. However, it is false, as it is premised on the false belief that Erôs is a god.

Socrates also believes that Erôs is desire. Since all desire is for good and beautiful things, it is logical to believe that Erôs desires beautiful and good things. However, Erôs cannot desire what he already has, and if he is a god, he possesses good and beautiful things. So, according to Diotima, at the same time as Socrates has the reasoned false belief that Erôs is a god, he has the reasoned true belief that Erôs is not a god:

> "And just how Socrates, could he be agreed to be a great god by people who say he's no god at all?"
> "Who are these people?" I asked.
> "You're one," she said, "and I'm one, too." (202c1–4, Rowe's translation)[18]

---

16. It is widely agreed that Socrates argues that all desire is for the good at *Men.* 77b3–78c2 and *Gorg.* 466a–468e.

17. At *Lys.* 217a–218c, Socrates argues that only those who do not have—who still long for—knowledge and happiness will continue to seek it.

18. ὁμολογοῖτο μέγας θεὸς εἶναι παρὰ τούτων, οἵ φασιν αὐτὸν οὐδὲ θεὸν εἶναι; τίνες οὗτοι; ἦν δ' ἐγώ. εἷς μέν, ἔφη, σύ, μία δ' ἐγώ.

Perhaps we can analyze Socrates's rich system of *doxa* into individual beliefs that are reasoned, unreasoned, and true, or false. His reasoned true belief might be superior to his unreasoned false belief. However even his reasoned true belief cannot be knowledge, for he assents to it at the same time as he holds a contradictory, false belief.

If we maintain that we can individuate beliefs along propositional lines, then we might want to say that there are unreasoned true and unreasoned false beliefs and there are reasoned true and reasoned false beliefs. However, can we agree that such beliefs can be arranged hierarchically? Perhaps it seems clear that the unreasoned false belief will be near the bottom. So far, it is not at all clear that we should deem any reasoned true belief knowledge, but perhaps they belong closer to the top—the superior end—of the hierarchy. Still, can we establish a hierarchy among the reasoned false and the unreasoned true beliefs?

Diotima has demonstrated that our contemporary understanding of belief as consisting of organically individuated propositional unities comes up short. She also frustrates any effort we might make to arrange knowledge, belief, and ignorance into a neat hierarchy that distinguishes both knowledge and ignorance from *doxa* even though she appeared to indicate they could be at 202a5-9. Besides, even if we could make a hierarchy among these beliefs, Plato seems to assume that it would not contain the entities that interest us; it would not be a hierarchy of *human epistemological states*. Propositional accounts would consider what Socrates is entertaining to be a number of beliefs at the same time. He is unaware of the fact that he holds a false belief (either reasoned or unreasoned) and a different reasoned true (and contradictory) belief, at the same time. This keeps him from having knowledge (despite his reasoned true belief).

How would we best describe Socrates's epistemic state? Where does it belong in the aforementioned hierarchy? Does Socrates not even recognize that his false belief is false (double ignorance)? Is his so-called reasoned and true belief insufficiently reasoned? If it really were reasoned, wouldn't he have considered it carefully enough to realize that it contradicts his belief that Erôs is a god? Can one or both of two contradictory beliefs be reasoned? Plato rubs our noses in judgments that seem designed to make us despair of forming any hierarchy whatsoever among them. Socrates's epistemic state, and whether it makes him knowledgeable, or ignorant, or something in between has to do with all of what would be considered his propositional beliefs *taken together*.

Doxa and the Individuation of Beliefs

Plato has shown that even if we could make a hierarchy of individual beliefs as separate, distinct, freestanding propositions, it would not be a hierarchy of human epistemological or cognitive states. To the extent that we can be said to have *individual* beliefs, we entertain many of them at the same time and it is these masses of beliefs that seem to be most readily identified with our epistemological state.

Further, as we see in Diotima's analysis of Socrates's own views, our beliefs do not, on their own, prior to analysis and reflection, fall into discrete unities. Is Socrates's belief that Erôs is a god a different belief from his belief that Erôs is beautiful? If they are two beliefs, does it make sense to say that one of them is reasoned and the other not if he also holds a third belief that all gods are beautiful? Plato is presenting *doxa* as a mass of things that do not naturally fall into discrete unities. Part of our making them reasoned is our reflecting and making critical judgments about where one belief begins and another ends. Individuated beliefs—if there are such things—are artifacts that are created by human reflection, judgment, and rationalization. Our manner of doing this will be sensitive to the inquiry we are making and the circumstances that necessitated our efforts to sort out our beliefs and sense experiences in order to answer that inquiry.

Clearly, Socrates needs to sort out the various elements of his system of beliefs about Erôs, beauty, desire, good, and happiness. Doing so will allow him to better appreciate how well they actually cohere and, hopefully, how well they map onto the way the world is. Still, Socrates has, at other times, considered his beliefs about desire and the good without thinking about whether or not Erôs was a god. I might think about whether or not my horse is muscular without thinking about how well it could nourish a wolf. However, when I consider whether my horse would make a good meal for a wolf, my beliefs about my horse's muscularity might be hard to disassemble from my beliefs about how much protein he would afford a predator. It might also turn out that I deem my earlier beliefs about his muscularity less reasoned when I am also assessing my beliefs about his protein content.[19]

---

19. To reprise my comment in n. 8, above, this seems to be a moment when the con-

Even though the English terms *belief* and *opinion* can be used to indicate discrete, individuated entities and are treated as such in some contemporary epistemological theories, that is not their only common use. For example, in English we say "public opinion" and "my belief in democracy," both of which treat the singular as something amorphous and lacking in definite boundaries. As students of philosophy, epistemology, and Plato, it could be that we drift into treating "belief" and "opinion" as indicating individual propositions in philosophical contexts because we are overly influenced by JTB theories in contemporary epistemology. I will proceed to use the English *belief* and *opinion* as well as the Greek *doxa* in both the plural and the singular with the advice that they be interpreted in this more amorphous manner.[20] I encourage us to think of "clouds" of belief—or if that is too vague—of interconnected, nonlinear, multidimensional structures of belief(s). We will see that this picture coheres best with this *Symposium* passage.

Does the Upward Path Help?

Symposium 201d1–212c3 appears to denote some kind of hierarchy among various relationships between a human inquirer and the Form of Beauty. It assumes that knowledge is the best epistemological relationship we can have with beauty. Might this shed light on that which lies in between

---

ception of *doxa* as a count noun rather than a mass noun fails us. It is as if we are asking where one drop of water ends and the next begins while the water is still in the hose just because the water becomes drops once it has gone through the sprinkler on the end of the hose.

20. In fact, it is common for translators to translate *doxa* in this way. See Grube's (Cooper 1997) translation of *Men.* 97a3–98d2. In Guthrie's (Hamilton and Cairns 1961) translation of the same passage, he mixes singular and plural with the result that there is at no place an implication of a single belief. The context at *Symp.* 204–212 expects us to treat *doxa* (translated "judgment" by some—see Nehamas and Woodruff [Cooper 1997]) in a manner that is parallel to the uses of the verbal and abstract nouns *love*, *desire*, and *happiness*, none of which seem comparable to any notion of individual judgments or beliefs. At *Rep.* 475e4–479e5, opinion is identified with a capacity (*dunamis*) and it is set over "opinable" (*doxaston*), which also seems to indicate an amorphous ill-bounded mass.

ignorance and knowledge and whether it is linear and hierarchical or, as I have argued, multidimensional and not susceptible to an ordinal ranking?

Diotima summarizes this ascent at 211c. Earlier in this section of the dialogue, she describes Erôs as poor and homeless, but a schemer after the beautiful and good, and resourceful in the pursuit of intelligence (203cd). He is declared a *philosophos*—a lover of wisdom. As he is a philosopher, she places him between wisdom and ignorance. For no one who is ignorant loves wisdom nor does anyone who is wise.[21] She clarifies the assertion that the ignorant do not love wisdom with a description of double ignorance stated in the language of desire (204a4–7).

After telling us that Erôs is useful to human beings because it motivates us to pursue our ultimate goal—happiness—Diotima cautions against loving beautiful *things* because "what everyone loves is really nothing other than the good" (205e7–206a1). People want the good to be theirs forever. This leads to a discussion that connects having the good forever with reproducing beautiful and, hopefully, immortal ideas—such as a blueprint for a just city (209a–b).

As we near the end of Diotima's speech, knowledge plays a greater and greater role and she, once more, shows us the difficulty of hierarchically categorizing complex epistemological states that consist of (or can be analyzed into) what we would think of as multiple individual beliefs. At 207e1–208a7, after describing the constant metamorphosis of an individual's body and soul, Diotima adds that we are never the same with respect to our epistemic states.[22]

> And don't suppose that this [always losing what one had before and always being renewed] is just true in case of the body; in the case of the soul, too, its traits, habits, opinions, desires, pleasures, pains, fears—none of these things is ever the same in any individual, but some are coming into existence, others passing away. It's much stranger even than this with the pieces of knowledge we have: not only are some of them coming into existence and others passing away, so that we are never the

---

21. The contention that the wise do not love wisdom and that, therefore, philosophers are not wise is also asserted at *Lys.* 217a–218c.

22. Note that Diotima uses the plural here (αἱ ἐπιστῆμαι [207e5] and τὰς ἐπιστήμας [208a2]), so some kind of network of "epistemic states" seems like an appropriate way to think about this.

same even in respect to the things we know, but in fact each *individual piece of knowledge is subject to the same process*. For what we call "going over" things exists because knowledge goes out of us; forgetting is the departure of knowledge and going over something creates in us, again, a new meaning in the place of the one that is leaving us, and so preserves our knowledge in such a way as to make it *seem the same*. (207e1–208a5, Rowe's translation; emphasis added)[23]

One part of our epistemic state comes to be in us while another fades away. We study because we always forget something and need to replace it with other things. This makes it *seem* as though we have maintained some, one, interconnected group of beliefs[24] when we have not. Thus, our epistemic states—our epistemic network—is shifting and changing. It is unstable.

Diotima's plural use of *epistêmai* and locutions that imply "pieces" of *epistêmê*[25] hearkens back to all of those beliefs, even ones that are reasoned and true, that we have at the same time as we have many others. These beliefs are so numerous that it is possible for them to become more and more internally consistent and more and more accurate, without ever completely closing in on all of what-is.

At 210e6–211b2, we get a description of the Form of the beautiful. We also get a contrasting description of the lover's epistemic state that is *about* the beautiful.

> [Whoever contemplates the various beautiful things] in order and in the correct way, will now . . . suddenly catch sight of a beauty amazing in its nature—that very beauty, in fact, Socrates, that all his previous toils were for: first, a beauty that

---

23. καὶ μὴ ὅτι κατὰ τὸ σῶμα, ἀλλὰ καὶ κατὰ τὴν ψυχὴν οἱ τρόποι, τὰ ἤθη, δόξαι, ἐπιθυμίαι, ἡδοναί, λῦπαι, φόβοι, τούτων ἕκαστα οὐδέποτε τὰ αὐτὰ πάρεστιν ἑκάστῳ, ἀλλὰ τὰ μὲν γίγνεται, τὰ δὲ ἀπόλλυται. πολὺ δὲ τούτων ἀτοπώτερον ἔτι, ὅτι καὶ αἱ ἐπιστῆμαιμὴ ὅτι αἱ μὲν γίγνονται, αἱ δὲ ἀπόλλυνται ἡμῖν, καὶ οὐδέποτε οἱ αὐτοί ἐσμεν οὐδὲ κατὰ τὰς ἐπιστήμας, ἀλλὰ καὶ μία ἑκάστη τῶν ἐπιστημῶν ταὐτὸν πάσχει. ὃ γὰρ καλεῖται μελετᾶν, ὡς ἐξιούσης ἐστὶ τῆς ἐπιστήμης· λήθη γὰρ ἐπιστήμης ἔξοδος, μελέτη δὲ πάλιν καινὴν ἐμποιοῦσα ἀντὶ τῆς ἀπιούσης μνήμην σῴζει τὴν ἐπιστήμην, ὥστε τὴν αὐτὴν δοκεῖν εἶναι.

24. . . . ὥστε τὴν αὐτὴν δοκεῖν εἶναι . . . (208a6).

25. . . . μία ἑκάστη τῶν ἐπιστημῶν . . . (208a3).

> always is, and neither comes into being nor perishes, neither increases nor diminishes; secondly one that is not beautiful in this respect but ugly in that, not beautiful at one moment but not at another, not beautiful in relation to this, but ugly in relation to that, not beautiful here but ugly there, because some people find it beautiful while others find it ugly; nor again will beauty appear to him to be the sort of thing a face is, or hands, or anything else in which a body shares, or a speech, *or a piece of knowledge.* (210e4–211a7, Rowe's translation; emphasis added)[26]

Beauty does not change, but the lover's epistemic state is an unstable bunch of *doxai*. As long as this contrast between beauty itself and the epistemic state of the lover remains—as long as the *doxa* remains unstable—it seems we should assume that some kind of belief that falls short of knowledge is being ascribed to the lover.

This contrasts with the stability that Plato generally associates with knowledge throughout the dialogues.[27] Further, it appears as though, to the degree that we can individuate them, we are at a loss to describe any individual belief as stable. This is because, even if it remains true, our assessments of the degree to which an individual belief is well reasoned shifts as elements that surround it in our epistemic structure shift. As noted before, my beliefs about my horse's muscles might seem true and well reasoned until I note that they are inconsistent with some of my beliefs about my horse's protein content. It looks like we must identify the entire doxastic structure with what counts as what we believe. To contrast this with JTB notions of knowledge, it seems unlikely that we will find any way to *identify* knowledge with an individual reasoned true belief if

---

26. . . . ἐφεξῆς τε καὶ ὀρθῶς τὰ καλά . . . ἐξαίφνης κατόψεταί τι θαυμαστὸν τὴν φύσιν καλόν, τοῦτο ἐκεῖνο, ὦ Σώκρατες, οὗ δὴ ἕνεκεν καὶ οἱ ἔμπροσθεν πάντες πόνοι ἦσαν, πρῶτον μὲν ἀεὶ ὂν καὶ οὔτε γιγνόμενον οὔτε ἀπολλύμενον, οὔτε αὐξανόμενον οὔτε φθίνον, ἔπειτα οὐ τῇ μὲν καλόν, τῇ δ' αἰσχρόν, οὐδὲ τοτὲ μέν, τοτὲ δὲ οὔ, οὐδὲ πρὸς μὲν τὸ καλόν, πρὸς δὲ τὸ αἰσχρόν, οὐδ' ἔνθα μὲν καλόν, ἔνθα δὲ αἰσχρόν, ὡς τισὶ μὲν ὂν καλόν, τισὶ δὲ αἰσχρόν· οὐδ' αὖ φαντασθήσεται αὐτῷ τὸ καλὸν οἷον πρόσωπόν τι οὐδὲ χεῖρες οὐδὲ ἄλλο οὐδὲν ὧν σῶμα μετέχει, οὐδέ τις λόγος οὐδέ τις ἐπιστήμη,

27. This is, perhaps, most clearly communicated in the comparison to Daedalus's statues at *Men.* 97a–98a, but is also implied in such places as *Euthd.* 280a6–8, and *Theaet.* 152c5–6.

we want what we say about belief to cohere with the impression of *doxa* that we get at *Symposium* 202–212. It could be that, for Plato, coming to have knowledge involves the transformation of an entire doxastic structure into something that is unified, stable, and, as a result, known. In which case, it would no longer be *doxa*.

Diotima describes the lover in the upward path as using beautiful things "like rising stairs" (211c3) in order to arrive at knowledge of beauty. Diotima presents knowledge of beauty as discontinuous with all of the accounts that lead up to it; it is different in kind. If anyone grasps beauty itself, it will no longer occur to him to judge beauty by these beautiful sights: not by gold, nor clothing, nor beautiful bodies (211d3–5). Diotima says that actual beauty is pure and unmixed, while—in perceptibles—it mixes with other properties (211d8–e2). Beliefs about beauty and ugliness will be reasoned and unreasoned, true and false. However, the beautiful things are not beauty itself. Further, *doxa*—whether about beauty itself, or beautiful things—is not knowledge.

The text suggests that beauty itself and knowledge of it are in a category unto themselves, and that their relationship to the beautiful objects and collections of beliefs that fall short of them is not simply a matter of degree.

> Beginning from these beautiful things here, one must always move upwards for the sake of that beauty I speak of, using the other things as steps . . . from beautiful bodies to beautiful sciences and finally from sciences to *that* [translator's emphasis] science, which is science of nothing other than beauty itself in order that one may finally *know*[28] [my emphasis] what beauty is itself. (211c1–211d1, Rowe's translation)[29]

---

28. If I were making an account of what Plato thinks knowledge is like, it would be worth noting that, here, we are no longer open to interpreting anything as pieces of knowledge. Also that perhaps there is some stability implied here—this knowledge of beauty cannot be forgotten and reconstructed in a similar manner to "knowledge" that only "seems to stay the same" at 208a5.

29. ἀρχόμενον ἀπὸ τῶνδε τῶν καλῶν ἐκείνου ἕνεκα τοῦ καλοῦ ἀεὶ ἐπανιέναι, ὥσπερ ἐπαναβασμοῖς χρώμενον . . . ἀπὸ τῶν καλῶν σωμάτων ἐπὶ τὰ καλὰ ἐπιτηδεύματα, καὶ ἀπὸ τῶν ἐπιτηδευμάτων ἐπὶ τὰ καλὰ μαθήματα, καὶ ἀπὸ τῶν μαθημάτων ἐπ' ἐκεῖνο τὸ μάθημα τελευτῆσαι, ὅ ἐστιν οὐκ ἄλλου ἢ αὐτοῦ ἐκείνου τοῦ καλοῦ μάθημα, καὶ γνῷ αὐτὸ τελευτῶν ὅ ἔστι καλόν.

130 | Opining Beauty Itself

Diotima acts as if Socrates and others might not be able to glimpse beauty itself:

> [Beauty itself], *if ever you see it.* . . . what then do we suppose it would be like *if* someone succeeded in seeing beauty itself [pure and not contaminated with mortal nonsense] but were able to catch sight of the uniformity of divine beauty itself? (211d2–212a1, Rowe's translation; emphasis added)[30]

There is no assumption that human beings actually succeed in reaching and seeing beauty itself. Similarly, it is unlikely that human beings ever entertain epistemological states that fix on all of, and only, what is true. Our doxastic systems will always be comprised of reasoned true beliefs that are mixed with other beliefs that are less true and less reasoned.

In the cases of both beauty and knowledge, it seems, the pure Form is the goal. It is an aspiration that leads us to recognize that there is a stairway to climb (it frees us from double ignorance). Further, it helps us maintain our motivation to continue to climb it, no matter how arduous it proves to be, as we recognize the advantages of improving our epistemological states—our doxastic mass—and therefore having a more true, more reasoned, doxastic structure. Nevertheless, Diotima hints that we might never reach the top and see beauty or have knowledge.

Doxastic Structures and Knowledge

Despite its lack of resonance with JTB theories, this analysis of *doxa* in the *Symposium* does resonate with what Plato says about true belief that has been tied down with a reasoned account at *Meno* 97a–98a. True beliefs about how to get to Larissa are, in that passage, represented as tremendously unstable; they disappear in the night like runaway slaves. The way to make them stable (and turn them into knowledge) is to tether them with a "causal account" (αἰτίας λογισμῷ). Our contemporary notion of justified true belief might incline us to interpret this passage as if the

---

30. ὃ ἐάν ποτε ἴδῃς . . . τί δῆτα, ἔφη, οἰόμεθα, εἴ τῳ γένοιτο αὐτὸ τὸ καλὸν ἰδεῖν εἰλικρινές, καθαρόν, ἄμεικτον, ἀλλὰ μὴ ἀνάπλεων σαρκῶν τε ἀνθρωπίνων καὶ χρωμάτων καὶ ἄλλης πολλῆς φλυαρίας θνητῆς, ἀλλ' αὐτὸ τὸ θεῖον καλὸν δύναιτο μονοειδὲς κατιδεῖν;

belief (an individual belief or a small number of individual beliefs) is to be tethered *to* a causal account. However, the Greek simply reads that they are not of much value until one ties them down "by (or with)" a causal account (*heôs an tis autas aitias logismô*). Most straightforwardly, this seems to indicate that the causal account is *itself the tether*, not that to which the tether is tied. To what is this belief (or group of beliefs) being tethered by a causal account? Again, it seems here that there is a notion of belief as a mass or structure where what increases its stability is the reasoning used to tether or *connect* those beliefs *to one another* to afford architectural integrity to that doxastic structure.

In fact, another passage that captures this picture of *doxa* as an undifferentiated cluster of interrelated commitments begins at *Theaetetus* 201d. There, Socrates and Theaetetus begin to entertain the proposal that knowledge is true belief plus an account. Socrates remembers someone saying that things of which there is no account are not knowable (*agnôsta*, 202b6), while things that have an account are. Socrates then goes on to pose problems that stem from the assumption that the belief itself and those things that account for it must be categorically different kinds of things—a complex and its elements.

Socrates goes on to show that one problem with the theory that says that knowledge is true belief plus an account is that it is agreed that a complex thing is known when it is accounted for by its simple elements. On the one hand, if we could give an account of the elements, we would end up with an infinite regression, so we assume the elements are simple and do not have an account (*Theaet.* 202b6).[31] However, on the other hand, since we agree that a thing cannot be known if it does not have an account, we are now stuck trying to know a complex by reducing it to unknowable elements. How can we know the complex by virtue of unknowables (203a1-d6)? So, true belief plus an account, where the account is elemental, is not going to get us knowledge.

Let us consider this part of the *Theaetetus*, Diotima's discussion in the *Symposium*, and the notion of tethered true belief in the *Meno*, together. Plato might be trying to make us question the assumption that the belief accounted for and the elements of the account must be different in kind. He might be trying to get us to question the notion that one is complex and the other is not. He might be trying to get us to reevaluate the notion of complexity. Must complexity indicate that a thing is *composed*

---

31. Ferejohn 2013, 172-74.

of a number of other things? Might it be that something is complex if it is only comprehensible by understanding its relation to the things with which it can be woven or mixed together?

The relevant *Meno* and *Symposium* passages suggest a different way of construing true belief plus an account. If we think of *doxa* as a mutually supportive structure whose integrity can be improved or reduced, then it looks like the account is not *made of* elements that are individual beliefs. Rather, the account is what remains of the structure after we have focused on the particular part for which we need to give an account. The entire structure is made of components of equal status that are not independent and can each serve as a focal thesis with the remainder consisting in the account—or part of the account—for this focal thesis.[32] The question of whether we have true belief plus an account might actually be determined by whether the entire doxastic structure maps onto the way the world is. I will place this aside as I am not arguing for any particular understanding of Platonic knowledge here. I do, however, want to observe that Plato might have a model in mind where any particular doxastic element upon which we choose to focus, if true, is true due to its relation to what-is, but is justified by how it coheres with, and is supported by, all of the other doxastic elements in which it is structurally embedded. On this model, the focal element and all of the others are of the same type. This would allow Plato to suggest that we have doxastic webs with better and worse degrees of structural integrity; thereby giving us lots of room to improve our doxastic structure's integrity. However, even with this improvement we might still be ignorant or at least not have something that Plato would deem knowledge, even if we have things that analytic theories would claim are justified true beliefs.[33]

---

32. The notion of a "tensegrity" structure as popularized by Buckminster Fuller comes to mind. See Pugh 1976.

33. In any case, tethering with a causal account as described here in the *Meno* seems far from what JTB advocates treat as justification. Most JTB theorists would say something like the following: I am justified in believing Fermat's last theorem because a mathematician I have good reason to trust told me that it is true. I also believe that the academic mathematical community (whom I also trust) has checked this proof and they agree with it. Most JTB theorists would say this is sufficient justification for me to *know* Fermat's last theorem. However, the discussion of reasoned true belief in the *Symp.* and the tying down of Daedalus's statues in the *Men.* do not seem to be talking about this sort of thing. What they describe seems more like understanding the proof. One would at least need to be able to reconstruct it and apply it. This

Doxastic Structures Are not Knowledge

Many (perhaps all) people entertain doxastic clouds that are only partly true and partly reasoned. Perhaps Plato wants to identify knowledge with a doxastic cloud that is altogether true and reasoned. The question of what knowledge is for Plato or Diotima lies beyond my focus in this book. However, it is worth looking at Diotima's assumptions about the relationship between *doxa* and ignorance in order to further clarify her thoughts regarding *doxa*.

At 202a5–9, Diotima says that unreasoned, true *doxa* cannot be identical to knowledge or ignorance,

> Don't you recognize . . . that having correct beliefs, even without being able to give a rational account of them, is neither a matter of knowing (since how could something irrational be knowledge?), nor of ignorance (how could something that hits on what is the case be ignorance?)? (Rowe's translation.)[34]

However, this does nothing to bar some kinds of *doxa* from being worse or further from knowledge than other kinds. In fact, a categorical separation of ignorance from *doxa* is impossible for Diotima because she never, in practice, equates individual, propositional beliefs with any epistemic state. Thus, there are better and worse doxastic structures, and doxastic structures can improve. This at least makes some of them more useful than others. The more useful a doxastic structure is, the more it functions the way knowledge functions. The less useful it is, the more it gives us the same result as ignorance.

In the upward path, Diotima speaks about *epistêmai* in the plural. She appears to be using the plural in a mass noun–like manner saying that parts of it can change while other parts stay the same. She is speaking of so-called knowledge (useful doxastic structures) as having multiple, simultaneous, pieces. Improving some of the pieces might improve the whole (*Symp.* 207e5–211a7).[35] In her analysis of Socrates's beliefs about

---

also seems more like what Plato has in mind in his discussion of true belief plus an account at *Theaet.* 201d. I am grateful to Ruth Saunders for suggesting this comparison.

34. Greek provided in n. 6, above.

35. ἐπιστῆμαι is literally translated "knowledges." This does not literally imply pieces of some, one "knowledge." But, Diotima speaks of even individual knowledges as

Erôs, she takes his epistemic condition to be some kind of sum value of all of his *doxa* taken together.

How exactly knowledge and *doxa* come together is a puzzle with which those who would like to develop a thorough interpretation of Platonic knowledge will have to contend. Of course, *doxa* that is true, but not completely reasoned, easily fails to be knowledge. But, it is also hard to construe any claim that Diotima is making as the sentiment that adding *logos* to an *individual proposition* turns it into knowledge.[36] We will also want to call some people's doxastic structures examples of ignorance. Many candidates for doxastic states smack of ignorance. They include many systems of belief that—as a whole—do not hit what-is because at least some parts of them are false or unreasoned even if other parts are of superior quality. Perhaps Plato has Diotima set us up with the naive expectation that we can make a linear hierarchy of individual propositional epistemic entities so that he can then rub our noses in the complexity of actual epistemic states and our efforts to evaluate them in an ordinal manner. Understanding what is in between knowledge and ignorance will not be easy.

Conclusion

The *doxa* that Diotima discusses in the *Symposium* is rich and complicated and it can be very disorganized and harmful rather than useful. These

---

changing (ἀλλὰ καὶ μία ἑκάστη τῶν ἐπιστημῶν ταὐτὸν πάσχει), so this does imply that even an individual branch or kind of knowledge is changing. Translators into English generally revert to speaking of "pieces of knowledge," I assume this is out of sensitivity to Diotima's employment of it in a mass-noun manner.

36. Even the road to Larissa example at *Men.* 97a9 does not make much sense when understood as an individual proposition becoming knowledge. It's more like the translation (perhaps into propositions) of an ever-changing satellite image, like Google Maps augmented by Waze. In fact, Plato's support for first-person experience in the case of the road to Larissa (if it is to provide something error free) seems well assimilated to the crowd-sourced real life experience of many people in real time as supplied by Waze. What knowledge needs, and what no ossified justification can provide, is the ability to strike the best balance between precision and generality. What does this will depend upon the actual circumstances in which one travels to Larissa. I am indebted to Nathan (2021, 267) for getting me to think about the pliability of what it is to be infallible with respect to striking a balance between precision and generality. I believe this concern looms large in Plato's elevation of knowledge to something that "never makes a mistake" (*Euthd.* 280a6-8, *Rep.* 477e6-7, *Theaet.*152c5-6).

doxastic structures can also be more organized, reasoned, and useful. They can be more like not-knowing (more like ignorance) or more like knowing (if they reflect what-is and possess structural integrity).

In contemporary analytic philosophy, "belief" has the connotation of a unitary and individuated propositional entity. The kind of *doxa* Diotima gives us at the beginning of inquiry and discovery and throughout these processes is more like a rich and undifferentiated cloud of epistemic experience.

The pre-investigatory, prephilosophical epistemic experience is this cloud of *doxa*. The activity of *making* one's belief system true and well reasoned is the process of isolating each of its content areas as they relate to what-is and to one another. In this process, the content will be changed and adjusted to fit better with the way the world is and what question one is trying to answer under what particular circumstances.[37] It may turn out that in the process of making our doxastic structure true and reasoned, we make ourselves more able to (artificially, but legitimately) divide it into nominally separate propositional beliefs. Even so, if we are never completely successful at rendering the entire cloud true and reasoned, we will be left with an interconnected network of artificially individuated propositional beliefs only some of which are true and accounted for. It is not clear that Plato would be willing to consider this knowledge. On the face of things, it is hard to avoid the impression that it is much easier for Plato to count our doxastic structures as continuing to be in between knowledge and ignorance, or as continuing to be ignorance even though it is the best and most useful kind of ignorance, than to count them as knowledge.

---

37. As I suggested in my above footnote (36) about going to Larissa using Google maps supplemented by Waze.

Chapter 6

Doxa, Ignorance, and False Judgment in the *Phaedrus* and *Theaetetus*

It does not look as if Plato wrote Diotima's speech in the *Symposium* in order to clarify his thoughts about *doxa*. In my discussion of that passage, I am either unpacking an argument that Plato attempts to make covertly, or diagnosing assumptions that he seems to be entertaining below the surface of the issues that he is overtly discussing. I think that this is actually a good way to reveal Plato's understanding of *doxa*, but only if it fits with, or even clarifies, his more straightforward examinations of *doxa*. I will now show that it does enlighten us with respect to other, more overt, discussions of *doxa* in two other dialogues. The *Phaedrus* contains Plato's third discussion of recollection. Here, Plato discloses why some souls' prenatal experience makes them have only *doxa* while others might at least eventually come to possess knowledge. I will then look at what is one of Plato's most prolonged discussions of *doxa*, his digression on false judgment in the *Theaetetus* (187d1-200c7).

Doxa and Ignorance in the *Phaedrus*

Several passages in the *Phaedrus* underline the notion that our entire spectrum of doxastic states includes those that count as ignorance and hence, that ignorance consists of *doxa(i)*. Because the *Phaedrus* is one of the three dialogues that talk about recollection, these same parts of the *Phaedrus* also contain evidence that Plato assumes that even those who are ignorant and have only *doxa* have an unwitting, cognitive connection to what-is.[1] As recollection is under discussion in this dialogue, here the unwitting cognitive connection is attributed to the soul's prenatal experiences. As a result, they provide further evidence that, for Plato, even mere *doxa* and ignorance are *about* what-is. I will go through these passages and present this evidence in the order in which it appears in the text. Thus, in our discussion of these passages we will move around a bit among the evidence for the thesis that all *doxa* is about what-is and the thesis that even those who are ignorant have unwitting cognitive contact with what-is.

All *Doxa* Is about What-is

At 248a–d, Socrates uses the image of a charioteer with two horses to describe souls that have various, and contrasting, appreciations of what-is. It is transparently evident in this text that what-is is to be identified with Form-like objects such as beauty itself:

> [The soul of the god] in its circuit sees justice itself, sees self-control, sees knowledge—not that knowledge to which coming to be attaches . . . but that which is in what really is and which is really knowledge (247d6–e3). . . . [O]f the other souls, the one that follows god best and has come to resemble him most raises the head of its charioteer into the region outside and is carried round with the revolution, [even] while being disturbed by its horses and scarcely seeing the things that are;[2] while another now rises, now sinks and because of the force exerted

---

[1]. Rather than to what both is and is-not as we will see in *Rep.* V. In chapter 7, I will argue for an interpretation that shows this passage to be consistent with what is said about the object of *doxa* in that part of the *Rep.*

[2]. I have modified Rowe's "meanwhile" to "even while" (supplied in any case: θορυβουμένη ὑπὸ τῶν ἵππων καὶ μόγις καθορῶσα τὰ ὄντα) in order to make sure we understand that this soul—though disturbed—is able to get the best grasp on what-is of any human soul (see Hackforth's far less literal translation). Ryan offers an apt analogy:

> The experience of the first soul is like that of a rail passenger who gazes out the window while traveling at high speed over a rough roadbed; the second is plagued by the same difficulties compounded by his carriage repeatedly, and quite without warning, plunging into tunnels. (2012: 194)

by its horses sees some things and not others. The remaining souls follow them, all straining to reach the place above but unable to do so. (248a1–7, Rowe's translation)[3]

Those souls whose horses are most controlled and least distracting have the best view of what-is (even if it is not a very good one), while those who are least able to control their horses are unable to see what-is at all. Those between the two extremes, the ones that both rise and sink, can become crippled (248b3–5). Some become so crippled that instead of relying on "the sight of reality" in order to carry on their lives, they have to depend on "opinion for sustenance."[4] The souls that never get to see what-is cannot be born as humans (249b6–249c4). Importantly, any souls born as human did get to see what-is, even if they became so crippled that they now must rely on *doxa*.[5]

Just as we will see, in the cave (*Rep.*, 514a–518b) and the divided line passages (*Rep.*, 509d–511d) in chapter 8, here those human souls who are in the worst epistemic condition do have *doxa*. The human souls who are in the worst epistemic condition are Plato's examples of ignorant individuals.[6] Ignorance consists in *doxa*, there is no separation between the two.[7] As we will see in chapter 7, this contrasts with some readings of *Republic* 475e4–479d5. I will argue in chapters 7–8 that those readings do not take some important contextual features of the uses of *doxa* in that *Republic* passage into account. These occurrences of *doxa* are in an argument that Plato says Socrates designed to console the lover of sights

---

3. ἐν δὲ τῇ περιόδῳ καθορᾷ μὲν αὐτὴν δικαιοσύνην, καθορᾷ δὲ σωφροσύνην, καθορᾷ δὲ ἐπιστήμην, οὐχ ᾗ γένεσις πρόσεστιν . . . ἀλλὰ τὴν ἐν τῷ ὅ ἐστιν ὂν ὄντως ἐπιστήμην οὖσαν: . . . αἱ δὲ ἄλλαι ψυχαί, ἡ μὲν ἄριστα θεῷ ἑπομένη καὶ εἰκασμένη ὑπερῆρεν εἰς τὸν ἔξω τόπον τὴν τοῦ ἡνιόχου κεφαλήν, καὶ συμπεριηνέχθη τὴν περιφοράν, θορυβουμένη ὑπὸ τῶν ἵππων καὶ μόγις καθορῶσα τὰ ὄντα: ἡ δὲ τοτὲ μὲν ἦρεν, τοτὲ δ' ἔδυ, βιαζομένων δὲ τῶν ἵππων τὰ μὲν εἶδεν, τὰ δ' οὔ. αἱ δὲ δὴ ἄλλαι γλιχόμεναι μὲν ἅπασαι τοῦ ἄνω ἕπονται, ἀδυνατοῦσαι δέ.

4. τροφῇ δοξαστῇ (248b5).

5. This is instructive regarding whether ordinary people can become philosopher kings. It looks like those who are so crippled that they forever rely on *doxa* are in E2, but cannot make a transition to E3, while those that both rose and sank, but did not become crippled, can.

6. I note that Hackforth also assimilates this piece of text in the *Phdr.* to the *Rep.*'s cave and line (1952, 81).

7. Unless we grant that there is ignorance that consists of a cognitive blank.

and sounds. This is why, in that *Republic* passage, Socrates contrasts *doxa* with ignorance in a striking and unusual way that is not common in the dialogues. The account I offer in chapters 7–8 *will* take the consolation of the lovers of sights and sounds into account in interpreting what Socrates says there about *doxa* and ignorance. In this *Phaedrus* passage, it is also useful to note that those who are most ignorant are straining to see what-is and are crippled by having misconceptions *of* what-is. This will also resonate with my reading of *Republic* 475e4–479d5.[8]

Everyone Has Unwitting Cognitive Contact with What-is

The *Pheadrus* further testifies to the notion that everyone who is born into a human body has had prenatal contact with the truth. It further corroborates that this prenatal contact with the truth provides an unwitting contact with the Forms that supplies the kind of reference that is a necessary precursor to recollection (the kind that we discussed in chapters 1–4). There is no evidence that it supplies something more than that, such as true beliefs or knowledge. The *Phaedrus* provides this testimony by alerting us to the fact that anyone who qualifies as human must have had some contact with the truth and, so, be able to use reason to bring many perceptible examples together under a reasoned unity. Everyone does this even if some humans possess souls that were crippled by their deficient experience of what-is. Therefore, some have souls that are not supremely equipped to achieve knowledge and must be sustained by mere belief instead. But, this must be mere belief that is still about the same things of which others had a more helpful fleeting glimpse while they themselves had a terrible one;

> For the soul which has never seen the truth shall not enter this shape of ours. A human being must comprehend what is said universally, arising from many sensations and being collected together into one through reasoning: and this is recollection of those things which our soul once saw when it travelled

---

8. Their misconceptions are not *of nothing at all* (which seems to be what Socrates says that ignorance has as its object in *Rep.* 475e4–479d5), as I will take pains to show in chapter 7.

in company with god and treated in contempt the things we now say are, and when it poked its head up into what really is. (249b6–249c4, Rowe's translation)[9]

Becoming a Philosopher: Recognizing One's Commitment to Thinking beyond Perceptibles

This same piece of text also makes it clear that the philosopher ("the one who uses the reminders of these things correctly" and "stands outside of human concerns" [249c6–d1]) deals with perceptibles, but understands that the point is to look beyond the perceptibles to the unities that they represent.[10] This previews for us the difference between the lovers of sights and sounds and the philosopher at *Republic* 475e4–479d5 and between the two middle sections of the divided line: *pistis* and *dianoia* (*Rep.* 509d–511d), which I will emphasize in chapters 7–9.[11]

This *Phaedrus* passage ends with a discussion of why, despite the fact that everyone has had previous contact with what-is, not everyone is equally good at recognizing that this is what they are thinking about when they do things such as use language. Furthermore, even those who have the advantage of having had a good look at what-is in their previous lives cannot always sort it out all at once and are likely to have some very good form of *doxa*, but one that falls short of knowledge.

> For as has been said, every soul of a human being has by the law of its nature observed things that are, or else it would not have entered this creature, man: but it is not easy for every soul to gain from things here a recollection of those other things, either for those which only briefly saw the things at an earlier time, or for those which fall to earth and have the

---

9. οὐ γὰρ ἥ γε μήποτε ἰδοῦσα τὴν ἀλήθειαν εἰς τόδε ἥξει τὸ σχῆμα. δεῖ γὰρ ἄνθρωπον συνιέναι κατ' εἶδος λεγόμενον, ἐκ πολλῶν ἰὸν αἰσθήσεων εἰς ἓν λογισμῷ συναιρούμενον· τοῦτο δ' ἐστὶν ἀνάμνησις ἐκείνων ἅ ποτ' εἶδεν ἡμῶν ἡ ψυχὴ συμπορευθεῖσα θεῷ καὶ ὑπεριδοῦσα ἃ νῦν εἶναί φαμεν, καὶ ἀνακύψασα εἰς τὸ ὂν ὄντως.

10. Here, we can think of this as a method of moving from E2 toward E3, once again (See chapter 3, above).

11. I have already introduced this comparison between lovers of sights and sounds and philosophers, in chapter 4.

misfortune to be turned to injustice by keeping certain kinds of company, forgetting the holy things they saw then. Few souls are left who have sufficient memory; and these, when they see some likeness of the things there, are driven out of their wits with amazement and lose control of themselves, though they do not know what has happened to them because they cannot properly see through it. (249e4–250b1, Rowe's translation)[12]

The souls with sufficient memory react to the likenesses, unaware of that to which they are truly reacting, which is what-is. This bespeaks the cognitive, but confused and, therefore, unwitting contact human souls have with the actual object of their *doxa*.

The fact that even the best souls cannot fully grasp what they are seeing seems to assign them some kind of doxastic structure that falls short of knowledge. This perhaps lends weight to my speculation concerning the end of *Symposium* 202–212, that Plato might think that no one who is embodied—not even the person who has seen beauty itself—enters a state of sufficient stability and infallibility that Plato is willing to deem it knowledge. This might, in turn, lend weight to my speculations that Plato thinks of knowledge as holistic and that, were anyone to have knowledge, it would have to be based on the condition of her entire doxastic structure all at once. But those are mere speculations, and I am not investing in any theses concerning knowledge in this book.

Ignorance Is Composed of *Doxa*

At *Phaedrus* 262c, the person who chases opinions rather than truth is called "ridiculous" and is shown to be so ignorant as neither to be able to fool others nor to be able to escape being fooled themself.

---

12. καθάπερ γὰρ εἴρηται, πᾶσα μὲν ἀνθρώπου ψυχὴ φύσει τεθέαται τὰ ὄντα, ἢ οὐκ ἂν ἦλθεν εἰς τόδε τὸ ζῷον: ἀναμιμνῄσκεσθαι δὲ ἐκ τῶνδε ἐκεῖνα οὐ ῥᾴδιον ἁπάσῃ, οὔτε ὅσαι βραχέως εἶδον τότε τἀκεῖ, οὔθ' αἳ δεῦρο πεσοῦσαι ἐδυστύχησαν, ὥστε ὑπό τινων ὁμιλιῶν ἐπὶ τὸ ἄδικον τραπόμεναι λήθην ὧν τότε εἶδον ἱερῶν ἔχειν. ὀλίγαι δὴ λείπονται αἷς τὸ τῆς μνήμης ἱκανῶς πάρεστιν: αὗται δέ, ὅταν τι τῶν ἐκεῖ ὁμοίωμα ἴδωσιν, ἐκπλήττονται καὶ οὐκέτ' ἐν αὑτῶν γίγνονται, ὃ δ' ἔστι τὸ πάθος ἀγνοοῦσι διὰ τὸ μὴ ἱκανῶς διαισθάνεσθαι.

Doxa, Ignorance, and False Judgment in the *Phaedrus* and *Theaetetus* | 143

> In that case, my friend, anyone who does not know the truth, but has made it his business to hunt down appearances, will give us a science of speech that will, so it seems, be ridiculously unscientific. (262c1–3, Rowe's translation)[13]

This would also seem to imply that those in the worst state of ignorance are among the opiners. Ignorance is not a cognitive blank, but it is a consequence of one's beliefs, how they cohere with one another, and how they map onto what-is.

More Unwitting Cognitive Contact

Phaedrus 265c–e, once more, appears to attribute an unwitting cognitive contact with what-is even to those who are ignorant to the point of using speech extremely poorly.

> S: [B]y chance two kinds of thing found expression, whose significance would be gratifying to express in a scientific way.
>
> P: What were these?
>
> S: First there is the perceiving together and bringing into one form items which are scattered in many places, in order that one may define each thing and make clear whatever it is that one wishes to instruct one's audience about on any given occasion. Just so with the things we said just now about what love amounts to when defined: whether what was said was right or wrong, because of it the speech was able to say what was at any rate clear and self-consistent.
>
> P: And what's the second thing you're talking about, Socrates?
>
> S: Being able to cut up whatever it is again, kind by kind, according to its natural joints, and not to try to break any part into pieces like an inexpert butcher. So too, the speeches

---

13. λόγων ἄρα τέχνην, ὦ ἑταῖρε, ὁ τὴν ἀλήθειαν μὴ εἰδώς, δόξας δὲ τεθηρευκώς, γελοίαν τινά, ὡς ἔοικε, καὶ ἄτεχνον παρέξεται.

regarded derangement as naturally a single form in us, and the one cut off the part on the left-hand side, then cutting it again and not giving up until it had found among the parts a love that is, as we say, "left-handed," and abused it with full justice, while the other speech led us to the parts of madness on the right-hand side, and discovering and setting forth a love that shares the same name as the other but is divine, it praised it as the cause of our greatest goods. (265c8–266b2, Rowe's translation)[14]

When we "define" (*horizomenos*) each thing we start out by gathering sense impressions that are scattered about everywhere, under one kind. Even if we do this incorrectly, this contact allows speech to proceed clearly and consistently. Furthermore, somehow—even if we did a bad job of it—this is cutting things up along their natural joints (correctly). This can only be the case if the reference of the natural kind that we claim to be defining begins by connecting us to whatever that natural kind actually is despite any incorrectness in our definition. Moreover, this only works if it continues to point to that thing through any process that refines that definition until it gets it right. That is what, in this case, happened with love: despite misconceptions, the interlocutors' unwitting grasp enabled them to sort out the fact that love is a madness and then to distinguish the sinister human obsessive madness from the divine one that is a great good. In the *Phaedrus*, this ability to cut nature at its joints due to our unwitting reference to the nature of each thing is a prequel to collection

---

14. . . . τούτων δέ τινων ἐκ τύχης ῥηθέντων δυοῖν εἰδοῖν, εἰ αὐτοῖν τὴν δύναμιν τέχνῃ λαβεῖν δύναιτό τις, οὐκ ἄχαρι. - τίνων δή; - εἰς μίαν τε ἰδέαν συνορῶντα ἄγειν τὰ πολλαχῇ διεσπαρμένα, ἵνα ἕκαστον ὁριζόμενος δῆλον ποιῇ περὶ οὗ ἂν ἀεὶ διδάσκειν ἐθέλῃ. ὥσπερ τὰ νυνδὴ περὶ Ἔρωτος—ὃ ἔστιν ὁρισθέν—εἴτ' εὖ εἴτε κακῶς ἐλέχθη, τὸ γοῦν σαφὲς καὶ τὸ αὐτὸ αὑτῷ ὁμολογούμενον διὰ ταῦτα ἔσχεν εἰπεῖν ὁ λόγος. - τὸ δ' ἕτερον δὴ εἶδος τί λέγεις, ὦ Σώκρατες; - τὸ πάλιν κατ' εἴδη δύνασθαι διατέμνειν κατ' ἄρθρα ᾗ πέφυκεν, καὶ μὴ ἐπιχειρεῖν καταγνύναι μέρος μηδέν, κακοῦ μαγείρου τρόπῳ χρώμενον: ἀλλ' ὥσπερ ἄρτι τὼ λόγω τὸ μὲν ἄφρον τῆς διανοίας ἕν τι κοινῇ εἶδος ἐλαβέτην, ὥσπερ δὲ σώματος ἐξ ἑνὸς διπλᾶ καὶ ὁμώνυμα πέφυκε, σκαιά, τὰ δὲ δεξιὰ κληθέντα, οὕτω καὶ τὸ τῆς παρανοίας ὡς ἓν ἐν ἡμῖν πεφυκὸς εἶδος ἡγησαμένω τὼ λόγω, ὁ μὲν τὸ ἐπ' ἀριστερὰ τεμνόμενος μέρος, πάλιν τοῦτο τέμνων οὐκ ἐπανῆκεν πρὶν ἐν αὐτοῖς ἐφευρὼν ὀνομαζόμενον σκαιόν τινα ἔρωτα ἐλοιδόρησεν μάλ' ἐν δίκῃ, ὁ δ' εἰς τὰ ἐν δεξιᾷ τῆς μανίας ἀγαγὼν ἡμᾶς, ὁμώνυμον μὲν ἐκείνῳ, θεῖον δ' αὖ τινα ἔρωτα ἐφευρὼν καὶ προτεινάμενος ἐπῄνεσεν ὡς μεγίστων αἴτιον ἡμῖν ἀγαθῶν.

and division. Thus, it is safe to conclude that collection and division (two further methods of inquiry) probably also require this unwitting cognitive contact with whatever the kind-itself actually is, as well.[15]

Ignorance Is Composed of *Doxa* (Reprised)

Phaedrus 269b–d also testifies to Plato's assumption that ignorance is composed of some kind of *doxa*:

> S: [If] some people who do not know how to converse prove unable to give a definition of what rhetoric is, and as a result of being in this state think that they have discovered rhetoric when they have merely learned the necessary preliminaries to the science, believing that when they teach these things to other people they have given them a complete course in rhetoric. (269b5–c2, Rowe's translation)[16]

> P: I rather think, Socrates, that the substance of the science that these men teach and write up as rhetoric is something like that. (269c6–8, Rowe's translation)[17]

Once again, we confirm that Plato does not imagine that *doxa* and ignorance are mutually exclusive; Plato hews to the ordinary seeming assumption that ignorance is, at least most often, composed of beliefs. Those in the worst epistemic state have many (preliminary and perhaps even appropriate)

---

15. Certainly, for division one must already grasp the part within the whole as the butcher, ideally, already somehow senses the boundaries of the cut of meat in the whole animal or as the sculptor frees the form from the marble. With collection, one must already be sensitized to whatever the disparate group of objects has in common so that there is some prior possibility that when one wants to examine what a bee is essentially one gathers together a group of sensible objects that are, arguably, bees.

16. . . . εἴ τινες μὴ ἐπιστάμενοι διαλέγεσθαι ἀδύνατοι ἐγένοντο ὁρίσασθαι τί ποτ' ἔστιν ῥητορική, ἐκ δὲ τούτου τοῦ πάθους τὰ πρὸ τῆς τέχνης ἀναγκαῖα μαθήματα ἔχοντες ῥητορικὴν ᾠήθησαν ηὑρηκέναι, καὶ ταῦτα δὴ διδάσκοντες ἄλλους ἡγοῦνταί σφισιν τελέως ῥητορικὴνδεδιδάχθαι . . .

17. ἀλλὰ μήν, ὦ Σώκρατες, κινδυνεύει γε τοιοῦτόν τι εἶναι τὸ τῆς τέχνης ἣν οὗτοι οἱ ἄνδρες ὡς ῥητορικὴν διδάσκουσίν. . . .

opinions about, for example, rhetoric.[18] Their problem is that they have nothing to look to in order to organize those beliefs or to deploy them in order to create a science that can be deployed in a reliable manner and that can be taught (269c9–d1). In the next chapter, we will be able to appreciate the similarity between this statement about the ignorant and the contention at *Republic* 477a9–10 that ignorant people set their epistemic capacities upon "nothing at all" while entertaining doxastic commitments that must be about something as those commitments do have truth values that are determined by what-is.

Phaedrus 269e4–270a1 again highlights the notion that even our worst epistemic states are about the nature of what-actually-is:

> All sciences of importance require the addition of babbling and lofty talk *about nature* (*phuseôs peri*); for the relevant high mindedness and effectiveness in all directions seem to come from some such source as that. (Rowe's translation, emphasis added)[19]

Without contact between even our low-value babbling and the natures of that about which we are babbling, we cannot move from ignorance to the development of a knowledge-laden practice rather than one that is "artless and empirical" (270b5–6).

Doxa and False Judgment in the *Theaetetus*

The first part of the *Theaetetus* (142a–186e) develops a line of argument against Theaetetus's proposal that knowledge is perception.[20] In opening the second part of the dialogue, Socrates contrasts the current project upon which he and Theaetetus will now embark with what they have just

---

18. They "think that they have discovered rhetoric when they have merely learned the preliminaries to the science" (Rowe's translation of τὰ πρὸ τῆς τέχνης ἀναγκαῖα μαθήματα ἔχοντες ῥητορικὴν [269b7–8]).

19. πᾶσαι ὅσαι μεγάλαι τῶν τεχνῶν προσδέονται ἀδολεσχίας καὶ μετεωρολογίας φύσεως πέρι· τὸ γὰρ ὑψηλόνουν τοῦτο καὶ πάντῃ τελεσιουργὸν ἔοικεν ἐντεῦθέν ποθεν εἰσιέναι.

20. While I believe that parts of that passage would provide additional fodder for my claims about what Plato thought about the nature of such internal states as perception and *doxa*. I do not think enough would be gained to make it worth going through those arguments here. Please see my 1994 for my view on the first third of the *Theaet.*

finished doing, saying that they will now look for knowledge in "whatever we call that activity of the soul when it is busy by itself about things that are" (187a4–6). Theaetetus responds that this activity must be *doxa*, and Socrates verifies that he is indeed talking *about doxa* (197a7–9). In other words, they are now confining themselves to the world of *doxa*. What is most important for the type of evidence that I am looking at regarding *doxa* is the fact that Socrates characterizes it as "about things that are" (*peri ta onta*). Plato here refers to *doxa* unqualified. We have a clear statement that, in this dialogue, Plato has no problem asserting that all *doxa* is about what-is. It is not (or at least not only) about what both is and is-not, which is what we will see he seems to assert at *Republic* 477a6–b1. Furthermore, when he proceeds to discuss false *doxa* at length, he does not make any exception for it. He does not claim that false *doxa* is about nothing at all.[21] The aforementioned passage in *Republic* V says nothing about false belief, but it does appear to assert that ignorance is about nothing at all. In chapters 7–9, I will address this seeming inconsistency and argue for a more nuanced interpretation of that section of *Republic* V–VII that is consistent with these assertions in the *Theaetetus*.

We should also note Plato's tacit reliance on the non-doxastic connection that I have diagnosed in the *Meno*, *Phaedo*, and *Republic*. It must underlie his claim that it is possible to entertain false beliefs. Again, when we look at *doxa*, and now at *doxa* that is false, we once again need to avail ourselves of the notion that there is a spectrum of better and worse doxastic states whose content does not necessarily determine what they are about. Thus, their aboutness (of what-is) comes from the same referential prerequisite that we saw applied to other ignorant states: an unwitting cognitive connection. In particular, in many cases of false *doxa*, it must be this connection that allows a judgment to be false *about* what-is.

Interpreting False Belief in the *Theaetetus*

In the middle of the *Theaetetus*, at 188a1–2, Plato has Socrates assert, "Everything is either known or unknown." This is reminiscent of (S1) from Meno's paradox (see chapter 1, 32–36, above). Once more, we are confronted with a statement that allows for the following two interpretations:

---

21. Certainly, a major thesis of the *Soph.* is that false statement is not about nothing at all, it is about otherness with respect to things that are (262e5–6).

(S1M) Every *x* is either something I know completely or something concerning which I am completely ignorant; knowing and not knowing is all or nothing, it does not come in stages or degrees.

(S1S) Knowledge obeys the law of excluded middle; there is some range of doxastic states with knowledge at one extreme and ignorance at the other and somewhere along this spectrum there is a cut-off point where everything to one side of it counts as knowledge and everything to the other side counts as not-knowledge, even if it counts as *mere* true belief.[22]

Recall that, in the *Meno*, some wanted to support (S1M) as the proper reading and others found (S1M) too implausible to be seriously contemplated by Socrates's character. They found it implausible because it involves saying that one either knows *x* or is cognitively blank concerning *x*, and it seems unlikely that anyone is cognitively blank concerning anything (and certainly, Socrates and Meno appear not to be cognitively blank about virtue). By contrast, here, in the *Theaetetus*, it is hard to find a commentator who does not go with the (S1M) reading. However, they do so for different reasons. Some do so because they think that Plato thinks of knowledge along the lines of what we today call "knowledge by acquaintance" and that, therefore, for Plato, knowledge is hit or miss and all or nothing.[23]

Fine (2003, 212) also grants that at this point in the *Theaetetus* we are to understand this thesis as (S1M). However, in contrast to those just mentioned, she does not think that Plato *believes* (S1M); she thinks that Plato has Socrates premise the false belief discussion with (S1M) because it is the kind of all or nothing theory of knowledge that must follow from Theaetetus's suggestion that knowledge is true belief (*Theaet*. 187b6). According to Fine, it is the suggestion that knowledge is true belief that Plato is really trying to undermine by showing that a theory that embraces (S1M) cannot fathom false belief. If (S1M) produces a theory that cannot

---

22. I am using (S1M) and (S1S) to follow Fine's (2014, 12, 71) proposal that (S1M) is how Meno understands (S1) initially and (S1S) is how Socrates reinterprets it. See chapter 1, n. 18.

23. For example, see McDowell 1973, 194; Cornford 1935, 110. See my discussion of knowledge by acquaintance in chapter 1, 49–50.

allow for false belief, then it is obvious that we must abandon (S1M) because it is obvious that there are false beliefs.

Perhaps Plato does intend for us to interpret *Theaetetus* 188a1-2 as (S1M). Just as we found a brute counterexample to (S1)—however construed—in the *Meno*, through the fact that the slave can learn something he didn't already know, in the *Theaetetus* (187b4-5, d1-4), Plato presents the obvious existence of false belief as a brute counterexample to (S1).[24] His argument will show that, if S1 is true, there can be no false belief, but clearly there is false belief. For example, Theaetetus earlier in the dialogue held the false belief that knowledge is perception (183c).

I also think that Plato is pointing us to *something like* (S1M), partly because it seems that he doesn't think much of (S1S). *Symposium* 200-212 offers resistance to the claim that there is a logical progression of doxastic states from better to worse, which are ordered in such a way that we can pinpoint some boundary where one side is *doxa* that amounts to ignorance and the other side is *doxa* that amounts to knowledge.[25] It seems to me that Plato might be championing the view that everything is either known or unknown in a manner that is in keeping with what we observed in the *Symposium* and the *Phaedrus*. That is, he might place the entire

---

24. Rudebusch (1985) does a nice job of summarizing Plato's deflation of the view that mistakes (false beliefs) can be explained through mismatches (misidentifications) and shows it to be a deflation of Frege's strategy of introducing senses in order to explain why some identities are surprising despite the fact that a = a is never a surprise. His article dovetails nicely with the point that I am making here. His thesis is that in order to explain a misidentification, we need to add at least one new object that wasn't considered in the first attempt at identification. For misidentification in our beliefs, we always add something that is contained within the sphere of *doxa* and since this is always something we will take ourselves to know incorrigibly (like a Fregean sense), it will remain mysterious how we managed to mismatch it with something else that we either know or don't know. It is mysterious because it requires us not to realize that a = a. It appears that I differ from Rudebusch. He thinks that Plato might be giving up the idea that there is false belief. However, since I am supposing that Plato's view of *doxa* is very different from the notion of false (propositional) belief assumed by the likes of Frege, I think I can agree with Rudebusch that Plato is not fumbling in his efforts to come up with Frege's answer but "clear[ing] the ground in preparation for his own strange theory" (537). Still, I believe that Rudebusch has in mind some stranger theory than the one I propose later in this chapter. See Rudebusch (1990) and pages 160-61, below.

25. S1S also ignores any consideration of the plausibility of the position for which the likes of Moss, Schwab, Gerson, and Vogt have argued, namely, that knowledge cannot be identified with any kind of *doxa*.

doxastic spectrum—including the entire range of doxastic structures of the best usefulness and quality—on the ignorance side of the knowledge versus ignorance dichotomy. Everything is either not-known (i.e., it is ignorance, which is a quick way to talk about every kind of *doxa* on the spectrum), or it is knowledge (which is not a kind of *doxa*).[26] While I will come to argue for this interpretation of how the not-knowing side of the (S1M) dichotomy should be understood, arguing for anything regarding the knowing side of the (S1M) dichotomy would take me too far into concerns about what knowledge is for Plato. I will not discuss that side of the dichotomy, as I am focused only on those epistemic states that fall short of knowledge in this book.

The Transition from "What Is Knowledge?" to "What Is False Belief?"

At 187b4–5, Theaetetus is quick to point out that belief cannot simply be identified with knowledge, as there is both true belief and false belief. Theaetetus then suggests that knowledge is *true* belief. The remainder of this section of the dialogue looks like a digression. Socrates claims to be dragging Theaetetus back to an "old point about belief" (187c7): the old point is that it is impossible to come up with an account of false belief. It is not that either Socrates or Theaetetus doubts that false belief occurs—it obviously does (Theaetetus used to believe falsely that knowledge is perception).

Socrates begins the investigation of false belief with the premise that, once learning and forgetting are set aside, each thing is such that we either know it or don't know it.[27] Since *everything* is something we either know or don't know, this must be true of the objects of our beliefs as well; they must be either things we know or things we don't know (188a1–4). As I shall show below, he then devises models that conform to S1, to see if they allow for false belief. When that fails, he follows with models that add back in things remembered and those recently introduced (objects of

---

26. This would show me to be sympathetic with some aspects of the kind of view encouraged by Gerson, Vogt, and, Moss and Schwab.

27. περὶ πάντα καὶ καθ' ἕκαστον, ἤτοι εἰδέναι ἢ μὴ εἰδέναι; (188a1–2).

Doxa, Ignorance, and False Judgment in the *Phaedrus* and *Theaetetus* | 151

learning) as a means for finding the alternative to the restrictions provided by S1, to see if that can allow for false belief.

The Argument from Knowing and not-Knowing

Socrates puts the claim that everything is known or not known as follows: "When a man believes, the objects of his belief are necessarily either things he knows or things he doesn't know."[28] Having assumed that each object of belief is either known or unknown, Socrates rehearses all of the situations in which we cannot have a false belief:

> (I1) You cannot mistake two things that you do know for each other. (188b2–5)
>
> (I2) You cannot mistake two things you do not know for each other. (188b7–10)
>
> (I3) You cannot mistake something that you do know for something that you do not know (and the other way around). (188c2–3)

Let us refer to these as the "three impossibilities." It is clear that false belief is impossible on the model where knowledge involves mistakes that relate what one knows to what one does not know.[29]

The Argument from Being and not-Being

Socrates quickly turns to another hypothesis: the hypothesis that false belief involves either (1) believing what is-not about one of the things

---

28. τὸν δοξάζοντα δοξάζειν ἢ ὧν τι οἶδεν ἢ μὴ οἶδεν; (188a7–8).

29. This is perhaps clearest in the case of Fine's understanding of (S1M) as it involves mistaking something one knows completely for something concerning which one is cognitively blank, or the other way around. This is why many people think that (S1M) should be treated as Socrates's understanding of S1 in this dialogue.

that are, or (2) believing what is-not (just by itself) (188d3–e2). However, Socrates decides that just as one can only see, hear, or touch something that-is, one cannot entertain beliefs about something that-is-not. One can only have beliefs about what-is, so false belief cannot be a judgment of what is-not. Again, if false belief can be identified with ignorance, this is strikingly inconsistent with the apparent claim at *Republic* 477a3–5 that ignorance is of what is-not.

Heterodoxy

Socrates next proposes that false belief is a kind of "heterodoxy" (other judging): a case where we accidentally substitute one of the things that-is for another of the things that-is. In order to do this sort of substitution, a person must set down something in her thought as something other than itself (189d7–8). In order to do that, the person in question must have both things that are to be confused before her mind, either at the same time or in sequence (189e1–3).

Socrates then describes thinking and something we will now call "judgment" (still referred to by Plato using the word *doxa*[30]) in relation to one another:

---

30. As mentioned in earlier chapters, *doxa* is translated variously as "belief," "opinion," and "judgment" by different people in different places in published translations of Plato's dialogues. As a general term, *doxa* seems to encompass all of these English terms and be wider than each of them separately. It is also wider than the disjunction of all of them. In general, I have been using whichever English word best fits with my English prose or corresponds to the translation used by a commentator on a particular passage. See Burnyeat (1990, 68–70), Bostock (1986, 156–158), McDowell (1973, 193), and Cornford (1934, 109–10) for similar comments about translating *doxa* into English. Here, at *Theaet.* (189e–190a), however, there is reason to get more technical with the term *judgment*. Socrates gets very specific about a species of *doxa*, saying that it is the outcome of *dianoeisthai*; it is the determination one makes as a result of a dialogue that one has silently with oneself. At *Soph.* (263e–264b) he makes a similar distinction between *dianoia* and *doxa*. This leads to the common practice of translating *doxa* as "judgment" in those two dialogues. I am following this practice and am agreeing that Plato is trying to make a distinction at this moment between a more generic kind of *doxa*, which I have described in the *Symp.* and *Phdr.*, and a more precise species of *doxa* that is the outcome of the dialogue the soul has with itself. Clearly, these terms are not used consistently with this distinction across all of the dialogues, as *dianoia* appears to be a higher cognitive state than *doxa* on the divided line (*Rep.* 509d–511e). I will address this in chapters 8–9.

A discussion that the soul conducts with itself concerning whatever it might consider.... For [the soul], it seems to me, when it is thinking (*dianooumenê*), does nothing other than to have a dialogue; asking itself questions and answering them itself and affirming and denying. But whenever it delineates something, whether gradually or in a sudden leap, and continues to affirm it without doubt, we call this judgment (*doxan*). (189e7–190a4)[31]

In distinguishing thinking from judgment, it seems Plato is describing a view concerning *doxa* of which we caught a more fleeting glimpse in the *Symposium* passage. Plato is presenting generic *doxa* as a mass or cloud of thinking activity. We are always dealing with a doxastic system that is rich and varied enough that it can have a "dialogue" among its parts (some of which are at odds with others). It goes through deliberations that are puzzling and slow even if it sometimes sees something all in one leap. Part of making our entire doxastic system reasoned is individuating it, via reflection, into particular "judgments" that we look at against the background of the rest of our doxastic structure. It is only then that we can, perhaps, come to see whether we should affirm or deny an individuated judgment. The individuation process is just as much a part of the deliberation as is the decision to affirm or deny that individual judgment. To echo what I said regarding the *Symposium* passage, individual judgments are artifacts that are created by human reflection, judgment, and rationalization. Our manner of doing this will work best if it is sensitive to the inquiry we are making and the circumstances that necessitated our efforts to sort out our beliefs and sense experiences in order to answer that inquiry.

At this point, Socrates concludes that when we judge we affirm or deny a statement silently to ourselves. But, he continues, how does this help us with false judgment? We judge falsely that the beautiful thing is ugly or that the animal before us is a cow when it is actually a horse. We all know that this kind of thing happens. However, it cannot be that we affirm statements such as, "Beauty is ugliness" or, "A cow is a horse" to

---

31. λόγον ὃν αὐτὴ πρὸς αὑτὴν ἡ ψυχὴ διεξέρχεται περὶ ὧν ἂν σκοπῇ ... τοῦτο γάρ μοι ἰνδάλλεται διανοουμένη οὐκ ἄλλο τι ἢ διαλέγεσθαι, αὐτὴ ἑαυτὴν ἐρωτῶσα καὶ ἀποκρινομένη, καὶ φάσκουσα καὶ οὐ φάσκουσα. ὅταν δὲ ὁρίσασα, εἴτε βραδύτερον εἴτε καὶ ὀξύτερον ἐπᾴξασα, τὸ αὐτὸ ἤδη φῇ καὶ μὴ διστάζῃ, δόξαν ταύτην τίθεμεν αὐτῆς.

ourselves. No one ever thinks carefully through their thoughts and ends up saying silently to themselves that x is something that is $\sim x$. So, what might other judging be? While this is a problem, note that Plato's solution to the beginning problem discussed in chapters 1–4 anticipates a way out: a judgment can have *content* that is independent of what it is *about*. *Doxa* that contains content that bespeaks cow-itself can be—unwittingly—in contact with horse-itself.

The Wax Block

All looks bad for other-judging and the existence of false belief at this moment, but at 191b, Socrates revives the project anew. There might be a way that one can judge something he knows to be something he does not know. Back at 188a, Socrates set aside learning and forgetting, and dealt only with what is known and what is not-known. Now he will reintroduce them.

His strategy seems to be to try to find a doxastic state that is weaker than the outcome of the silent dialogue that produces what he calls judgment.

I suggest that Plato's strategy is as follows. Learning something new and forgetting something are modes of *doxa(i)* that are weaker than what he has just identified as "judgment." They are not the considered outcome of debates with the self. They can be less than fully formed or, if fully formed, their truth values are suggested to us from other sources, rather than our own deliberations. My doxastic structure contains scraps about various constellations of stars that I've seen, concerning which I have never tried to adjudicate let alone make affirmations or denials. It also contains affirmations such as, "The square of a negative number is a positive number," which I affirm but have never deliberated about or tried to integrate with the rest of my *doxa(i)*. Learning from others can give me some pre-individuated statements the truths of which I have not yet judged for myself. Forgetting can leave me with some *doxa* that is too scrappy to be verifiable. This inferior quality of *doxa* affords us a fuzziness regarding both its content and what it is about.

In reprising learning and forgetting, I suggest that Plato wants something that is not a cognitive blank but is still a case of not-knowing. Something that has content but is on the not-knowing side of (S1M). His

Doxa, Ignorance, and False Judgment in the *Phaedrus* and *Theaetetus* | 155

hypothesis is that this would enable us to confuse something we don't know but have some other relationship with, with something we do know. This hypothesis will not be right, but it will get him partway to his goal.

Plato has Socrates reintroduce memory and learning by devising a model upon which the soul contains a wax block. The action of stamping an image upon the wax block constitutes learning something new, and the maintenance of the image within the wax block symbolizes memory. Now we are to consider a person who has a wax block with imprints in it and who, at the same time, perceives things.

Next, Socrates rehearses all of the three impossibilities multiplied by all of the different ways in which mistakes might occur: if we stick only with the imprints, we will not be able to confuse them in any of the three ways mentioned (two imprints with one another, an imprint with nothing—and the reverse, and two nothings with one another) (192a).[32] Moreover, if we stick only with our perceptions, we will be similarly unable to confuse them (192b).[33] Nevertheless, Socrates has a further suggestion: he increases the sophistication of this new model by introducing the notion of having an imprint and perception of the same thing *where the imprint and the perception are held in line with one another*:

> Yet, again, it is not possible to think that a thing that you both know and are perceiving, where you are holding its imprint in line with its perception [your perception of it] is another

---

32. It is hard to capture this with English here: where I am saying "nothing," Socrates is saying, "something which you don't know and of which you don't have an imprint" (καὶ ὅ γε οἶδεν αὖ, οἰηθῆναι εἶναι ὃ μὴ οἶδε μηδ' ἔχει αὐτοῦ σφραγῖδα, 192a5-6). While you can confuse an imprint with *something* that *is*, but of which you do *not have an imprint*, mismatching can occur (and can only occur) between two different kinds of things (imprints and perceptions, for example) (see Rudebusch 1985 and n. 33, below). The idea is that if you, for example, had only *one* imprint, you would not be able to *confuse* it in any way—you cannot confuse something with nothing).

33. Another way to put this is to say that in none of these cases would this confusion be a "mismatch." These would be "mistakes" or "misidentifications" of a thing with itself. This type of mistake requires both knowing and not knowing the same thing (somehow getting a = a wrong), which seems impossible. See Rudebusch (1985) for the distinction between mismatching (which must happen between an imprint and a perception) and mistaking (which is a misidentification of an imprint and an imprint [or a perception and a perception]).

thing that you know and are perceiving and are also holding its imprint in line with its perception (192b2–5).³⁴

Socrates rehearses cases where false belief cannot occur on this model. All are extensions of the three original impossibilities at 188ab. In fact, these same three impossibilities are translated to the wax block model at 192d. To summarize, the upshot is that whenever one is comparing two things, where, for at least one of them, one has both a perception and an imprint and, in at least that one case, the imprint and the perception are being held in line with one another, false belief cannot occur. None of these affords us an alternative to knowing and not-knowing.

To clarify for the baffled Theaetetus, Socrates applies the wax block model to an actual case. The clarification is premised upon the observations that, (1) when it comes to things we know, we sometimes perceive them and sometimes do not perceive them, and (2) when it comes to things we do not know, we often do not perceive them. Nevertheless, we sometimes do perceive them and, further, in the case where we do perceive them, we *only perceive them and do not know them*:

> Then as regards the things we don't know, we often don't perceive them either, but often we only perceive them? (192e5–6)³⁵

This strategic variation is, again, Plato's effort to add some nuance and complexity to the description of things we do not know in order to make them available for participation in our false judgments.

Note that at this stage he must lean on the assumption of unwitting cognitive contact that solved the beginning problem in chapters 1–4. Plato wants an object to enter into our epistemological discussion as an object of cognition but not an object of knowledge, partial knowledge, or true belief. This is, or is analogous to, that object's being perceived but not known. We are cognitively connected to it while continuing to be ignorant of it. This relationship is designed to be one of not knowing while giving us some sort of contact with the object it is actually *of*, but

---

34. καὶ ἔτι γε αὖ καὶ ὃ οἶδε καὶ αἰσθάνεται καὶ ἔχει τὸ σημεῖον κατὰ τὴν αἴσθησιν, οἰηθῆναι αὖ ἕτερόν τι ὧν οἶδε καὶ αἰσθάνεται καὶ ἔχει αὖ καὶ ἐκείνου τὸ σημεῖον κατὰ τὴν αἴσθησιν. . . .

35. οὐκοῦν καὶ ἃ μὴ οἶδε, πολλάκις μὲν ἔστι μηδὲ αἰσθάνεσθαι, πολλάκις δὲ αἰσθάνεσθαι μόνον;

unwittingly so. The contact with the perception does not require *any* absorption of content into our thinking. Our perception is successful in that it is *of* a specific object but is not required to have any content. This kind of perception would involve our having unwitting cognitive contact with whatever it is (actually) a perception of.

Once again, Plato rehearses all of the ways that the three impossibilities will prevent false belief from emerging on this model: If we have imprints of both Theaetetus and Theodorus, but perceive neither, we cannot confuse them; If we have an imprint of only one of them, and perceive neither, we cannot confuse them (and also if we have a perception of only one of them, and an imprint of neither); If we have neither an imprint nor a perception of either one of them, we cannot confuse them. But finally, here's a case that seems to work: suppose that we have an imprint of each of them and have a perception of each of them. However, our perception is faulty—they are far away, or poorly lit, or we only get to look for a very short time—we might mismatch the faulty perception of Theaetetus with our imprint of Theodorus and vice versa (193b9–d2). This could also happen if we have an imprint of each and a substandard perception of only one.

At 194b1–4, Socrates gives a rather dissatisfying mid-argument assessment:

> [I]t is in cases where we both know things and are perceiving them that judgment is erratic and varies between truth and falsity.[36]

Socrates says that only in cases where we both have an imprint and perceive can our beliefs vary between truth and falsity, because it is only in this case that we can bring our perceptions and imprints together in this crosswise fashion. However, Socrates's summary leaves out something important: it is only in the case where we have both an imprint and a perception *and the perception is substandard* that this other-judging can occur. I emphasize this because a substandard perception seems designed to play the role of something that is not a case of knowing but has been introduced as an epistemological state that is weaker than knowledge or even judgment. It is likely that this kind of doxastic state can only *be* about

---

36. . . . περὶ δὲ ὧν ἴσμεν τε καὶ αἰσθανόμεθα, ἐν αὐτοῖς τούτοις στρέφεται καὶ ἐλίττεται ἡ δόξα ψευδὴς καὶ ἀληθὴς γιγνομένη. . . .

what it is *actually* about through an unwitting cognitive connection (since we have no idea, or are wrong about, what the perception is *actually of*). Thus, it is only in the case where we have this unwitting cognitive connection that we can relate the object our perception is about to another, falsely, in a judgment.

Socrates has gone beyond the possibilities of knowing *x* or being a cognitive blank. He has expanded his palette concerning what is contained on the not-knowing side of the dichotomy. Now there are things we do not know and only perceive (as when I see a person I have never met) (192e6) and substandard perceptions of things concerning which we already have imprints (such as when I catch such a fleeting glimpse of my mother that I do not recognize her). It seems that, in order to account for false beliefs, Socrates has to introduce a kind of *doxa* that is not even judgment let alone true belief, partial knowledge, or knowledge. Further, he has to claim that people who make mistakes do it through this more amorphous kind of *doxa* that must be related to (be *of*) the object concerning which they are mistaken in a manner that is content independent.

Knowledge Cannot Be Part of the Analysis of False Belief

The text continues in an even more surprising vein. While the above discussion focuses on the poverty of the perception, it now becomes clear that Plato thinks this model works because the *imprint* is substandard.[37] At 194c5–d7, Socrates says that wise men who have wax that is deep, abundant, smooth, and well constituted will never mismatch a perception with an imprint not its own. Those who have knowledge will not mismatch an imprint with a perception, no matter how quickly they gained their impression. It is in cases where there is an indistinct impression (because the wax was too hard, too soft, or too lumpy 194e1–195a9) that this mismatch occurs. So, despite Plato's recent development of a palette that contains some weaker epistemological relationships, heterodoxy cannot make use of any of them in a person who has good wax and, therefore, good imprints. Presumably, good imprints—ones that constitute knowledge (whatever that is)—overcome weak perceptions and do not allow for con-

---

[37]. Thus, I would take the liberty of translating ἴσμεν (we know) as "we have an imprint of" at 194b1. See Fine (2014, 50–53, 131) for Plato's casual use of many verbs that might appear to be claims of knowledge.

Doxa, Ignorance, and False Judgment in the *Phaedrus* and *Theaetetus* | 159

fusion about them. One needs *both* weak imprints *and* weak perceptions in order for heterodoxy to occur. Heterodoxy—the only kind of false belief for which Plato has been able to devise a model—only happens when even the *imprint* does not allow for knowledge. A faulty imprint is another case of generic *doxa* that is neither knowledge nor judgment and that seems to have the same content-independent relationship to what it is about that those faulty perceptions do. Those with knowledge (which, here anyway, seems to involve—at least—good, distinct imprints) do not make these mismatches, those without knowledge do.

Plato will now turn away from this model—ostensibly for other reasons. Still, we should note the following: if this model has done anything for providing an account of false belief, it has done so by making both imprints and perceptions doxastic elements that are neither deliberated judgments nor knowledge.[38]

Let's labor over something that seems a bit odd here. Plato develops a model upon which—at least at first blush—false belief can occur. At first it looks as though he does so by weakening the epistemological strength of the perception, but he claims that it results from a weakening of the imprint that learning has placed, and memory has retained, in the block of wax. Plato goes on to surmise that only those who do not have knowledge can have false beliefs (due to heterodoxy) on this model.

Why did Plato come to this conclusion? Why not be content that a person can have an excellent imprint (i.e., knowledge) and still get the perception and the imprint misaligned (because the perception, not the imprint, is faulty)? At 194b, we get a textual hint at a possible answer to this question: Throughout the discussion of the wax block, Plato refers to the imprint as a "sign" (*sêmeion*) and to the perception as such (*aisthêsin*), suggesting that only the imprint is found in the wax. Yet, at 194b4–6, he refers to both of them using variations on the same term for "print" (*tupos*):

---

38. This fits well with any proclivity Plato has for treating knowledge as infallible and stable. Although I am not making any positive pronouncements about what Plato thinks knowledge is here, this might set some constraints. It might be that Plato is thinking that those who have knowledge cannot make mistakes. It might make sense to assume that Plato thinks this is because knowledge is so holistic that knowing any part of what-is will require knowing all of it. Plato maintains that people who have good wax do not have false beliefs (194c5–d4), so the only model upon which false belief is possible is one upon which there is no knowledge. That is, false belief is only possible on a model where we have faulty imprints and cannot improve them because we have poor quality wax.

> When [judgment] brings together appropriate impressions (*apotupômata*) and imprints (*tupous*) it is true, when it does so skewed and crosswise it is false. (194b4–6)[39]

This suggests that they are both in the wax. Plato appears to be using the wax as an analogue for whatever it is in the soul (194c6) that is the seat of all cognition. Thus, he understands both the learned/remembered/known impression and the newly received perception as imprinted in the wax.[40] If the wax is of good quality, they will both be of good quality and mistakes will not be made. If the wax is of poor enough quality that one is faulty, then the other will be faulty as well. Thus, if heterodoxy can occur, that is a sign that the wax is not good enough to sustain a veridical imprint of either kind. Heterodoxy has to occur in those without knowledge and has to be a mismatch of faulty perception with faulty imprint. Perhaps false belief only occurs in those who have no hope of knowledge!

To summarize, the importance of this passage to the picture of doxastic structure that we started to form in the *Symposium* is this: Plato only sees heterodoxy begin to work when he briefly puts our *doxa(i)* about the two things that need to be confused on the not-knowing side of the equation. In other words, he hints to us that false judgment can only occur when our *doxa* that is not judgment is about two things, neither of which is known to us, regardless of the content of that *doxa*.

False judgment will only work on the heterodoxy model if Plato assumes that our whole doxastic spectrum is on the not-knowing side of the (S1M) dichotomy. This would have us only making false judgments about things concerning which our cloud of *doxa* is neither accurate nor fully reasoned, or is neither. Our *doxa* concerning these confused objects counts as not-knowing but also counts as being *about* those objects con-

---

39. καταντικρὺ μὲν καὶ κατὰ τὸ εὐθὺ τὰ οἰκεῖα συνάγουσα ἀποτυπώματα καὶ τύπους ἀληθής, εἰς πλάγια δὲ καὶ σκολιὰ ψευδής.

40. Thus, Burnyeat (1990, 100) is mistaken when he says that Locke's use of the wax block in *An Essay Concerning Human Understanding* (II 29.3) differs from Plato's in that it treats perception as an imprint. In contrast with Burnyeat, Campbell understands both to be imprints at this point (as I do):

> ἀποτυπώματα καὶ τύπους (1) τύπος is here the present impression, which we endeavour to fit into the mark left by the former one (ἀποτύπωμα). τύπος can scarcely be (2) "the form of the object." This would be inconsistent with the previous use of the word, 192 A. (1883, 189 n. 3)

cerning which we are confused, because we are in contact with them no matter what the content of the *doxa* that is about them is.

The picture of *doxa* that emerges from the one (fleeting as we will see) "positive"[41] note in the heterodoxy discussion is that there is a bunch of thinking that is not judgment, only some of which develops into judgment through deliberation. When we do birth judgments from our deliberations regarding our more generic *doxa*, it can be false because we are making judgments about things that we don't know. Not only are the objects of these judgments things we don't know, but they involve the elements of our *doxa* that have not yet, themselves, been clarified and formed into judgments—our imprints and perceptions. For those of us with suboptimal wax, all of our *doxa* will involve some degree of bad imprints and bad perceptions, and so will be confused to that same degree. So, when we say that everything is either known or not-known, the not-known side of that dichotomy refers to our entire rich doxastic structure. What is known is not identified with that type of structure (and, so far, Plato has not figured out how to identify it).

So, Plato is reducing the notion of (S1M) where everything is either known or not-known to absurdity in the case where the not-known side is some sort of cognitive blank. However, he is replacing that notion with an (S1M) in which "not-known" refers to our entire doxastic cloud; Our entire spectrum of doxastic states that range from best to worst (but cannot be ordered hierarchically). Presumably, Plato thinks that some of what is not-known is more useful or more like knowledge than other things that are not known. Also, he presumably thinks that some people's entire doxastic structures are more useful and more like knowledge than other people's doxastic structures are. That is, some people's wax, while suboptimal in quality, will still be better than others. Still, everything is either known or is not-known (and, if not-known, is *doxa*).

Further Problems with False Belief

This heterodoxy model of false belief is no panacea. Socrates says that it cannot account for a large number of cases of false belief. For instance,

---

41. I put "positive" in scare quotes because, while it does represent a step toward accounting for false judgment, it does so by showing how dismal is the doxastic state of anyone who is capable of entertaining false judgments. I imagine that Plato thinks most if not all people fall into this category.

it implies that we never confuse two things that we have learned and remembered. He stated above (193a, 192d) that, if we are thinking of both Theaetetus and Theodorus, but we perceive neither, we cannot confuse them. But, Socrates claims that it is clear that we can; he considers the case of two numbers that we hold only in thought: when we think to ourselves that $7 + 5 = 11$, we think falsely that $12 = 11$. Therefore, false judgment cannot simply be a mismatching between a thought and a perception because we have false beliefs in the absence of relevant perceptions.

However, it is important to recognize that Socrates does not criticize the wax block for what it does do. He seems satisfied that it can explain how we come to have false beliefs due to mismatching substandard perceptions and conceptions. His complaint is that it does not account for a significant category of false beliefs: those that take place when we confuse two things that we are entertaining only in thought. That is, it does not account for when we confuse two things about which we are thinking at a time when we are not also entertaining perceptions of those same things that we are currently confusing in thought.

The Aviary

Socrates worries that his investigation suffers because he has used the word *knowledge* when he does not know what knowledge is. Nevertheless, he decides that he must proceed and must do so by saying something about knowledge anyway (196d8–197a4). He will now attempt to produce a model upon which we believe falsely because we confuse two things that are only in our minds, such as the numbers 11 and 12. Socrates distinguishes between possessing knowledge (having it at one's disposal) and having knowledge (using it). He uses the image of an aviary to model this distinction. Each of us has an aviary. Learning is symbolized by catching a bird and putting it in the aviary. Thinking about something we know is symbolized by hunting down a particular bird that is already in the aviary and catching it. Thus, the aviary contains what is known and the act of holding a bird in one's hand is the act of thinking about one of the things known.

On the aviary model, false judgment occurs when a person, who has both an 11 and a 12 bird in his aviary, catches the 11 bird in an effort to hunt down the 12 bird. This is what happens when we think $7 + 5 = 11$. So, the person has knowledge—he knows both 11 and 12—and he has false judgment—he believes that 11 is 12. Rather than glorying in an apparent success, however, Socrates finds a problem with the implications that this model holds for knowledge: false belief has been accounted for through an interchange among pieces of knowledge. Here, a person who has knowledge is ignorant, not through lack of knowledge, but in virtue of the knowledge that he has (199d). The example has this person confusing two things that he knows. Socrates and Theaetetus agreed that this could not occur when they listed the three impossibilities. Socrates points out the absurdity in all of this:

> It means that, knowledge being present, the soul knows nothing, but is completely ignorant. For from this argument, nothing prevents both that the presence of ignorance will make someone come to know something and blindness will make one see, if knowledge is ever going to make one ignorant. (199d4–8)[42]

Theaetetus makes a valiant attempt to save the metaphor by placing birds of ignorance in the aviary as well. But then, false judgment would have to be the mistaking of something one knows for something one doesn't know and that was also disallowed by the three impossibilities. The aviary has revealed itself as a model upon which everything is either known or unknown where being unknown has no doxastic status. Notice that there is nothing in the aviary that has a status of being *doxa* but not knowledge. Nothing is said about what is outside of the aviary. It seems that Socrates has gone back to a model that deals with the (S1M) that identifies not-knowing with cognitive blankness and—as might have been predicted—it cannot account for the brute evidence of false belief.

Conclusion

We have now corroborated salient features of the picture of *doxa* that I diagnosed from below the surface of the Diotima speech in the *Symposium* with claims made more overtly in the *Phaedrus* and the *Theaetetus*. The *Phaedrus* contains evidence for the claim that ignorance consists of *doxa(i)*.

---

42. ἐπιστήμης παραγενομένης γνῶναι μὲν τὴν ψυχὴν μηδέν, ἀγνοῆσαι δὲ πάντα; ἐκ γὰρ τούτου τοῦ λόγου κωλύει οὐδὲν καὶ ἄγνοιαν παραγενομένην γνῶναί τι ποιῆσαι καὶ τυφλότητα ἰδεῖν, εἴπερ καὶ ἐπιστήμη ἀγνοῆσαί ποτέ τινα ποιήσει.

It also demonstrates Plato's conviction that all *doxa*, from the best kind to the worst, is about what-is. All human souls are trying to have the best *doxa* they can regarding the truth (whatever it is) but, in the *Phaedrus*, their prenatal experiences either limit or make possible their capacity for *doxa* of high quality or for knowledge. We also see how much Plato's picture of the legacy of recollection relies upon each person having the capacity to intentionally refer to what actually is even if what actually is escapes the content of any beliefs they have that are about it.

The digression on false judgment in the *Theaetetus* shows Plato distinguishing between an amorphous and generic brand of *doxa* that is about what is, despite its primitive nature when compared to the more explicit notion of *doxa* that is judgment. He also conveys the notion that even the most amorphous and unevaluated kind of *doxa* that each person has is about what-is. Furthermore, in order to solve the puzzle of false judgment, we see Plato move *doxa* of all different kinds of qualities onto the ignorance side of the knowing versus not-knowing dichotomy. Plato's three impossibilities and the way they play out in every case but the wax block make it clear that false judgment cannot involve knowledge of any kind. Since false judgment occurs regularly, Plato must think that most people do not have a sufficiently stable "wax block" to maintain impressions in a manner that amounts to knowledge. It seems anyone who is capable of false judgment has a doxastic structure that is less than optimal. Furthermore, people differ in their abilities to assess what actually is, due to the differences in the integrity of their intermingled beliefs, the quality of the sum of which varies between those that are highly accurate about what-is and those that we would want to claim are most ignorant.

In the next chapter, I begin to bring these theses together with Plato's most well-known and most controversial discussion of *doxa* in the middle books of the *Republic*. In doing this I will show that Plato thinks that we all opine beauty itself, even though he says in *Republic* V that *doxa* is "over" (*epi*) what is and is-not.

Chapter 7

Opining Beauty Itself in *Republic* V

With some insight into the structure of *doxa* and what Plato shows it to be about from other dialogues, the stage is now set for us to struggle with Plato's confusing, but ultimately insightful, declaration that knowledge is of what-is, *doxa* is of what both is and is-not, and ignorance is of what is-not in *Republic* V. The task is to fit this three-part distinction into the same picture as the many other commitments we have already seen Plato make in other dialogues regarding *doxa* and what it is about. I have argued that in the *Meno* and *Phaedo* all *doxa* is about such things as virtue itself and equality itself. I have shown that it is about beauty itself even in this same *Republic* passage, regarding which—in chapter 4—we looked at an argument that is concurrent with, but less overt than, the one we are about to examine.

As I have interpreted these three passages, Plato suggests that we can neither inquire nor have beliefs that end up being false about what-is, unless we are—at least unwittingly or confusedly—intending to have our *doxa(i)* be about the particular Form that characterizes that particular aspect of what *actually is*. We need to be, somehow, hitting the right Form with our intentions when we try to answer inquiries or come to judgments that are true or false about that which we intend them to be about. In fact, in chapter 4, we saw that even people who claim that only perceptibles exist (like lovers of sights and sounds and "the many") can come to rely upon additional beliefs that they *already* have, to which they are even more strongly committed, that are about imperceptibles such as the double itself (as opposed to the half itself, *Rep.* 479b3–4) and thickness itself (as opposed to thinness itself, *Rep.* 523e–524a). In this process, they sometimes come to realize that they *already* have these beliefs and are *already* committed to the existence of these abstract entities.

We have also seen Plato present *doxa* as a rich and complicated intersecting bunch of thinking that, once sorted out through a process of reflection and individuation, usually contains many internal inconsistencies. We have further seen him assume that only some of the contents of our doxastic structure are individuated and judged at any given time. Thus, there is nothing to be gained from evaluating one individual "piece" of *doxa* for its truth and reasonableness. To do this is not to examine a human epistemic state, as it does not reflect the way humans opine or reason. As a result, no such exercise can reflect the doxastic state of a human or allow us to affirm their epistemic competence.

Even further, it now looks to us as if the integrity of a person's doxastic structure can be so poor that their *doxa* should be deemed ignorance, while others might have doxastic structures of such high integrity that they track the truth and interact with what-is relatively well, particularly if restricted to a narrow range of cases. Plato has also made it apparent that we should give up on making ordered hierarchies of *doxa(i)* that move unambiguously from *doxa* of the lowest quality to that of the highest. A doxastic structure that is especially well suited for one endeavor is unlikely to be equally well suited for many other endeavors—I don't hire a Nobel Prize winner in economics to fix my plumbing.

So how can we put all of this together with the above claims regarding the respective objects of knowledge, opinion, and ignorance? There appear to be some inconsistencies. For example, the three-part distinction makes it seem that *doxa* cognizes something other than that which is cognized by ignorance. An apparent second inconsistency is that, in this passage, only knowledge has any relationship with "what-is," while I have argued that, in the other texts we have examined, Plato assumes that both good and bad *doxa* are always *about* "what-is."

The Overt Argument of *Republic* 475e4–479d5: The Consolation of Lovers of Sights and Sounds

At *Republic* 475e4–479d5, Socrates describes *doxa* as inferior to knowledge. He repeats this often, using many different locutions. While not as willing to disparage lovers of sights and sounds as Glaucon is, he says that these lovers of *doxa* live in a dream state even while awake (476c2–7). He contrasts *doxa* with knowledge, saying that, while knowledge is infallible, *doxa* is fallible (477e6–7). *Doxa* is shadowy compared to knowledge (478c13–14).

In this passage, Socrates also separates the object of knowledge from the object of *doxa*. He says that the object of knowledge is *what-is*. In contrast, the object of *doxa* is what *both is and is-not*. Socrates also calls the object of *doxa* deficient when compared to the object of knowledge. It is ambiguous (479c3) and wandering (479d9). Socrates goes on to identify a third epistemic capacity: ignorance. Ignorance is even more obscure than *doxa*, and its object is nothing at all. Certainly, what I have already said about *doxa* in the chapters leading up to this one makes it easy to see that *doxa* is inferior to knowledge (even though I have been careful not to make commitments about the nature of knowledge). Still, it will take some work to square both the claim that knowledge has a different object than *doxa* does and the claim that ignorance is inferior to *doxa* with what I have already assessed as Plato's commitments regarding ignorance and *doxa* in all of my earlier chapters.

Generally, in this passage, Plato expresses the relationship between each capacity and its unique object using the Greek word *epi*. Translators often use the locution "set over" to translate *epi* in the context of this passage. However, later in the *Republic* (533e3–534a8), Socrates also says that *doxa* concerns (employing a different Greek word, *peri*) what comes to be. So, it seems correct to conclude that Plato is differentiating capacities according to their objects or according to what they are about.

It is straightforward that Plato separates knowledge, *doxa*, and ignorance as different capacities each of which is set over its own unique object. Generations of scholars have said that Plato limited *doxa* to being only about what both is and is-not and limited knowledge to being only about what-is. In other words, Plato said that we cannot have both *doxa* and knowledge about the same things. I agree with this on one level. There is a very important way that *doxa* is about what both is and is-not, while knowledge cannot be. There is also an important way in which knowledge, but not *doxa*, is about what-is. Neither *doxa* nor knowledge can be about nothing at all. This important way of *being about* relates to what I will call a "first-degree object." What-is, is the first-degree object of knowledge. What both is and is-not is the first-degree object of *doxa*. Nothing at all is the first-degree object of ignorance.

However, I will argue that Plato is assuming a "second-degree object" for each of these capacities as well. I will elaborate upon what this second-degree object is, and how it fits with Plato's text, when we examine his analogy to the senses (*Rep.* 477c1–d1), below (176–180). It is only if we assume a second-degree object for *doxa* and ignorance that we can understand why *doxa* is deficient as compared to knowledge and why ignorance is even worse than *doxa*. For, if *doxa* is well suited to capturing what-is and is-not, and that is its only object, why should we call it confusing and problematic? Further, if ignorance is doing something appropriate—something it is supposed to do—with what is-not, why should it be viewed it so negatively?

Plato's point is that *doxa* is really bad at capturing what-is (its second-degree object). Further, ignorance isn't even on the map when it comes to capturing what-is (which is also its second-degree object). Knowledge stands out because it is really good at capturing its first-degree object, which is also its second-degree object. Plato is rating these three capacities with respect to how well they capture such things as beauty itself (these are what Plato eventually calls his Forms). Ignorance is ignorant about (second-degree object) beauty itself. *Doxa* is deceptive concerning (second-degree object) beauty itself. Knowledge stands out because its first-degree object and its second-degree object are the same. Knowledge captures beauty itself.

In what follows, I will argue that, while *doxa* wittingly directs itself only at what both is and is-not, it is decreed deceptive and obscure because it is importantly and intentionally also *about* what-is. It is shadowy and fallible about beauty itself, which is what the person experiencing *doxa* intends it to be about. That is why it is inferior to knowledge.

An Ongoing Debate

Before going farther, allow me to situate my thesis with respect to a continuing debate concerning the objects of *doxa* and knowledge in this *Republic* passage. Perhaps I can characterize the debate most simply and with the least historical baggage by saying that the debate revolves around a disagreement over whether Plato thinks we can come to know that which we earlier only opined: Can an object of *doxa* come to be an object of knowledge?[1]

---

1. I am narrowing the focus of the debate over the "two world" or "distinct objects" (Moss 2021) view to the question of whether *epistêmê* and *doxa* have mutually exclu-

In her 2012 book, *Truth and Belief*, Katja Vogt summarizes the debate between the "Traditional" view and the "Countertraditional" view as follows:

> Traditional (T1) There is no knowledge about the objects of belief (perceptible things), and no belief about the objects of knowledge ("what-is"). Each cognitive power is exclusively related to its objects.
>
> (T2) "What-is" refers to the Forms.[2]
>
> Countertraditional (C1) We can have knowledge about perceptible things, and beliefs about "what-is." Knowledge and belief engage with propositions—true propositions in the case of knowledge, and true and false in the case of belief—not with this or that kind of object.
>
> (C2) "What-is" does not refer to the Forms, but rather to what is true.[3]

In her 2012, Vogt rejects (C1) and (C2). She embraces (T2) but not (T1).[4]

I will also reject (C1) and (C2), while I embrace (T2) and not (T1).[5] However, I do this for different reasons than Vogt does and disagree with her on several points.[6] I believe that *doxa* does have what-is (or, to be precise, Plato's Forms) as what I will call a "second-degree object." In fact, I argue that Plato thinks that *doxa* is inferior because "what-is" is *always* its

---

sive objects. See Moss (2021, 18–26) for a more nuanced appreciation of the range of views on each side of this debate. See also ch. 10, below.

2. Vogt (54, n. 9) associates this most closely with Cornford (1933).

3. Vogt (54 n. 10) associates this most closely with the interpretation proposed by Fine (2003).

4. Moss and Schwab (2019), Gerson (2009), Harte (2017), Schwab (2016), Szaif (2007), and Smith (2000, 2019) are others who have recently engaged in this debate. I will note any important similarities and differences between my interpretation and theirs in notes as I proceed.

5. While I am not discussing knowledge here and thus am not developing a view on T1, I do express some thoughts on whether Plato thinks that perceptibles can become known in chapters 8 (191–192, 197 n. 12) and 10 (229), below.

6. Which I will also note as I continue.

second-degree object.⁷ I argue that Plato thinks we can improve our *doxa* so that it becomes better quality *doxa*. That is, *doxa* can do a better or worse job at capturing its second-degree object (the Forms)—it is not all equally bad at this. So, Plato thinks *doxa* is importantly concerned with doing its best to capture "what-is" (which it can do only deficiently). *Doxa* is not at its best when it is content with dealing only with what-is and is-not (the perceptibles).⁸ The point is to be a good deliberator concerning one's *doxa*, so as to correct for its shortcomings and develop a higher quality *doxa* (perhaps on the way to gaining knowledge).⁹ Still, I disagree with those who claim that Plato thinks *doxa* is just true and false propositional beliefs, where the true beliefs later become knowledge through some kind of justificatory exercise.¹⁰ While I will not be arguing for this position here, I do not think

---

7. Vogt thinks that *doxa* can sometimes have a Form as its (first-degree, according to me) object (although that situation is less than ideal), and also that knowledge can sometimes have perceptibles as its (first-degree, according to me) object (although that is less than ideal). She says this is like when one tries to appreciate a sonata by looking at the written music rather than hearing it (64–65). Harte (2017) also makes this general type of claim.

8. Vogt presents *doxa* as adequate for capturing what-is and is-not (64). I would argue (more along the lines of Moss and Schwab, I believe) that what is and is-not cannot be captured—it is too amorphous and unstable for this. *Doxa* is best deployed when it is trying to see beyond perceptibles to what-is. For, example, at *Rep.* 523e3–524a4, Socrates says that even the ordinary people will have to summon the understanding to comprehend the thickness and thinness of fingers (see ch. 4, 105–108).

9. Some of this revolves around the difficult issue of why *dianoia* is on the part of the divided line (*Rep.* 509) that is *epistêmê* rather than *doxa*, since it involves the making of hypotheses (which seem to be beliefs rather than knowledge). I will not deal with this controversy here and will treat the recognition that one's *doxa* is *doxa* and not knowledge as a superior kind of *doxa* (rather than a form of *dianoia/epistêmê*). This is the kind of *doxa* that Socrates singles himself out for having in the *Apol.* (23b). It is a better kind of *doxa* than the kind that those he examines have. See Gerson (2009, 34) to appreciate the difficulties with *dianoia*'s placement on the divided line. Vogt appears to distinguish *doxa* from hypothesis, but does not say whether hypothesis counts as something other than *doxa* or knowledge, or whether she thinks it is former *doxa* transformed into knowledge (17).

10. At *Men.* 97a6–98a8, Socrates appears to assert, and at *Theaet.* 187b4–c5, 202c–210d, he appears to examine, the hypothesis that knowledge is some sort of enhanced true belief. Thus, he implies that a belief can become known. While I am not making commitments about knowledge in this book, I lean against the view that Plato thinks that *doxa* remains *doxa* and becomes known. Knowledge replaces and overrides *doxa*.

that Plato's *doxa* can be mapped onto our contemporary analytic notion of belief, where beliefs are individuated according to their propositional content and an individual proposition can be known to be true.[11]

The *Epi*-locution

"Over" is a literal translation of the Greek word *epi*. Plato uses the Greek word *epi* to connect each of the three epistemological capacities under discussion in this passage to what-is, that which is in between what-is and what is-not, and what is-not, respectively. I will call Plato's use of *epi* in this context the "*epi*-locution."[12] My thesis concerning *Republic* 475e4–479d5 is that, while each of these capacities is unique in what it is *epi* and thus unique in what is its first-degree object, Plato must have thought that all three epistemic capacities had the same second-degree object. They are all—also and equally—*about* what-is. What-is is their second-degree object in each case. I will illustrate this shortly.

This is consistent with what is stated in the *Men.* and with my understanding of the end of the *Theaet.*

11. See Moss and Schwab (2019) for a rehearsal of some of their reasons that resonate with mine. My reasons are in chapters 5 and 6, above.

12. Smith (2000, 2019) emphasizes the *epi* locution. Harte (2017, 145–48) and Vogt (62–63) both emphasize Plato's use of *epi* with the verb *tassô*. Harte emphasizes his use of *epi* and *tassô* with the dative and compares it to *Rep.* 345d1–353a11 (150–54). All also emphasize that Plato uses it at times with *pephuken* ("naturally"). My interpretation is certainly consistent with recognizing that this is an atypical way for Plato to articulate a verb and its object. However, as I note, Plato does say, later at 533e3–534a8, that *doxa* is *peri* what "comes to be" (see also Moss and Schwab, 6). Further, he refers to the "opined" (*doxaston*) and the "known" (*gnôston*) alternatively with what-is and what is and is-not. Thus, I think it's most consistent with textual evidence to notice the *epi* locution, but not to treat it as categorically different from other ways that Plato might specify the object of a verb. Furthermore, both Harte and Vogt argue that in nonstandard situations, what-is can be what I call the first-degree object of *doxa* and what-is and is-not can be the first-degree object of knowledge. My point is that *doxa* and knowledge always have different first-degree objects and always have the same second-degree objects (I will explain this soon). So, *doxa* can have the same second-degree object as knowledge. I speculate that knowledge can only know what-is and is-not derivatively from knowledge of the Forms (but am making no commitments regarding knowledge here). See ch. 8, n. 1.

At 476e7–8, Plato has Glaucon play the role of the lovers of sights and sounds and, as such, Socrates leads him through the exposition of the division of the epistemic capacities into knowledge, ignorance, and opinion.[13] They agree that these three capacities are "over" (*epi*) what-is, what is-not, and that which is in between what-is and what is-not respectively.

Later, Glaucon returns to speak in his own voice about the object of *doxa*:

> Those things too are ambiguous, and one cannot know for certain either that they are or that they are not, or that they are both or neither. (479c3–5, Grube's translation)[14]

Socrates returns to address Glaucon as himself and not as a stand-in for the lover of sights and sounds:

> Then do you know how to deal with them? Can you find a better placement for them than halfway between being and not-being? (479c6–7)[15]

Glaucon agrees that Socrates has shown that all particulars are as ambiguous as the subjects of the riddles used for entertainment at dinner parties.[16]

Between Being and Nonbeing

Socrates's consolation of the lovers of sights and sounds begins at 476e5 with the question, "Does the person who knows know something or nothing?" to which the lover of sights and sounds (played by Glaucon) answers "something," and further agrees to "something that-is" and "that which-is completely is known completely." He also agrees that "what is-not

---

13. I agree with Vogt that Glaucon is supposed to answer as an enlightened lover of sights and sounds—the way a lover of sights and sounds *should* answer. Her arguments against Fine's dialectical requirement are well taken by me (58–62).

14. καὶ γὰρ ταῦτα ἐπαμφοτερίζειν, καὶ οὔτ᾽ εἶναι οὔτε μὴ εἶναι οὐδὲν αὐτῶν δυνατὸν παγίως νοῆσαι, οὔτε ἀμφότερα οὔτε οὐδέτερον.

15. ὅτι χρήσῃ, ἢ ὅποι θήσεις καλλίω θέσιν τῆς μεταξὺ οὐσίας τε καὶ τοῦ μὴ εἶναι;

16. Riddles that call a bat a "bird that is not a bird" and a eunuch a "man who is not a man" (Cooper 1997, 1106 n. 18).

in any way is altogether unknowable."[17] Then, at 477a6–7, Socrates's next question is,

> [I]f anything is such as both to be and not to be, then won't it be intermediate between purely being and not being at all?[18]

The lover of sights and sounds assents *(metaxu)* to this conditional. Socrates's next question is:

> Since knowledge is set over what-is and ignorance has to be set over what is-not, mustn't we search for something in between knowledge and ignorance if there be such a thing? (477a9–b1)[19]

They have agreed that were there to be something in between being and not-being it would be the domain of a capacity in between knowledge and ignorance.

Between 477b and 478d, Socrates and the lover of sights and sounds commit themselves to the existence of opinion and deem it a capacity. Socrates asks, "Do we say that opinion is something?"(477b3) and the lover of sights and sounds agrees that they do. In fact, they deem it a capacity and figure out that it lies in between knowledge and ignorance. It is in between because, while knowledge is infallible, it is fallible—so it is not knowledge and is inferior to knowledge. It does not opine nothing at all—for it must opine something, so it is not ignorance and is superior to ignorance. It is "darker than knowledge, but clearer than ignorance" (478c4–5).

They then return to discuss what opinion is *epi*:

> We said earlier that if something should be shown *(phaneiê)* to be the sort of thing that both is and is not at the same time *(hama)* then it would lie *(keisthai)* between what purely is and what altogether is-not. Neither knowledge nor ignorance would

---

17. . . . μὴ ὂν δὲ μηδαμῇ πάντῃ ἄγνωστον[.] (477a3–4).

18. εἰ δὲ δή τι οὕτως ἔχει ὡς εἶναί τε καὶ μὴ εἶναι, οὐ μεταξὺ ἂν κέοιτο τοῦ εἰλικρινῶς ὄντος καὶ τοῦ αὖ μηδαμῇ ὄντος;

19. οὐκοῦν ἐπὶ μὲν τῷ ὄντι γνῶσις ἦν, ἀγνωσία δ᾽ ἐξ ἀνάγκης ἐπὶ μὴ ὄντι, ἐπὶ δὲ τῷ μεταξὺ τούτῳ μεταξύ τι καὶ ζητητέον ἀγνοίας τε καὶ ἐπιστήμης, εἴ τι τυγχάνει ὂν τοιοῦτον;

be set over it (*ep' autô esesthai*), but something in between knowledge and ignorance. (478d5–9)[20]

Next, Socrates says that it remains for them to find what participates in both being and not-being, so that if such a thing comes to light, it can rightly be called the opinable (478e3).[21] Subsequently, Socrates questions the lover of sights and sounds and brings him to agree that each of the things that he calls beautiful (each beautiful sight and sound) is also ugly and that this is true for what he calls just/unjust, pious/impious, double/half, big/small, and light/heavy as well. Glaucon concludes,

> [T]hey are similarly[22] ambiguous (*epamphoterizein*) and one cannot conceive of them as steadily being or not being, or as both (*amphotera*), or as neither (*oudeteron*). (479c3–5)[23]

Socrates checks with Glaucon, asking, "Do you have a [better] way to deal with them? Can you find a more appropriate place than in between being and not-being?" and he reiterates the requirement that they be less than what-is and more than what-is-not, clearer than what-is-not and darker than what-is (479c6–d1). Glaucon agrees that there is no more appropriate place and Socrates concludes that,

> According to the many conventions of the common people about beauty and the others, they [piety, justice, etc.] are rolling around in between what-is and what-is-not. (479d3–5)[24]

He further notes that they earlier agreed that "if something of this sort came to light" (479d7) they would have to call it the opinable.

---

20. οὐκοῦν ἔφαμεν ἐν τοῖς πρόσθεν, εἴ τι φανείη οἷον ἅμα ὄν τε καὶ μὴ ὄν, τὸ τοιοῦτον μεταξὺ κεῖσθαι τοῦ εἰλικρινῶς ὄντος τε καὶ τοῦ πάντως μὴ ὄντος, καὶ οὔτε ἐπιστήμην οὔτε ἄγνοιαν ἐπ' αὐτῷ ἔσεσθαι, ἀλλὰ τὸ μεταξὺ αὖ φανὲν ἀγνοίας καὶ ἐπιστήμης;
21. ἵνα, ἐὰν φανῇ, δοξαστὸν αὐτὸ εἶναι ἐν δίκῃ προσαγορεύωμεν.
22. Glaucon is alluding to the riddles and puzzles that he describes earlier in this sentence. See, n. 16, above.
23. καὶ γὰρ ταῦτα ἐπαμφοτερίζειν, καὶ οὔτ' εἶναι οὔτε μὴ εἶναι οὐδὲν αὐτῶν δυνατὸν παγίως νοῆσαι, οὔτε ἀμφότερα οὔτε οὐδέτερον.
24. ὅτι τὰ τῶν πολλῶν πολλὰ νόμιμα καλοῦ τε πέρι καὶ τῶν ἄλλων μεταξύ που κυλινδεῖται τοῦ τε μὴ ὄντος καὶ τοῦ ὄντος εἰλικρινῶς.

An Analogy to the Senses

Plato introduces the three epistemic capacities by saying that the person who has knowledge knows something that-is (476e7–10). He later expresses this as "knowledge is *set over* (*epi*) what-is."[25] The same *epi*-locution is used for ignorance (and nothing at all) and opinion (and that which is in between something and nothing). Plato clarifies his use of this locution by having Socrates make an analogy to the capacities of sight and hearing. He says that he distinguishes powers from one another by what they are "set over" (*eph' hô*) and what they produce (*ho apergazetai*) (477c1–d1). Using this analogy, we can get some clarity about how to interpret the thesis that opinion is set over what-is and is-not and ignorance is set over what is-not.

Let's think, along with Plato, about how we distinguish seeing from hearing. When I look at an operating electric fan, my sight is set over the fan. If we wanted to use a literal translation of the *epi*-locution into English, we might say, "I *set* my sight *upon* the fan." Our sight then *produces* a visual image or impression. When I set my hearing upon the fan, I set it upon a different aspect of the fan, and it produces an auditory impression. This is how I know that seeing is different from hearing—I have to set (aim or cast) these two different capacities upon different "things": light waves in one case and sound waves in the other. Light is a different kind of entity from sound. Their products—auditory and visual impressions—differ from each other, so, hearing is different from seeing.

Let us apply this back to the three epistemic capacities: Knowledge is set over what-is. It produces knowing. Ignorance is set over nothing at all, producing ignorance. *Doxa* is set over what-is and is-not, producing opinion or belief. What are we supposed to make of this? What is this supposed stuff that is in between what-is and what is-not upon which *doxa* is cast? The description of the lover of sights and sounds as in a dream state at 476c5–9 has already suggested that the lover of sights and sounds has only opinion because he sets his epistemic capacity upon the perceptibles. For recall that the lover of sights and sounds is the dreamer, the one who "whether asleep or awake, takes what is similar for what is not [merely] similar but identical" (476c5–7).[26] Furthermore, this is what has distinguished him from the philosopher: the philosopher looks to beauty itself to answer questions about beauty itself. In contrast, the

---

25. This is the most common translation of *epi* in this passage.
26. See my discussion of this passage in ch. 4, 91–92.

lover of sights and sounds looks to beautiful sights and sounds—to perceptibles—to answer questions about that same thing—*about beauty itself*.

The philosopher's capacity for knowledge is set over what-is. The lover of sights and sounds' capacity for *doxa* is set over what only participates in beauty itself: the perceptibles. Socrates identifies the perceptibles with what both is and is-not. They are the first-degree objects of *doxa*. *Doxa* is inferior because its first-degree objects are entities that are not reliable indicators of beauty itself. They participate in *beauty itself*. However, they are not identical to beauty itself (476d1–3). Furthermore, they participate in ugliness itself at the same time (479a5–b2). *Doxa's* first-degree objects confuse and mislead it concerning beauty itself. One must look beyond these ambiguous perceptibles if one wants to come to understand beauty itself. This is why we should regard what-is and is-not (the perceptibles) as the first-degree object of opinion, but we should see what-is (beauty itself) as *doxa's* second-degree object. Plato regards the perceptibles as epistemically inferior to the pure (479d2–4) beings, such as beauty itself, in which they participate because they are impure (they are characterized by more than one Form)[27] and, therefore, confusing examples of beauty itself. Thus, things like beauty itself must also be some kind of object of *doxa*; one that *doxa* tries but fails to capture. Plato is not casting aspersions on *doxa* because it gives confusing information about perceptibles—perceptibles are appropriately represented as confusing—they *are* confusing! That is Plato's point, perceptibles cannot be known, because they don't have the kinds of properties that make them knowable. Lovers of *doxa* make the mistake of thinking that the perceptibles are beauty itself and that they know something about the perceptibles. They are wrong on both counts.

First and Second-Degree Objects of Sense Experience

Let's go back to the analogy with sense experience to clarify this. Socrates states it as follows:

---

27. I will emphasize this in my discussion of how we to understand that they both are and are-not in the next chapter (193–200).

In the case of a capacity, I can look only to this: to what it is directed and to what it achieves, and in this way I call it a capacity; if it is related to the same object and achieves the same result I call it the same, while that which is related to a different object and achieves a different result I call a different capacity. (477c9–d5, Grube's translation).[28]

First, let us parse this English sentence:

I set my sight on light waves and get visual information about the fan.

This sentence has a compound verb and singular subject. "I" is the subject. "Set" and "get" are both verbs. "Sight" is the direct object of "set" and "information" is the direct object of "get." "Light waves" is the object of the preposition "on." "Fan" is the object of the preposition "about." I am calling the object of the preposition "about" ("fan") the *second-degree object* [O2] of the capacity "sight."

Let us again consider an electric fan:

I $\underline{see}_A$ the $\underline{light\ waves}_{O1}$ emanating from the fan, I get $\underline{sight}_{A*}$ about the $\underline{fan}_{O2}$.

I $\underline{hear}_A$ the $\underline{sound\ waves}_{O1}$ emanating from the fan, I get $\underline{hearing}_{A*}$ about the $\underline{fan}_{O2}$.

I $\underline{feel}_A$ the $\underline{airwaves}_{O1}$ emanating from the fan, I get $\underline{tactility}_{A*}$ about the $\underline{fan}_{O2}$.

Note that I distinguish my senses by what they are set over (*epi*). I distinguish them by what fills in O1. Also, by what they produce—by what fills in A*. Each sense naturally interacts with a specific kind of first-degree object [O1]. This is how we verify that they are different capacities.

---

28. δυνάμεως δ' εἰς ἐκεῖνο μόνον βλέπω ἐφ' ᾧ τε ἔστι καὶ ὃ ἀπεργάζεται, καὶ ταύτῃ ἑκάστην αὐτῶν δύναμιν ἐκάλεσα, καὶ τὴν μὲν ἐπὶ τῷ αὐτῷ τεταγμένην καὶ τὸ αὐτὸ ἀπεργαζομένην τὴν αὐτὴν καλῶ, τὴν δὲ ἐπὶ ἑτέρῳ καὶ ἕτερον ἀπεργαζομένην ἄλλην.

However, notice that in every case the second-degree object—what fills in O2—is the same. The second-degree object is always the fan. We might say that the first-degree object is the sensory object and the second-degree object is the object of cognition (the intellectual object).[29] Given what Plato says about the inferiority of *doxa* and ignorance, I think that we have to assume that he is talking about how poorly *doxa* captures the intellectual object, and the fact that ignorance misses it altogether.

Allow me to anticipate what will need clarification. The analogy I am about to use might be confusing because Plato is contrasting sense experience, which results in *doxa*, with some kind of nonsensory cognition that results in knowledge of what-is. However, both his analogy and mine use sense experience for all of the analogues. So, in order to appreciate the analogy, we need to compare different kinds of sense experience to each other in a way that this passage tells us is not theoretically agreeable to Plato. So please bear in mind that the following is only an analogy.

Let us isolate the sense of sight and show what would make one person's sight superior to another's. For the sake of the analogy, allow me to stipulate that perfect vision (20/20 eyesight) and perfect color sensitivity allow a person to see the truth about a visual object. Let's consider three people: J has perfect vision and color sensitivity. K is red/green color-blind. We don't know what L's vision is like; she never opens her eyes.

1. J sets her vision on the traffic light and gets good visual information about the traffic light.

---

29. I owe this general strategy for parsing the *epi*-locution to Smith (2000; 2019, 59–62) and I am grateful to him for several discussions on this topic. I am agreeing with him that just as the object of sense (of the capacity of sight) is not the object of cognition, Plato is presenting the object of each epistemic capacity as different from what you might call its intellectual object. However, I depart from him when I say that the object of intellect is the Form in all cases (in fact, he does not think it is the Form in any case). I believe that I am stricter than Smith is about what he calls "mixed cognition" (2019, 64–65). I certainly agree that Plato thinks the philosopher applies knowledge to the perceptible world (when, for example, he returns to the cave), but I believe the philosopher is applying knowledge *of the Forms* to perceptibles. That is, any knowledge of perceptibles is derived from knowledge of the Forms in which they partake. Neither Smith nor I embrace a "two world" theory, nor does either of us embrace Fine's veridical interpretation. I think that both the predicative interpretation (which Smith does embrace) and a veridical interpretation that works for *doxa* can be derived from an ontological interpretation, I will discuss this in ch. 8.

2. K sets her vision on the traffic light and gets faulty and confusing visual information about the traffic light.

3. L doesn't open her eyes and gets no visual information about the traffic light.

J's epistemic situation is clearly the best. She is (analogically, anyway) equivalent to the philosopher who has the capacity of knowledge. She looks at the object that she is trying to capture (albeit with vision, in this analogy) and gets it just right. She sees how things are with the traffic light. K is in an inferior epistemic situation with respect to J. She can interact with only some of the wavelengths emanating from the traffic light. She thus gets less than true information about the traffic light. What she gets is misleading and confusing. It is not misleading and confusing about the wavelengths of light with which she can interact (O1)—that's not the problem. Her position is inferior because it gives her confusing information about the traffic light itself (O2). That is why it is inferior. If there were no one traffic light that both were trying to capture, we could not explain why K's experience is inferior to J's. So, in order to call K's experience and her O1 inferior to J's, we have to assume that each of their epistemic capacities is importantly about O2 in addition to being about O1. Thus, when we are talking about O1, we can say that their capacities have different sensory objects, but O2 forces us to admit that their different capacities have the same object of cognition. It makes sense to think that even though Plato has Socrates say that knowledge and *doxa* have different objects, he would agree that they have different "sensory" or "target" objects, but the same intellectual object.

Let's think about L, who doesn't open her eyes in the presence of the traffic light. She has not set her vision on anything at all and ends up ignorant about the traffic light. Even in her case, the traffic light is featured as the object about which she has no cognition. Her ignorance is about the second-degree object (O2). She has altogether failed to capture it. So even L's epistemic condition shares a second-degree object with J's and K's epistemic conditions.[30]

---

30. This might make it seem as though no one is ignorant on Plato's view as all one needs to avoid being L is to (metaphorically) open their eyes. Recall from chapters 5 and 6 that, outside of *Republic* V, where *doxa* and ignorance are distinguished by Plato

Back to the Example at Hand

So now, let's look at what we were trying to analogize from *Republic* 475e4–479d5. I will use "capacitizes" as a made-up verb here to stand in for the exercise of the capacity that we are distinguishing in each case. I will call the lover of sights and sounds the *doxophilist* ("lover of *doxa*") to fit better with the spacing below:

The philosopher "capacitizes$_A$" *epi* what-is (Forms)$_{O1}$ and gets knowledge$_{A*}$ about what-is$_{O2}$.

The doxophilist "capacitizes$_A$" *epi* what-is and is-not (perceptibles)$_{O1}$ gets opinion$_{A*}$ about what-is$_{O2}$.

The ignorant person "capacitizes$_A$" what is-not (nothing)$_{O1}$ and gets ignorance$_{A*}$ about what-is$_{O2}$.[31]

What fills in A* is different in each case, as is what fills in O1, this information is what Plato uses to conclude that we are taking about three different capacities: The philosopher's capacity is "knowing," the doxophilist's is "opining," and the ignorant person's is "ignoring." This same information is what allowed us to realize that seeing, hearing, and feeling are different in our analogy. However, this doesn't contradict the notion that there is an object that each person and their capacity is succeeding or failing to capture that is the same in all cases. That object is an object of intelligence and is "what-is"—something like beauty-itself.

---

for artificial reasons (in order to console the Lover of Sights and Sounds), everyone is in E2 and is capable of *doxa*. However—outside of *Rp.* V—*doxa* is co-extensive with ignorance, and ignorance comes by degrees. *Doxa/ignorance* is a spectrum of states that fall below knowledge. So, there is a very low bar for *doxa*. There are ignorant people, and they all have *doxa*, and some of them are more ignorant than others. The concern is to possess "good" *doxa* or "better" *doxa*. But, it is likely that everyone possesses *doxa* and falls somewhere on the spectrum of ignorance (even those who seem most well-informed are on the closer-to-knowledge end of the *doxa/ignorance* spectrum).

31. I have stated this awkwardly in order to make the three cases parallel. Clearly, the ignorant person is not "capacitizing nothing." She is failing to capacitize anything at all. The important point is that ignorance is ignorance *of* what could be known or opined through the other two capacities (O2).

Doxa wouldn't be inferior if we were only comparing its ability to interact with what-is and is-not with knowledge's ability to interact with what-is. It is the fact that knowledge succeeds, and *doxa* fails, to capture "what-is" that makes *doxa* inferior and unreliable. Likewise, it is not its lack of contact with what is and is-not nor its relationship with what is-not that makes ignorance bad. It is the fact that it cannot get to what-is (or what-is and what is-not). My conclusion is that Plato's evaluation of these three capacities makes it clear that he was not principally trying to tell us that *doxa* and ignorance are trying to capture different things. Yes, *doxa* interacts only with perceptibles, and ignorance does not interact with any objects, but they are all being measured against each other because they all have the same second-degree object or object of cognition. However, only knowledge manages to have a successful relationship with that intellectual object. *Doxa* has a relationship with it, albeit a bad one. Ignorance is related to it by ignoring *it*. When it comes to second-degree objects, they are all trying to capture the same thing. This is what they intend to do whether they notice that this is where their intention lands or not.

The Quality of *Doxa*

Doxa interacts with perceptibles and produces something that is inferior to knowledge. However, the fact that Plato has given us a three-part evaluation that includes ignorance seems to imply that Plato thinks it is better to keep our eyes open rather than shut. It is, at least in principle, better to be like K above, than like L. Plato surely thinks that it is always better to have knowledge than *doxa*. Still, especially because he introduces this entire three-part distinction as a "consolation" of the lover of *doxa*, Plato is indicating that *doxa* is, in principle, better than ignorance. He is saying that looking to perceptibles is better than not looking at all. I believe that he is also indicating that *doxa* can be useful and can be improved.

Let us think about why all of this is supposed to be a consolation to the doxophilist. Socrates tells the doxophilist that he is importantly similar to the philosopher and importantly different from those who are ignorant. The similarity between the lovers of sights and sounds and philosophers is that they both understand that they must interact with *something* and conduct inquiries concerning it in order to improve their epistemic situation. Lovers of sights and sounds differ from philosophers in how they seek to do this. While the lover of sights and sounds looks to perceptible particulars, the philosopher looks beyond the perceptible particulars to the Forms. Still, in recognizing that he must look to something, the lover of sights and sounds shows himself to be importantly different from the ignorant person.

Some of the scholars who wish to say that *doxa* is significantly different from knowledge and that knowledge cannot be some sort of enhanced *doxa* emphasize the fact that *doxa* is dangerous.[32] *Doxa* is misleading and confusing. I agree that Plato thinks our ultimate goal is to get rid of *doxa* altogether and to replace it with knowledge.[33] This goes hand in hand with the view that *doxa*, as used in this part of the *Republic*, is not translatable to the notion of "belief" that is found in contemporary "justified true belief" analyses of knowledge. The countertraditional interpretation holds that to believe is to hold a certain unit of propositional content to be true. This belief will become knowledge if it is indeed true and if one can ensure that its truth is not simply a matter of chance. There is much disagreement about what is required for this last criterion to be fulfilled and much of the work in contemporary analytic epistemology revolves around what this criterion is and whether or not it can be fulfilled.

Those who argue that Plato exhorts us to *replace doxa* with knowledge, rather than to *enhance doxa*, point out that *doxa* lacks the kind of clarity of content that would allow it to reflect units of propositional content: it is dreamlike, unstable, and elusive. Something that has no precise content cannot go on to have its content justified and stabilized. I agree with this general description of *doxa* in *Republic* V.

Indeed, this might lead one to argue that it is more dangerous to have *doxa* than to have nothing. The person with unchecked *doxa* might be encouraged to be bold and act based on shifty and deluded impressions. It is reasonable to venture that, for Plato, acting on unchecked *doxa* is more dangerous than not acting at all. Plato does point out in other dialogues that it is better for those who lack knowledge to have fewer resources, as they are then less likely to act on their mistaken beliefs. Those who act on mistaken beliefs do more damage than those who do not act at all.[34]

Still, *doxa can* be, and here, Plato is saying that it—in principle—*is*, better than nothing. Socrates also says this elsewhere. Clearly, Plato thinks

---

32. Vogt, 66–69.

33. Vogt, 82–92; Moss and Schwab, 4–13.

34. *Euthd.*, 280e5–6.

that most people do not have knowledge. Socrates, in the *Apology*, is in a superior position to others despite the fact that neither he nor his fellow citizens have knowledge (22e6–23b4). Plato does not seem to recommend that anyone who is ignorant cease inquiry, and he seems to recognize that inquiry will result—at least initially—in *doxa* and not knowledge.[35] The lesson that we learn from both the *Apology* and *Republic* 475e4–479d5 is that the first way to improve one's own or another's *doxa* is to recognize or point out that it is *doxa* and not knowledge.

I have shown that Plato impugns all *doxa* because it comes up short in capturing the same second-degree objects that knowledge succeeds in capturing, namely, "what-is." I have also disagreed with others regarding *doxa*'s adequacy with respect to perceptibles.[36] Still, I believe Plato shows us *that doxa*'s falling short can come in degrees. This is not only because one person's *doxa* might be truer than another's (or truer than that same person's *doxa* was at an earlier time).[37] I say this because Plato has his characters use myths, models, and analogies in order to better come to understand things that might otherwise be ineffable.

To take an example that is not in Plato, the periodic table is a deficient picture of "what-is" when it comes to the elements. First, it might not represent all elements and the notion of an element might be incoherent.[38] Elements have many different properties. Proposals for how we draw the periodic table have varied over the years. Conflicting priorities concerning which properties to emphasize result in different tables. Still, I think that someone could put together a periodic table that all chemists would agree is inferior to any of those about which they currently disagree. I also think some chemists would choose to use one periodic table for one purpose

---

35. *Men.*, 85c9–d1.

36. See my n. 7–8, above. Vogt argues that *doxa* is the right thing to use to decide whether a piece of cake is large or small (64), but at *Rep.* 523e3–524a4, Socrates argues that this is just the kind of exercise that provokes the understanding (even in nonphilosophers [523d3–5], see ch. 4, 105–108, above) because *doxa* is inadequate to deal with it.

37. I will leave this possibility aside as it would force me to examine whether *doxa* can be more true or false without reflecting propositional content. I think that it can, but that would require too much argument that is outside of Platonic interpretation.

38. Do apparently synthesized elements count or only those found "in nature"? See Scerri (2007) for an exhortation to philosophers of science to treat the periodic table as neither a model nor a theory, but as an organizing principle (xvii–xviii).

(introducing children to chemistry) and a different one for other purposes (to reflect chemical periodicity as an objective fact).[39] All versions of the periodic table are simplified, misleading, and confusing when it comes to capturing "what-is." However, some are better than others, and some are better for some projects than for others.

Another example of improved *doxa* is what results from comprehension of Plato's divided line. It is common for commentators to point out that since the divided line is a representation using mathematical proportions that are translated spatially, it cannot itself occupy the *noêsis* section of the line. Depending on how one interprets the text in this section of the *Republic*, the line must be the (first-degree) object of either *pistis* or *dianoia*.[40]

I believe that Plato does not intend for his three-part distinction at *Republic* 475e4–479d5 to override the many places in the dialogues where he encourages us to think that it is better to hypothesize (using images, myths, models, and other manipulations of *doxa*) than it is to refrain from hypothesizing. He encourages us to do this provided that we recognize that we are dealing with hypotheses and treat them as such. Nor does the three-part distinction among capacities and their objects override the evidence found throughout the dialogues that we do well to revise our hypotheses, even if they remain hypotheses. Plato thinks that we must revise our hypotheses as we find that some appear to be more useful than their predecessors in capturing and helping us deal with a world that includes both perceptibles and intelligibles, and where we do not and cannot know the perceptibles.

Another Anomaly: Three Capacities or One?

Another anomaly of *Republic* V is the treatment of knowledge, opinion, and ignorance as three distinct capacities in line with the metaphor concerning the sensory capacities at (475c9–d5). A few pages into *Republic* VII (518a1–519a6), Plato expresses something that appears different. He talks about the "eye of the soul" (518c6) by analogy with the way our

---

39. See Scerri's (2007, 282–86) discussion and comparison of the "conventional medium-long form," the "left-step" table, and the "modified pyramidal" version.
40. See for example Smith (1996; 2019, 106–16) and Ferrari and Griffith (2000, 219 n. 32).

sense organs work. The very same eyes can be confused in two ways: first, by coming from darkness to light, and second, by going from light to darkness (518a2–3). The first is like a person at the bottom of the cave (without knowledge) looking to what-is, the second occurs when a person who has seen what-is (and thus presumably has knowledge of the Forms) goes back down into the cave to look at perceptibles. The first group of people would be parallel to the lovers of sights and sounds. I have already suggested identifying these prisoners with the lovers of sights and sounds in chapter 4 (103–104), and will say more about it in the next chapter (ch. 8).

In this later passage of the *Republic*, Socrates goes on to say that education takes it for granted that the capacity that sees the shadows (a metaphorical "sight" from the "eye of the soul") *could* see what-is if it (and the entire soul) were "turned" (518c7) toward the proper objects. He also restates this as the notion that *phronêsis* ("intelligence," 518e2) is always there even if other virtues are added as a person develops epistemically (518d3–e3). The eye of the soul is always there, as is the power of intelligence, but it is useful and beneficial if turned one way and can be vicious and harmful if turned the other (518e3–519a1). At 519b4–5, Socrates says that once they are turned, "the same soul of the same person" will see what-is as sharply as it earlier saw the shadows. Intelligence appears to be the capacity to acquire *epistêmê* under the right circumstances, but to acquire *doxa* under less than ideal circumstances.

Is this inconsistent with what Socrates has said in the earlier *Republic* passage in which he consoles the lover of sights and sounds? The fact that the earlier passage is supposed to be a consolation should encourage us to resist seeing them as inconsistent. Telling the lovers of sights and sounds that they have an irreparably different capacity from philosophers would not be much of a consolation. It would make far more sense for Socrates to say that the lovers of sights and sounds take the same "eye of the soul" and—through a misunderstanding concerning what-is—look at perceptibles instead of "turning" to look "through" them to what lies "beyond" them that both creates and governs them. While there is no talk of "turning" at 475c9–d5, we do have the *epi*-locution, which gives us a similar metaphor: lovers of sights and sounds *set* their epistemic capacities *upon* perceptibles, while philosophers *set their* epistemic capacities *upon* what-is. The same intelligence and eye of soul that produces knowledge for philosophers can do no better than be a capacity for *doxa* and produce *doxa* when set upon perceptibles—so, given how they deploy it, the lovers of sights and sounds have a capacity that can only offer them *doxa*. The philosophers will not make the mistake of setting their intelligence and eye of the soul on perceptibles qua perceptibles. As a result, the eye of their soul combined with their intelligence is a capacity for knowledge and produces knowledge. My suggestion is that we take the turning locution at 518c4–10 and the *epi*-locution as analogous. The three-part distinction is not a metaphysical one concerning the *ontological* mutual exclusivity of capacities in the soul, it describes the mutual exclusivity of what one capacity (the eye of the soul directed by intelligence) is capable of in those who have different understandings of metaphysics and ontology—those whose souls are turned in different directions. It describes how intelligence differs in usefulness and benefit in the hands of these two different kinds of people, while encouraging us to see that these two kinds of people are not, terminally, mutually exclusive.[41]

Conclusion

My goal in this chapter has been to show that Plato's three-part distinction between ignorance, *doxa*, and knowledge, and the parallel distinction among their respective objects, deals appropriately with what I have identified as each capacity's first-degree object. This is crucial to our understanding of this passage as a consolation of the lovers of sights and sounds. They have been told that they live in a dream state even while waking and that they don't have knowledge, but only have opinion. Socrates fears they might get angry (476d5–6), so he consoles them by saying that what they have—opinion—while worse than what philosophers have, is better than ignorance. Further, the primary object of their opinion is misleading when it comes to what beauty is, but it is a better starting place than what the ignorant person starts with—which is nothing at all. I understand Socrates to be approving of the fact that doxophilists at least aim their capacities at perceptibles, which is better than not looking to anything at all when forming their opinions. Furthermore, as we learned from the concurrent argument (chapter 4), because they look to perceptibles, while also harboring beliefs about beauty itself that are not consistent with beauty being identical with beautiful sights and sounds, they are

---

41. This general point has already been made by Szaif (2007, 266). He does not discuss any relationship between turning at 518c4–10 and the *epi*-locution.

in a position (E2) to advance along the path from lovers of sights and sounds to philosophers (E3).

Thus, when Plato evaluates knowledge, opinion, and ignorance with respect to one another, he is looking at, and comparing, their ability to capture their second-degree object, which is the same thing in all three cases, namely "what-is" or Plato's Forms: things such as beauty itself. For this reason, we must understand each capacity to have a relationship with, and to be attempting to deal with, "what-is." It is due to the degree to which they are able to appreciate what-is that Plato deems knowledge better than *doxa,* and *doxa* better than ignorance.

I have argued that no capacity ever takes something other than its natural (*pephuken*) object as its first-degree object, not even in an uncharacteristic or uncommon manner. Neither does any capacity take anything other than what-is as its second-degree object. Furthermore, the fact that *doxa* is naturally set over what-is and is-not (or what is becoming) is an accident of the fact that we must interact with everything external to us through our senses. Plato does not say that our senses are, on their own, good at taking in the properties of perceptibles or that *doxa* is adequate for sense experience of large and small things. In fact, he expressly says that perception cannot deal with perceptibles on its own (*Rep.* 523e3–524a4). In Plato's view, our goal should be to use sense experience and deal with perceptibles in such a way that we can compensate for sensation's inability to give us precise information, so we can then get some (albeit deficient) grasp on what-is. His evaluation of *doxa* as compared to knowledge and ignorance shows us that this is what Plato thinks good epistemic agents think of *doxa* as being *for.* To the extent that they fail to recognize this, they will fail to deal well with large and small perceptibles. As human epistemic agents get better at using their intellect to compensate for their *doxai,* they will improve their *doxai,* both by better appreciating what-is and by recognizing that *doxa* is limited.

The consolation of the lovers of sights and sounds leads Plato to deal with *doxa* and ignorance differently at *Republic* 475e4–479d5 than he does elsewhere in the dialogues. But this is not because he is using the terms differently from the way he does elsewhere.[42] What we learned about doxastic structure in the *Symposium* and *Theaetetus* (chapters 5 and 6) is consistent with what we see here: lovers of sights and sounds have

---

42. Compare Szaif (2007, 254) who suggests that Plato is using different, yet compatible, concepts of *doxa* and *epistêmê* in *Rep.* V.

clouds of *doxa* that lack integrity and contain many inconsistencies (such as believing that largeness = large perceptibles, and smallness = small perceptibles, while believing that largeness ≠ smallness) because they don't recognize their own investment in the existence of smallness itself and largeness itself *in addition to* large and small perceptibles.

What is really exceptional in *Republic* V, as compared to the *Symposium*, *Phaedrus*, and *Theaetetus* passages that we examined in chapters 5 and 6, is that Plato appears to be comparing *doxa* to ignorance in a way that implies that the two are mutually exclusive. In the *Phaedrus* and in the middle section of the *Theaetetus*, we saw evidence that ignorance consists of poor quality *doxa*. This contrast is the most striking of any anomaly that Plato appears to have constructed in service of consoling the lovers of sights and sounds. Plato must contrast *doxa* and ignorance in order to console them. In chapter 9, we will see that the appearance of mutual exclusivity is so particular to this passage that it is not even maintained in *Republic* VI–VII. Still, even here, the appearance of mutual exclusivity is only an appearance and need not result in a substantive difference in Plato's local conception of the human epistemic state we call "ignorance." Ignorance can still be composed of *doxa* even at *Republic* 475e4–479d5. Ignorance is *doxa* that is acquired through looking to nothing at all—not even perceptibles—and it results in *doxa* that is *about* what-is but that cannot help but be utterly misguided about what-is. I will speculate about how Plato might be thinking about this in the next chapter (8) by bringing in some evidence from the *Cratylus* and the *Theaetetus*. These are passages that discuss Protagoreanism. Plato portrays Protagoras as someone who thinks we need not even look to perceptibles (or that we at least needn't worry about inconsistencies among our perceptions) in order to develop *doxai* about what-is.[43]

While Plato thinks that *doxa* is set over perceptibles (what both is and is-not), he also thinks that *doxa* is *about* what-is and that is why it is inferior to knowledge. Doxophilists (i.e., lovers of sights and sounds, ordinary people, folks like Plato's readers—you and I) opine beauty itself. The

---

43. Here, it would be good to compare my use of *doxa* to the generic *doxa* I called "thinking" rather than judgment at *Theaet.* 189e–190a (ch. 6, 152–154). The ignorant person looks to nothing, and never even has to have a dialogue with herself. She never tries to match her "thinking" with something outside of her thinking, such as a perceptible or a Form. As a result, she has no need for dialogue with herself or to separate out judgments from the rest of her less considered thinking—everything she thinks is of equal integrity. That is, to her mind, everything she thinks is equally true.

notion that *doxa* is set over what both is and is-not presents an ontological puzzle that cannot help but trouble any interpreter of Plato's dialogues. The designation of *something* that both exists and doesn't exist—or lies somewhere in between existence and nonexistence, flies in the face of Plato's habit of checking many of the things he investigates against the Parmenidean claim that everything that exists must be something because not to exist is to be nothing at all.[44] For some, the designation of the primary object of *doxa* as what both is and is-not also flies in the face of common sense. Thus, before going on to speak more about *doxa* and ignorance in the second part of the next chapter, I will begin that chapter with a discussion of this bizarre claim.

---

44. *Euthd.* 291d7–e1; *Charm.* 161d1–4; *Prot.* 330c1; *Lys.* 218d7–8; *Phdo.* 74a12; *Symp.* 199d1–2, e6–7; *Rep.* 476e10, 478b6–c1 (which I will discuss in ch. 8); *Theaet.* 188e5, 166e9, 163e4–7; *Soph.* 237a3; *Parm.* 132b3–c7.

Chapter 8

Doxa, Ignorance, and the Consolation of the Lover of Sights and Sounds

I have presented my reasons for claiming that Plato thinks we can and must opine beauty itself in *Republic* V. Now I put this passage and my interpretations of both the overt argument (discussed in chapter 7) and the concurrent argument (discussed in chapter 4) found at *Republic* 475e4–479d5, into a wider context. Focusing on the context of the argument as a consolation of the lover of sights and sounds lends clarity and consistency to Plato's descriptions of *doxa* throughout the dialogues. I will first discuss several theses concerning the status of the locutions "what-is," "what is-not," and "what both is and is-not" in an effort to leave behind some existing debates regarding how we can read this passage. I think this will also afford those who study *epistêmê* (knowledge) throughout the dialogues a complementary clarity and consistency even though I am not engaging in such a project at this time.[1]

---

1. One of the consistencies I believe it affords for knowledge is that Plato allows us to have *knowledge* of perceptibles insofar as it is derived from first knowing the Forms in which the perceptibles partake. Knowing perceptibles is not knowing "things" (as will become clear later in this chapter); it is knowing the Forms, which includes knowing how they are being partaken in. Szaif (2007) rightly states that there would otherwise be a troubling inconsistency between this passage and others (254) and attempts to resolve it (262). In fact, his proposal of distinguishing between the formal and the material objects of *doxa* and *epistêmê* seems to share territory with my claims about primary and secondary objects in chapter 7, but this is hard to assess, as his focus and expansion on this suggestion is limited. However, in contrast to my interpretation,

In arguing for the clarity and consistency that is gained from regarding the three powers of knowledge, opinion, and ignorance as having the same secondary object (the Forms), I must further discuss the notion of ignorance and how we are to understand its primary object as what is nothing at all. This intensifies the need to talk about how to take all three of the locutions that describe the primary objects of knowledge, opinion, and ignorance.

My conclusions in chapter 7 relate to what I said about *doxa* in chapters 5 and 6 as follows: knowledge aims at what-is and produces knowledge *about* what-is; it is about such things as beauty itself, equality itself, and the diagonal itself. The capacity for opinion, while it might be aimed at perceptibles and produce a doxastic structure that is not knowledge and is inferior to knowledge, still yields a doxastic structure that is *about* the same things that knowledge is about—Forms. It is only because opinion is—and is intended to be—*about* what-is, that it can be identified as falling short of knowledge. It falls short of capturing the same secondary-object that knowledge captures. It is faulty, we presume, because it is a messy combination of beliefs that fall short to various degrees and that are variously integrated or incoherent. Ignorance will also have to be *about* these same things: Forms such as beauty itself.

Knowledge might be *doxa* that has been rationalized in such a way that it is no longer *doxa* at all, but is knowledge, or this rationalizing might make it so that it is no longer mere *doxa*, but is also knowledge.[2] In any case, lovers of sights and sounds are stuck with mere *doxa*. Their *doxai* do not possess enough integrity to be or become knowledge. Ignorance must also be *doxa* (as we have already surmised from *Symposium* 203c–212d

---

his resolution involves making technical distinctions between the ways in which *doxa* and *epistêmê* are used here as compared to the way they are deployed in the rest of the dialogues (254, 256, 258, 266). Furthermore, it does not consider the consolation of the lovers of sights and sounds, which leaves open a number of questions about the relationship between ignorance and *doxa* in the images of the sun, the cave, and the divided line. Szaif also assumes a veridical reading and a resulting universal literal self-predication regarding the Forms (on which I will comment in n. 14, below). I believe my interpretation lends more plausibility and overall clarity to this passage and to Plato's theory of Forms.

2. This is what is under dispute between those who think knowledge has a distinct object from *doxa* and those who don't. As this dispute is about knowledge, I am not adjudicating between these two views here. See chapter 10, below, for a brief comparison between each of these views and my own.

and passages from the *Phaedrus* in chapters 5 and 6). It is a capacity that is set upon (*epi*) nothing at all. In the last chapter, we interpreted this as when a person does not look to anything (looks to nothing at all) in developing and evaluating their doxastic structure. Further comprehension of this will be my focus later in this chapter. I will argue that Plato is saying that it is worse to be someone who bases their opinions on nothing at all (understood in a particularly Protagorean way) than it is to be a lover of sights of sounds. That is, what consoles the lovers of sights and sounds, even though Socrates has dismissed them as living in a dream state and being inferior to philosophers. When a person looks to nothing at all in order to form her opinions, she ends up having no resources or motivation to improve those opinions. A person who looks to nothing at all is committed to the view that there is no such thing as the integrity of a doxastic structure: there is no criterion by which to evaluate a doxastic structure or to make it better or worse. Such a person has no potential for improving her doxastic structure so that it becomes better and more useful. She cannot inquire or benefit from inquiry or education. Below, I will fill this in by examining other texts where Plato contrasts the assumption that inquiries have objectively better and worse answers with the assumption that everyone's opinion is equal and how things seem to each person is true for them. First, however, let's look at how we are to understand the notion that the object of opinion can both be and not-be.

To Be and Not Be

There is scholarly controversy over whether Plato intended the notion that something can both be and not-be in any of three general ways. On the "ontological" reading, we assume that Plato really is saying that a thing can have an ontological status that is in between fully existing and not existing altogether. This certainly seems to be what walks off the page in this part of the *Republic*, but commentators are reluctant to attribute this kind of view to Plato at least, because it seems anti-Parmenidean. I will explain this more fully below. As a result, many have followed Vlastos (1965), who does not see how Plato could have intended the ontological reading and instead proposes that "being and not being" is intended to imply a predicate, and that some predicate must always be supplied. For example, *doxa* is *epi* those things that are [beautiful] and not [beautiful] (as seems to be demonstrated in Socrates's discussion with the absent lover of sights and sounds at 475e4–479d5). This is the "predicational" reading.

Among those who find both the ontological and predicational readings problematic, Fine (1978, 2003) has championed a veridical reading supplying "true" where Vlastos argued for a range of predicates: "*Doxa* is set upon what is true and not true." Fine thinks Plato intends to say that while knowledge must be set upon true propositions, belief is set upon both true and false propositions.

Which of these readings we should favor is beyond the scope of this book. I believe that there is an ontological reading that is Parmenidean. However, an argument for that view would take us deep into Plato's metaphysics and beyond the scope of this project.[3] However, I believe that this ontological reading will allow us to say that perceptible objects are, for any F, both F and not-F, as Vlastos wants to say. In chapters 5 and 6, I argued that conceiving of our cloud of *doxa* as a bunch of individuated true or false *propositions* is a simplistic and misleading way to understand Plato's assumptions about what kind of cognitive states human belief and knowledge are and how they might be related to one another. Still, it is the case that if a person has knowledge, she will have an epistemic structure that might be able to be—artificially—rendered into what seem to us to be known propositions. Furthermore, in the case of knowledge, all of those propositions would have to be true. So, for the time being, since I am not going to present and argue for an ontological reading of this section of the *Republic*, I am content that what I present can be consistent with any of these three types of readings.[4]

Ontological Concerns and Parmenideanism

Even though I will not argue in favor of a particular ontological reading, I will give some indication of why I think an ontological reading need not conflict with Plato's Parmenidean sentiments. It's important to note that the all or nothing nature of existence that we understand Plato to have adopted from Parmenides is present in this very passage. Each

---

3. See Penner (1987, 206–231) for a sketch of this sort of view.

4. See Gonzalez (1996, 1998) for arguments against both the predicational and veridical readings with which I sympathize and for an ontological reading that is somewhat different from the one I would champion.

time Socrates introduces a new item for discussion, he asks whether it is "something or nothing" and follows up with the admonition that it could not be nothing or there would be nothing about which to ask the question. I propose that the key to reading this passage ontologically is to take Plato to be saying that whatever both is and is-not is on the *something* side of the something or nothing dichotomy.[5] Anything that both is and is-not cannot be nothing at all. The ontological puzzle is how something that both is and is-not gets to be *something that is*. I will offer a potential, Parmenides-friendly, answer to this puzzle: what both is and is-not is something—but not a free-standing, independent, unified, *thing*. I think we can say this in the same way that we would say that the stuff between the banks of the Mississippi River is something (it is certainly not nothing at all), but it is not a free-standing, independent, unified, *thing*. That mass's not being nothing at all is due to the fact that its existence is dependent on a number of abstract objects that are each some one thing. I will elaborate on this shortly.

In fact, just after it is reiterated that opinion cannot be of what-is (478b1–2), the "something or nothing" question is aimed at the stuff that *doxa* is set upon (478b7–8) and even there it is agreed that opinion opines something, because it is impossible to opine nothing. So, we enter into the conversation about that which both is and is-not having recommitted ourselves to the Parmenidean doctrine that anything worth talking about is something because the only alternative would be for it to be nothing, and it is impossible to talk about nothing.[6]

Just after the fact that opinion must opine something is affirmed, a new qualification is added to what it is to be something. Before, what was completely knowable was said to "purely be" (478d6–7)[7] and what did not exist in any way was said to be "utterly unknowable" (477a4).[8] Now, after asking if the person who opines, opines something, Socrates goes on to ask, "But the person who opines, opines some *one* thing?" (478b9),[9] to which

---

5. Note the similarity to the way, in my view, Plato dealt with the known/not-known dichotomy at *Theat.* 188a1–195b8 in chapter 6, 161.
6. See Kirk and Raven (1957, 268–72) for this well-accepted Parmenidean view.
7. τοῦ εἰλικρινῶς ὄντος
8. μηδαμῇ πάντῃ ἄγνωστον
9. ἀλλ' ἕν γέ τι δοξάζει ὁ δοξάζων;

the lover of sights and sounds answers, "Yes." After that, Socrates points out that it would be inaccurate to say that what is-not is *one* thing, for it is nothing. Next, Socrates goes on to make some comparisons, saying that opinion is clearer than ignorance and darker than knowledge. These comparisons persuade them to place what is opined in between that which is and that which is-not.

We have just seen Glaucon agree to two things that seem to be at odds with each other. He agreed that opinion opines some *one* thing. But, he also agreed that opinion opines something in between what *purely is* (what is *some one thing*) and what is *nothing at all*. This tension can be resolved as follows: Plato takes opinion to be set over (to take as its primary object) *existent* stuff, but not *discretely unified, and determinately identified* stuff. *Doxa* opines perceptibles. A perceptible is a mashup of "parts" of partakings in Forms (abstract unities). These abstract unities, in which the perceptibles partake, *are* some *one* thing—they are objectively unified, individuated, and determinate. Sense experience cannot take in an objective unity. The only objective unities are the abstract, intelligible, ones in which what is opined partakes. *Doxa* looks to the perceptible world, but only discrete, determinate, unchanging, and unified things count as some one thing. These unified and unchanging things cannot be perceived through human senses. Perceptibles fall on the "something" side of the something/nothing dichotomy. They exist, but they exist as temporarily and subjectively bounded, spatiotemporal conglomerations of partakings in abstract things. Perceptibles are amorphous globs of partakings in objective unities. They are globs that cannot be individuated into objective, unified, things. No perceptible can. What it is to exist "purely" (*eilikrinôs*, 477a7) is to exist as an unmixed, unchanging, unity with a unique, determinate identity. When we opine, we are opining something (not nothing at all) and ultimately, we are opining concerning what partakes in the only pure and objective individual beings (beings like beauty itself or the Forms).

Republic 475e4–479d5 is not the only passage that forces us to reconcile Plato's Parmenidean tendencies with some apparently bizarre existence claims. In the *Theaetetus*, Plato has Socrates distinguish between being and becoming.[10] There, the claim is:

---

10. Penner (1987, 206–31) makes the case for understanding the *Rep.* passage and the *Theat.* passage as the same theory and argues that the predicative theory cannot accommodate the claim in the *Theat.* that physical objects have no fixed identity. For, in order for there to be predicates, there must be some definite character underlying the predication (208).

[T]here is nothing which in itself is just *one* thing: nothing which you could rightly call *anything* or any *kind* of thing. If you call a thing large, it will reveal itself as small, and if you call it heavy, it is liable to appear as light, and so on with everything, because nothing is anything or any kind of thing. The things of which we naturally say that they "are," are in the process of coming to be, as the result of movement and change and blending with one another. We are wrong when we say they "are," since nothing ever is, but everything is coming to be. (152d2–e1, Levett's translation in Burnyeat [1990]; emphasis added)[11]

Here, Plato has Socrates move from saying that perceptibles are not some *one* thing to saying that they are not a *kind* of thing. Because they fall under both small and large, for example, they cannot be identified as a large kind of thing or a small kind of thing—they cannot be identified with one property to the exclusion of its opposite.

The idea that the things we take to exist (perceptible objects) are only in the process of becoming resonates with the present *Republic* passage. The lovers of sights and sounds, the common people, assume that perceptible objects exhaust what-is—but it turns out that perceptibles do not exist as individual objects; they are temporarily amassed stuff in flux. This mass of stuff partakes in multiple Forms simultaneously, it partakes first in one group of Forms and then in another, it partakes in a particular Form to a greater degree and then to a lesser degree. The becomers are not unified *somethings* that have determinate boundaries and unchanging identities. The becomers in this *Theaetetus* passage and the globs of partakings that are opined in the *Republic* V passage are described in much the same way. The becomers cannot be separated, bounded, and individuated—thus, they cannot be known. Only the Forms in which they partake are objective, determinate, unities with unchanging identities. If there is knowledge of perceptibles, it must be derived from first knowing the Forms.[12] The

---

11. ὡς ἄρα ἓν μὲν αὐτὸ καθ' αὑτὸ οὐδέν ἐστιν, οὐδ' ἄν τι προσείποις ὀρθῶς οὐδ' ὁποιονοῦν τι, ἀλλ' ἐὰν ὡς μέγα προσαγορεύῃς, καὶ σμικρὸν φανεῖται, καὶ ἐὰν βαρύ, κοῦφον, σύμπαντά τε οὕτως, ὡς μηδενὸς ὄντος ἑνὸς μήτε τινὸς μήτε ὁποιουοῦν· ἐκ δὲ δὴ φορᾶς τε καὶ κινήσεως καὶ κράσεως πρὸς ἄλληλα γίγνεται πάντα ἃ δή φαμεν εἶναι, οὐκ ὀρθῶς προσαγορεύοντες· ἔστι μὲν γὰρ οὐδέποτ' οὐδέν, ἀεὶ δὲ γίγνεται.

12. Szaif (2007, 257) points out that Plato seems to say that once Forms are known the perceptibles can also be known at both *Tim.* 37b (254) and *Rep.* 476d.

perceptibles taken all by themselves (which can only be done misleadingly and *per impossible*) exist only as temporary instances of Form partakings that are all mixed together in ever-changing combinations with no clear reasons why they should be "cut up" along the boundaries of one Form's partaking as opposed to another's.

Let's illustrate this with a perceptible "object": This perceptible apple to which I now point partakes in many different Forms at the same time. Apple-ness of course, but also redness, sweetness, pectin-ness, 68°F-ness, and roundness, among others. This conglomeration of Forms will not stay together over time. It does not and will not maintain the same boundaries in space. Pectin-ness can remain without apple-ness, apple-ness can remain without roundness or redness. The space where we find apple-ness does not map precisely onto the place where we find 68°F-ness (the exterior of the apple is likely to be the same temperature as the air touching it and the interior of the apple is likely to be a different temperature from the exterior). The space where redness is does not have the same boundaries as the space where apple-ness is (the interior of the apple is not red). Thus, when I point to the perceptible "apple," I am, artificially (for reasons having nothing to do with some objective metaphysics about what-is), choosing to pick out the boundary of one partaking over others. Were a worm living inside the apple able to point to and articulate the contents of its perceptible world, it would think much differently from the way we do about the proper way to individuate the "things" it perceives, and would choose the boundaries of different Forms in this conglomeration that we identify as an apple than we do, and focus on very differently bounded "things." The worm could do this in ways that are objectively better and worse for the worm. But what is objectively the best way for the worm to individuate perceptibles will not be what is objectively the best way for a person to individuate them. That doesn't force one of them (the worm or the person) to be wrong, as long as they are both relying on actual boundaries of actual partakings in actual Forms. The same would go for the human pharmacist who wishes to extract pectin from an indiscriminate bunch of fruit in order to make an anticholesterol drug. The pharmacist might be content to carve out the space where two different "apples" overlap or take a scoop that combines apple-ness and orange-ness indifferently. The goal with which one approaches dividing conglomerations of Forms into perceptible "things" will determine the adequacy of one's individuation of those "things."[13]

---

13. I take this view to be an expansion of Penner (1987, 218–31).

Thus, what the lover of sights and sounds points to as an individual apple is not—all on its own—objectively some one thing, but it is certainly not nothing at all! The temporarily and artificially individuated "apple" is a "becomer" or "rolls around between" being some one thing and not being some one thing. I have a screen saver on my computer that gradually, ingeniously, and in an organic seeming way, turns one of the photos in my computer's memory into another one by temporarily maintaining certain lines, shapes and colors while changing others. Plato is thinking that the "apple" singled out by the ordinary person has a being that is analogous to the kind of being possessed by the image of my cat, which I see almost completely become the image that it is before it transforms slowly into almost being the complete image of Mount Hood, before beginning to transform into the next image, on my screen saver.

What walks off the page of this part of the *Republic* V text is not a clear and simple assertion with which we can all simply agree. That is why there is so much argument in the literature over whether something needs to be supplied ("is F" or "is true") in order to make the text say something that seems to make more sense. I think that most would agree that these further locutions have been supplied because what *does* walk off the page is an *ontological* view, but one that does not seem to add up. So, making the ontological view add up by seeing its resonance with what is said elsewhere in the dialogues is the preferable way to go.

However, I offer this interlude on ontology in order to explain how, when it comes to both being and not-being, my interpretation does not keep anyone who holds either the predicational or veridical readings of the passage from verbalizing something that is either predicationally or veridically sensible: the apple is both red and not-red, partly because "it" is both an apple and not an apple at the same time. It is incredibly likely that if I try to assert a number of propositions about "it" some will be true and some will be false—in fact the same proposition can be both true and false of "it" because "its" identity is not determinate at any moment *and* changes over time. Meanwhile, this is not true about the Forms, whatever is properly predicated of them will be and remain predicated of them without qualification.[14] True propositions about the identities of

---

14. I should add that this does not commit Plato to Universal Literal Self Predication. Redness itself (the Form of Red) does not remain visually *red*, it remains *redness*: the visual property "red" is never truly predicated of it, but whatever predicates are predicated of it and give it its determinate identity, remain the same and never change. Some Forms, such as Beauty, may endure literal self-predication (of course, what

Forms are true without qualification and will remain so. The rest of what I want to say is not dependent upon any argument that one of these three is the preferred reading. Thus, after the next brief comment that takes advantage of the veridical reading, I will put ontology aside as I proceed.

Parallels between *Doxa* in the *Symposium* and the *Republic*

To my mind, any validity possessed by the veridical reading is due to the fact that it can be derived from the ontological reading. Still, some version of the veridical reading does help us to see that the talk about *doxa* that is unreasoned at *Symposium* 202a5–9 is paralleled by the talk of *doxa* being set upon what both is and is-not at *Republic* 475e4–479d5. We will recall from chapter 5 that the *Symposium* passage initially seemed to encourage us to think that we could form a neat hierarchy among all kinds of ignorance, beliefs, and knowledge. Nevertheless, in the end, we saw that *doxa* is complicated, messy, and so multidimensional that there is no way to compose a clean hierarchy of individual propositional beliefs, let alone of systems of beliefs. This is at least because it is not clear how to rank the individuated propositions that are believed and true but not reasoned against those that are not true but are well reasoned. We cannot rank entire doxastic systems because each one contains a variety of beliefs with a variety of truth-values and degrees of justification, and there is no single rubric according to which we can compare them and make an ordinal ranking. All of these beliefs vary along many different dimensions when it comes to their epistemic quality. In addition, we noticed that ignorance is also composed of beliefs. We would have to include these ignorant cases of *doxa* in our attempts to elucidate a hierarchy.

---

makes Beauty beautiful is not any physical property, nor is it physically beautiful), but that needn't be true of all Forms in order to make the predicational reading work as a surface reading of the text. Vlastos (1965) did not propose the best wording or conception of a possible predicational reading. The apple both does and does not have every property that it has. Redness itself always has the properties that make it what it is. Perceptible red things are both red and not red; their identities with respect to whether or not they are red *things* is indeterminate. Redness itself is always Redness, its identity insofar as it is Redness does not change.

Thus, while *doxa* that completely misses the mark of what-is, and is wholly unreasoned, is ignorance (at least theoretically, even if this never describes any actual human being's doxastic system). And, while *doxa* that completely matches up with what-is and is justified and coherent (at least theoretically, even if this never describes an actual human being's doxastic system) is the most like—or can become—knowledge. All other *doxastic* systems are as described by the veridical reading. They are variously composed both of *doxa* that hits what-is and that does not hit what-is, and composed of *doxa* that is reasoned and *doxa* that is not reasoned.

This rehearses the way that the *Symposium*'s (203c–212e) wide range of doxastic clouds, some of which count as ignorance, and some of which count as something in between knowledge and ignorance, are related to the fact that *doxa* is of what both is and is-not at *Republic* 477a–479a5. *Doxa* that is not knowledge contains some elements that are true and some that are false, and some that are reasoned, while others are unreasoned. But all of this totality of *doxai* must still be about what-is—otherwise none of its elements could be true or false.

At *Symposium* 202a5–9, Diotima says that true belief that is unreasoned is in between knowledge and ignorance. At *Republic* 477a5–479d5, Socrates says that opinion (*doxa*) is in between knowledge and ignorance. We now see that there is something to be gained by associating these two passages with one another and looking for parallels. I now put the ontological status of what is in between what-is and what is-not, at *Republic* 477a5–479d5, aside.

Further Consolation of the Lover of Sights and Sounds from Other Dialogues

All of this is proposed as a consolation to the lover of sights and sounds. Why is it consoling? The lover of sights and sounds is being told that he is importantly similar to the philosopher and importantly different from those who are ignorant. The similarity between the lovers of sights and sounds and philosophers is that they both understand that they must look *to something* and conduct inquiries concerning it in order to improve their epistemic situation. They must look *outward* to something that they take to be an *external* reality—something other than—or at least in addition to—*their own* thoughts (the contents of their own internal doxastic structure). Lovers of sights and sounds differ from philosophers in that to which they look. Or, to use the *epi*-locution, they differ from philosophers in what their capacity is set upon. While the lover of sights and sounds looks to perceptible particulars, the philosopher looks beyond the perceptible particulars to the Forms. Still, in recognizing that he must look to something other than what is in his own mind, the lover of sights and sounds shows himself to be importantly different from the ignorant person. The ignorant person looks to *nothing at all*—or, more accurately—does not look to anything *external* that he takes to be a governing and objective reality with respect to which he could be wrong, for guidance in order to come to understand the world.

To round out this description of the difference between lovers of sights and sounds and those who are ignorant, we might make a comparison to something that happens in the *Cratylus*. If we add "nothing at all" into the mix, the notion of looking to different kinds of things and getting more or less valuable results is consistent with a comparison Plato makes between looking to a true and natural form (*eidos,* 389b3, c3–8) as opposed to perceptible objects in the *Cratylus*.

The *Cratylus*

At *Cratylus* (385d7–e3), Socrates asks his interlocutor, Hermogenes, whether he sees any correctness to names. Hermogenes replies that there is no correctness to names and that "anyone can give a name" equally well. Socrates then asks Hermogenes whether he thinks that the "things differ as the names differ" and are "relative to individuals," as Protagoras says. According to Socrates, those who disagree with Protagoras must think that things have a "permanent essence of their own" (385e4–386a4). When Hermogenes admits that he finds Protagoreanism tempting at times, Socrates gives a very quick argument against it: if Protagoras were right that things are as they appear to each person, then no one could be wiser than anyone else, as each person would always be correct. On Protagoras's view, *thinking* that something is true *makes it be true* (386c2–d1). Protagoreans are the epitome of those who look *to* nothing at all in order to come to understand the world. Whatever they come to think about the world is true (for them) simply because they think it, so there is no need to look around, inquire, and explore. Protagoreans seem to be modeling the capacity of ignorance from *Republic* 475e4–479d5.

Although both Hermogenes and Socrates act as if Protagoras has been laid to rest at this point, Socrates goes on to make an argument that is at least as much an argument against Protagoras as it is an argument against Hermogenes. Hermogenes has supposedly adopted a less radical type of conventionalism than that proposed by Protagoras—one in which things do not differ as their names differ. However, Socrates ends up demonstrating there is no less radical position upon which it is also true that just anyone can give a name. The claim that "anyone can give a name" is not consistent with the claim that "things have a permanent essence of their own."[15]

Plato shows this by pointing out that words are the tools by which we speak just as knives are the tools by which we cut. I cannot simply pick up any old object, decide that it is a knife (call it a "knife") and then cut something with it. I will only succeed in cutting if I use the correct tool—calling something a knife does not make it a knife. I will cut most effectively if I use a tool that was fashioned by someone who understands the nature of cutting—someone who knows what kinds of materials can be used to cleave what other kinds of materials. I need a knife that is designed by someone who looks to what the world (metal, stone, wool, etc.) is like, not someone who just takes whatever seems to him as if it will cut. Likewise, if I wish to inform someone using speech, I will find that words that are well chosen or designed by someone who understands the things I am trying to talk about will be more effective. It will be better, for example, if the word for "help" is relatively short and distinct from other words that denote, "Look at that interesting thing over there," or, "Leave me alone." This is not to say that there is only one word that can be used for "help" just as there is not only one material out of which a knife can be made (389d8–390a3). Nevertheless, it is definitely the case that it is possible for some words to be better than others and that the more understanding of reality that the legislator of names has gleaned from the dialectician, the better names they will craft (390d9–e5).

---

15. To put the argument starkly and a bit differently from the way Plato makes it: as soon as one allows for even one permanent essence, effective naming will become restricted to those who are better at capturing (even by accident) that permanent essence, and it will no longer be the case that all names are equally good and that all people are equally good at naming. The argument assumes that names are tools for communication and a name is better if it allows for better communication (388b7–389a3).

In describing how the legislator of names will fashion them, Socrates draws a comparison to the maker of shuttles. Concerning the legislator of names, he asks, "To what does he look? (*episkepsai poi blepôn ho nomothetês?*)" (389a5) and in order to find an answer, he asks to what the carpenter "looks" in making a shuttle (389a6–8). He suggests that the carpenter will look to "that which is naturally fitted to act as a shuttle (*pros toiouton ti ho epephukei kerkizein*)" (389a7–8). Socrates follows this by suggesting two distinct things to which one might look,

> And suppose the shuttle be broken in the making of it. Will he make another, looking to the broken one? Or will he look to that form to which he looked in making the broken one? (389b1–3)[16]

The lover of sights and sounds would look at the broken shuttle—or other particular shuttles—to make a new shuttle. And, if he were really a lover of sights and sounds, in making new ones, the best he could do would be to duplicate the shuttles that already are; he could not improve upon them. He would look at perceptible particulars in order to understand the world. But the person who is best at making shuttles would be the one who looks beyond the broken shuttle—beyond particular instances of shuttles—to the [F]orm (*eidos*, 389b3) according to which all shuttles are made.[17] This shuttle maker might be able to make new, improved, particular shuttles by making ones that better approximate the nature of the shuttle. To look at the Form according to which all shuttles are made is to look to what completely is. To look to perceptible and temporary shuttles, or to broken shuttles, is to look to what both is and is-not. Lovers of sights and sounds do not look to what philosophers look to, and will get a worse result in fashioning a shuttle, *but at least they look to something*. They are not like Protagoreans who look to nothing (beyond their own thoughts). Anything Protagoreans *call* or *believe* is a shuttle *is* a shuttle in a manner that cannot fall short of being a shuttle, as far as Protagoras is concerned. But not anything they believe or call a shuttle

---

16. ἂν καταγῇ αὐτῷ ἡ κερκὶς ποιοῦντι, πότερον πάλιν ποιήσει ἄλλην πρὸς τὴν κατεαγυῖαν βλέπων, ἢ πρὸς ἐκεῖνο τὸ εἶδος πρὸς ὅπερ καὶ ἣν κατέαξεν ἐποίει;

17. In the next few lines, Socrates says that the form of the shuttle is the "shuttle-itself," so we would perhaps be justified in writing "Form" using the capital "F" here (389b5–6).

will get equally good results when it comes to weaving. By looking at the nature (Form) of the shuttle, the good carpenter (the philosopher) obtains knowledge of shuttles and weaving and makes an effective shuttle. By looking at perceptible shuttles, the lover of sights and sounds makes shuttles that will have varying degrees of effectiveness. If they look at a bad or broken shuttle, they will not make an effective one. The lovers of sights and sounds get only opinions about shuttles from looking where they do. Even worse, however, by looking at nothing (external) in order to create the shuttle, the Protagoreans end up just as ignorant about shuttles and weaving as they were before. Each of these three persons sets their capacity for knowledge, opinion, or ignorance on a different object, respectively. Still every one of the three is getting an objectively better or worse result, because they are all, wittingly or unwittingly, seeking to create the same thing—a shuttle (or the tool that is best at weaving, whatever that is). Thus, even the lover of sights and sounds and the ignorant person are unwittingly trying to get at—and referring to—the true natures of weaving, yarn of different types, woods of various sorts, and the human hand in all its various shapes and sizes. The lover of sights and sounds and the ignorant person are doing a bad job of the same thing concerning which the philosopher does a good job. However, even though the lovers of sights and sounds are being chastised for looking to the wrong thing, they are looking to *something,* and that is better than what the ignorant persons do, and that is their consolation.

A Further Note on Ignorance and *Doxa*

The *possession* of *doxa* cannot be what Plato thinks distinguishes the lover of sights and sounds from the ignorant person. Even those who look to nothing at all in the manner upon which I have just elaborated, still possess *doxa*. The weakness of their doxastic structure is what constitutes their ignorance. This example, from the *Phaedrus*, shows that even if someone like the ignorant person at *Republic* 475e4–479d5 looks to nothing at all in order to manifest their ignorance, there is no denying that ignorance is—most plausibly—a manner of entertaining *doxa*:

> [J]ust as a musical expert, if he met someone who thought he knew all about harmony just because he happened to know how to produce the highest and lowest notes with strings, would

not say savagely "you're off your head you wretch," but, being a musician, more gently, "My dear fellow, the person who means to be an expert in harmony must certainly know that, too. But there is nothing to prevent someone in your condition from having not the slightest understanding of harmony; for what you know is what has to be learned before harmony itself, not the elements of harmony as such." (268d6–e6, Rowe's translation)[18]

The ignorant have many opinions about, for example, how to play the highest notes on the strings. The problem is that this string player has no clue that he needs to look to the natures involved in the ruling science of "harmony" in order to organize and deploy his string-playing beliefs as a means to creating harmony. Plato shows that people's ignorance is due at least as much to the presence of their *doxai* as it is to its absence.

Conclusion

If we arrive at *Republic* V without having made a careful examination of inquiry and *doxa*, we risk misunderstanding the *epi*-relation and taking it to describe both opinion and ignorance as having no connection to the way things actually are and the abstract objects—things such as beauty itself and equality itself—that make up what-is. It is true that opinion and ignorance are not "set upon" things such as beauty itself. But it is also true that beauty itself and the other Forms both create the perceptible becomers and determine what each perceptible is and is-not. Consequently, opinion is true or false belief *about* things like beauty itself and ignorance is ignorance *of* beauty itself. Lovers of sights and sounds would be better off if they could be brought to set their epistemic faculties beyond the perceptibles and upon such things as beauty itself and equality itself. However, those who do not even question the coherence and consistency

---

18. ὥσπερ ἂν μουσικὸς ἐντυχὼν ἀνδρὶ οἰομένῳ ἁρμονικῷ εἶναι, ὅτι δὴ τυγχάνει ἐπιστάμενος ὡς οἷόν τε ὀξυτάτην καὶ βαρυτάτην χορδὴν ποιεῖν, οὐκ ἀγρίως εἴποι ἄν· 'ὦ μοχθηρέ, μελαγχολᾷς,' ἀλλ' ἅτε μουσικὸς ὢν πρᾳότερον ὅτι 'ὦ ἄριστε, ἀνάγκη μὲν καὶ ταῦτ' ἐπίστασθαι τὸν μέλλοντα ἁρμονικὸν ἔσεσθαι, οὐδὲν μὴν κωλύει μηδὲ σμικρὸν ἁρμονίας ἐπαΐειν τὸν τὴν σὴν ἕξιν ἔχοντα· τὰ γὰρ πρὸ ἁρμονίας ἀναγκαῖα μαθήματα ἐπίστασαι ἀλλ' οὐ τὰ ἁρμονικά.'

of their impressions of the perceptibles are even farther from having any useful beliefs. Plato has Socrates account for why they are in even worse shape than lovers of sights and sounds by calling them ignorant and saying that they set their faculty over nothing at all.

Plato is not making a technical claim here. He is not saying that lovers of sights and sounds alone possess beliefs. If we look at other passages where *doxa* is used as a generic term, as it is in the *Meno* and *Symposium* (and everywhere outside of *Theaet.* 189e–194d), it is clear that the difference between lovers of sights and sounds and those who are ignorant is a difference in the quality and the integrity of the structure of their mass of *doxa*. In the next chapter, we will see Plato again use *doxa* in a way that does not distinguish between the ignorant and those common people like the lovers of sights and sounds in books VI and VII of the *Republic*. The cave and the divided line create images that seem like they should be summaries of the epistemic contents of *Republic* V and the passages that follow in these middle books of the *Republic*. Both focus on the contrast between knowledge (*epistêmê*) and mere belief (*doxa*). However, neither of these summarizing images refers to ignorance as a third member of some sort of epistemic triad. Neither refers to ignorance as an absence of *doxa*. In fact, both treat ignorant states as composed of *doxa*.

Diotima's pronouncement that *doxa* that is true but unreasoned lies in between knowledge and ignorance at *Symposium* 202a5–9 sets us up to expect a linear hierarchy of mutually exclusive epistemic states that go from ignorance to belief to knowledge. But, by looking more carefully at how Plato designed her discussion with Socrates in chapter 5, we concluded that Plato has Diotima set us up with the naive expectation that we can make a linear hierarchy of individual propositional epistemic entities only so that he can rub our noses in the complexity of actual epistemic states and our efforts to evaluate them in an ordinal manner. A misguided interpretation of epistemic states at *Symposium* 203c–212e that takes them to be propositional and linearly ordinal might appear to underwrite a reading of *Republic* 475e4–479d5 that takes knowledge, *doxa*, and ignorance to be *about* separate and mutually exclusive things. However, once we let go of the naive notion that epistemic states are unidimensional, as the *Symposium* passage nudges us to do, we also let go of any mutual exclusivity of *doxa* and ignorance. This allows us to see that Plato holds the far more intuitive view that all epistemic states that fall short of knowledge are composed of doxastic systems of various degrees of quality and integration. Many other texts, especially in the *Phaedrus*, confirm that Plato sees no harm in conceiving of the worst epistemic states as composed of *doxa*.

None of this does anything to prevent us from understanding the distinction made between knowledge, *doxa*, and ignorance at *Republic* 475e4–479d5. In fact, the passage is easier to comprehend once placed in the context of the consolation of the lovers of sights and sounds. This framework allows us to see that, when Plato says that each of knowledge, belief, and ignorance is set upon something different, he is not necessarily talking about the cognitive contents of the state (it can still be beliefs in both *doxa* and ignorance) or what the truth-makers for that content must be (it must be what-is in every case). Rather, Plato is congratulating the lovers of sights and sounds for realizing that they must look to some sort of external criterion for the veridicality of their *doxa* if they hope to be able to inquire, learn, and improve their doxastic systems. However, he is also pressing them to look to the appropriate kind of thing rather than to those sights and sounds that they mistake for beauty itself and for every other nature about which they want to learn. In order for any of these ordinary people to have knowledge, opinion, or ignorance, their knowledge, opinion, or ignorance must be about what-is. Thus, Plato further assumes that all these people have a non-doxastic, unwitting, cognitive connection to the Forms. They all opine beauty itself.

Chapter 9

Doxa and Ignorance in the Cave and the Divided Line

We are now ready to interpret the famous images of the divided line and the cave in the context of our investigation of how Plato thought about all of those epistemic states that fall short of knowledge. Much has been written about these striking, but all too briefly described, Platonic images and there is much controversy and confusion concerning how to interpret them. Nothing that I say here will allow me to adjudicate among these many interpretations. The point that I wish to emphasize is not controversial. These (supposedly summarizing) images compare only *doxa* (belief or opinion) and *epistêmê* (knowledge); neither one even mentions (uses a Greek word that can be translated as) ignorance as a distinct epistemic condition that is separate from *doxa*.[1] Given that both the cave and the line are attempts by Plato to summarize and categorize human epistemic states or experiences, it is surprising that there is this striking disagreement between the three-part distinction in *Republic* V and these images in books VI and VII.

In contrast with the line and the cave, the discussion of epistemic capacities at *Republic* 475e4–479d5 *does* mention a triad of epistemic conditions: it includes ignorance in addition to knowledge and opinion. The contrast between how the consolation of the lovers of sights and sounds treats ignorance and *doxa* and the way *doxa* is discussed—while ignorance is ignored—in the cave and the line, underwrites the observation that I have already made about *doxa*: it is not, according to Plato, a distinct epistemic condition from ignorance. *Republic* 475e4–479d5 treated it that

---

1. For the sentiment that they are summarizing, see Annas (1981, 242), Ferejohn (2006b, 217–19).

way anomalously as a means for consoling the lovers of sights and sounds. In fact, as I concluded after close readings of *Symposium* 201d1–212c3, passages from the *Phaedrus* and the discussion of false judgment in the *Theaetetus*, *doxa* and ignorance can be two different descriptions of the same doxastic clouds and structures. In the *Symposium* passage, a surface reading of some of Diotima's preliminary statements might also, mistakenly, lead us to believe that Plato considers *doxa* and ignorance distinct. But a reading that goes on to make sense of the messiness of any spectrum of doxastic states that Plato is alluding to in the *Symposium* will reappraise the possibility of a clean, linear, hierarchy among epistemic states that fall short of knowledge. This reappraisal resonates with the midsection of the *Theaetetus* and the passages that discuss recollection and *doxa* in the *Phaedrus*. There, we found that the worst doxastic states count as ignorance and are *about* what-is rather than nothing at all.

Within twenty Stephanus pages of the three-part distinction at *Republic* 475e4–479d5, in *Republic* VI, Plato reverts to a discussion that contrasts only two epistemic conditions—*doxa* and *epistêmê*. An examination of *Republic* 509d–511d and 514a–518b will help us to see that this earlier *Republic* passage is designed chiefly to console the lovers of sights and sounds and not to lay out the metaphysical coordinates of Plato's epistemology. These passages confirm that the consolation of the lovers of sights and sounds does not contain evidence that overrides the evidence for Plato's conviction that ignorance is composed of, and overlaps with, *doxa*.

The Divided Line

The image of the divided line closes book VI of the *Republic*. Warning that much will be omitted, but agreeing to give as full an explanation as possible (509c9), Socrates distinguishes the intelligible from the visible and proceeds to give an image of these two realms as a line divided first into two unequal parts with each part again unequally divided.[2] The four

---

2. The text specifies the proportions of the division so roughly that many translators and commentators who try to draw the line draw it differently. Compare for example Hackett's original Grube translation (1974, 164) with the one revised by Reeve (1992, 183), which both differ from Smith (1996, 46). It is mathematically impossible for the two middle sections to be unequal in size, but some say it is not at all clear that this was Plato's intention (Ferrari and Griffith [2000, 219 n. 32]). That these two sections are the same size lends support to Smith's interpretation. He thinks they contain the

parts—working from the intelligible end—are labled *noêsis, dianoia, pistis,* and *eikasia.* The first two are intelligible, the second two are visible. Any effort to reconcile the divided line with the *Republic* 475e4–479d5 passage must be tempered by the fact that these are not the same terms that Plato uses there: *epistêmê, gnôsis, doxa,* and *agnôsia* do not appear in the four subsegments of the line and only *gnôsis* and *doxa* are on the line at all.

Setting aside the segment's proportions (their relative sizes represent clarity and obscurity), let's label the four sections ν, δ, π, and ε, according to their Greek names. ν is supposed to be clearer than δ and π is supposed to be clearer than ε, just as ν + δ is supposed to be clearer than π + ε. Working from least to most clear: in ε, *eikones* is cashed out as shadows (*skias*) and also reflections (*phantasmata*) in water and on reflective surfaces. These seem to be images of sensible objects. π contains the things that create those images—living creatures, plants, and artifacts—the sensible objects themselves. This is the visible realm, which has the same relationsip to the intelligible realm as π and ε have to each other. This is established when Socrates and Glaucon agree to the following summary, which now introduces the terms *doxa* and *gnôsis*. The section that contains *doxa* bears the same relationship to the section that contains *gnôsis* (the known) as that which is similar (an image) does to its model.

In talking about ν + δ and π + ε, we have returned to the terminology of the superior two cognitive states in the three-part distinction at *Republic* 475e4–479d5 as illuminated in chapter 7 (above). ν + δ are, together, *gnôsis*. π + ε are, together, *doxa*. We should expect the things in π + ε to be the things *doxa* is set upon, and indeed they are. Similarly, we should expect ν + δ to be that upon which *gnôsis* (*epistêmê*)[3] is set.

Secondary Objects versus the Primary Objects upon Which our Capacities Are Set

Distinguishing between what knowledge, belief, and ignorance are *set upon* (*epi*, this term is not used here, however) and what secondary object they

---

same things (perceptible objects). It also lends support to mine, as I think that they involve seeing or sensing the *same* things, but doing so with different agendas.

3. At *Rep.* 475e4–479d5, *epistêmê* and *gnôsis* are used interchangeably. *Gnôsis* is the opposite of the word used for "ignorance" (*agnôsia*) in that same passage. Many commentators identify *epistêmê* with ν + δ (Ferejohn, 2006b, 218).

are *about*, as we did in chapter 7, will also clarify our interpretation of the divided line. The divided line is a division of that upon which *gnôsis* and *doxa* are set—it is a division of their primary objects, for which the *epi*-locution was used in the three-part distinction. It's not a division of the secondary objects that our epistemic states are *about*. It is not illustrating what *metaphysical objects* are the truth-makers for all of these *cognitive states* (*noêsis, dianoia, pistis,* and *eikasia*)—we have already confirmed, in chapters 1–4 and 7, that these epistemic states must ultimately be about the Forms. Otherwise they will not have any degree of value with respect to one another. It is only by being, ultimately, about such truth-makers as beauty itself and equality itself that these epistemic states can, for example, have components that have truth values. $\nu + \delta$ covers those primary objects upon which the philosopher's capacity is set in order to gain knowledge. $\pi + \varepsilon$ (which is here called *doxa*) covers the primary objects upon which the lovers of sights and sounds (doxophilists) set their merely doxastic capacities in their—unsuccessful—attempts to know things. Ignorance and that to which it looks at *Republic* 477b are *not* mentioned, and have *no separately assigned place,* on the divided line.

We are back to the understanding of the bifurcated relationship between *doxa* and ignorance that we diagnosed in the *Symposium, Phaedrus,* and *Theatetus,* as elaborated in chapters 5–6. Epistemic states are dichotomous: each counts as *either* some degree of lack of knowledge (ignorance) *and* is identified with *doxa, or* it is knowledge. The use of "ignorance" at *Republic* 475e4–479d5 was specific to the consolation of the lovers of sights and sounds. The divided line represents a description of what we encounter in trying to gain epistemic access to the world we inhabit. Philosophers use "images" of Forms to explore the Forms. They stay on the $\nu + \delta$—the *gnôsis*—segment of the line. This is why they are *philosophers,* lovers of knowledge. Lovers of sights and sounds think of perceptibles as the ultimate substances, subordinate to nothing and superordinate to (and truth-makers for) anything that might naturally or intentionally resemble or represent them. Lovers of sights and sounds stay on the $\pi + \varepsilon$—the *doxastic*—part of the line. That is why they are doxophilists; lovers of opinion. Nowhere is the line devoted to ignorance; it is completely exhausted by *doxa* and *gnôsis/epistêmê.* The worst epistemic states, which would be the kinds that Plato might think should be called "ignorance" are on the $\pi + \varepsilon$ part of the line and thus overlap with *doxa.*

The Contents of *Dianoia*

These realizations, especially our understanding that the line represents what knowledge and *doxa* are *set upon,* rather than their secondary objects, can help us resolve some existing confusions about the contents of δ. It seems straightforward to agree that ν contains the Forms, π contains perceptible objects, and ε contains images of perceptibles. But there has been much debate and consternation over the contents of δ. The two supersegments of the line are supposed to be analogous and proportional to one another. Further, it is clear that the doxastic supersegment contains a subordinate subsegment that consists in the images of the contents of its superordinate subsegment. Thus, we are safest if we assume that the same relationship holds of the subordinate and superordinate subsegments of the epistemic supersegment: the contents of δ must be the analogue for images of the contents of ν. ν is the Forms, so δ is "images" of the Forms. Furthermore, in describing the *gnôsis* supersegment of the line, Socrates says that in its subordinate segment,

> the soul, using as images what before were models, is compelled to investigate from hypotheses, not toward a first principle, but toward a conclusion. In the second segment, which leads to a first principle that is not hypothetical, the soul proceeds from a hypothesis without using the images of the other [first] segment, by means of the Forms themselves and proceeding methodically through them. (510b4–9)[4]

So what is in δ? Philosophers and lovers of sights and sounds both cast their senses upon perceptibles in trying to understand their world. While lovers of sights and sounds just see them as perceptibles, philosophers understand the perceptibles (and the images that resemble them) via a self-aware reference to the Forms. Thus, in the case of *dianoia,* philosophers use perceptibles as a means for looking beyond those perceptibles at hypothesized abstract objects. In other words, philosophers use perceptible

---

4. ᾗ τὸ μὲν αὐτοῦ τοῖς τότε μιμηθεῖσιν ὡς εἰκόσιν χρωμένη ψυχὴ ζητεῖν ἀναγκάζεται ἐξ ὑποθέσεων, οὐκ ἐπ' ἀρχὴν πορευομένη ἀλλ' ἐπὶ τελευτήν, τὸ δ' αὖ ἕτερον—τὸ ἐπ' ἀρχὴν ἀνυπόθετον—ἐξ ὑποθέσεως ἰοῦσα καὶ ἄνευ τῶν περὶ ἐκεῖνο εἰκόνων, αὐτοῖς εἴδεσι δι' αὐτῶν τὴν μέθοδον ποιουμένη.

objects as a means to make hypotheses about which Forms exist. While they might not end up actually knowing those Forms, or being right about which ones exist, they do demonstrate that they understand that the point of looking at perceptibles is to look beyond them to knowable (determinate, immutable, unified) objects—to Forms.

The perceptibles are the vehicles for those with *dianoia* to look to the Forms. Lovers of sights and sounds, on the other hand, mistakenly, think the perceptibles are themselves knowable and as a result look only to the perceptibles. They do not, knowingly, refer the perceptibles to the Forms even though, as discussed in chapters 1–4, they do unwittingly rely on such things as equality itself to make their beliefs coherent enough to begin to adjudicate among them. They intentionally refer to whatever, for example, beauty *actually* is, but are clueless regarding where their reference lands.[5] So they look at the same perceptibles the philosophers do, but since they regard them as the objects of their inquiry, lovers of sights and sounds are left with mere *doxa* of the things that—unbeknownst to them—their *doxa(i)* is actually *about*: the Forms. This is why Socrates takes pains to mention that "shadows and reflections in water" are images of the figures looked to in *dianoia* (510e2–3). Thus, even the shadows and reflections in water (the primary objects on the least reliable part of the line) are images of the Forms and any veridicality or usefulness that results from (foolishly) looking to these images is due to the Forms. The lover of sights and sounds *looks to* the same perceptibles that the philosopher *looks beyond*. The philosopher might cast her eye on the perceptibles, but she is, wittingly, using them to see beyond them in an effort to set her epistemic capacities upon abstract objects.

Returning to our textual information about the epistemic supersegment of the divided line, we can make sense of the rest of it relatively straightforwardly: it says that, in dealing with δ, the soul is compelled to investigate from hypotheses and proceed to a conclusion (*teleutên*) rather than a first principle (*archên poreuomenê*, 510b4–9). When Glaucon asks for more explanation, Socrates points out that students of geometry agree upon a wide array of suppositions, which they take as given and for which they do not argue (510c2–d1). Because they all posit the same such things as the odd, the even, three kinds of angles, and many others, when they

---

5. For example, when pressed by Socrates, Plato assumes they choose between their belief that (beauty itself ≠ ugliness itself) and their belief that (beauty itself = beautiful sights and sounds), since they think they hold both and they now see that the two contradict each other. See chapter 4 (98–101), above.

investigate the same things using these hypotheses as their starting points, they reach the same conclusions. Socrates next associates the visible figures that geometers draw and use with these conclusions (511d5–7). But Socrates also makes it clear that this dianoetic process is limited: because all parties to the conversation agree on what seem to be obvious presuppositions, they end up arriving at the thing they were originally motivated to investigate. Thus, they hypothesize with regard to which abstract objects it seems reasonable to commit themselves. However, this doesn't allow them to know whether their hypotheses are correct. *Dianoia* might lead to good hypotheses about the Forms, but it can equally lead to misguided ones and does not lead to knowledge of them. It always, however, leads to hypotheses that are *wittingly about* Forms.

The Contents of *Noêsis*

Socrates continues, saying that the geometers do not talk about the visible figures themselves, but use the visible figures to talk about their models—the square itself and the diameter itself. They use what used to be models as images in order to talk about what cannot be seen "except in thought" (510e1–511a1). What Glaucon, confirmed by Socrates, goes on to express about the contents of ν further affirms my earlier theses concerning what Plato takes to be the actual objects of knowledge and their use to human beings.

> I understand . . . but not completely, for you seem to be speaking of a mighty task—that you wish to distinguish the intelligible reality contemplated by the science of dialectic as clearer than that viewed by the so-called sciences (*tôn technôn kaloumenôn*), for which their hypotheses are first principles. The students of these so-called sciences are, it is true, compelled to study them by thought and not by sense perception, yet because they do not go back to a first principle but proceed from hypotheses, you do not think that they have *nous* of their subjects, although these could be known if approached from the first principle. You seem to call the attitude of mind of geometers and such "*dianoia*" but not "*nous*," *dianoia* being midway between opinion (*doxês*) and *nous*. (511c3–d5, following Grube)[6]

---

6. μανθάνω, ἔφη, ἱκανῶς μὲν οὔ—δοκεῖς γάρ μοι συχνὸν ἔργον λέγειν—ὅτι μέντοι βούλει διορίζειν σαφέστερον εἶναι τὸ ὑπὸ τῆς τοῦ διαλέγεσθαι ἐπιστήμης τοῦ ὄντος

216 | Opining Beauty Itself

It is not clear who can practice dialectic, where one gets to engage with the Forms themselves and is not restricted to accessing them via referring perceptibles to them. In dialectic, one sees that the Forms must be there making the perceptible world the way it is. But, this is something about which this project will not speculate further as we are only talking about those epistemic states that, according to Plato, fall short of knowledge. Thus, we are more concerned with the practitioners of the so-called sciences who, while they do not have *nous* of their subjects, do not have the worst kind of *doxa* either. They are doing something right: they are intentionally studying things such as beauty itself and equality itself while admitting that they cannot approach them directly and must do so by making hypotheses about which ones exist, and then trying—somehow or other—to confirm those hypotheses. Consequently, while they don't know them, they are better off than mere lovers of sights and sounds. The practitioners of science are wittingly looking to the right kinds of things in order to try to figure out how their world works. They are far from having the least useful kind of not knowing. So the divided line confirms both that *doxa* and ignorance are not separate but are overlapping and that ordinary people—everyone from Meno's slave to Plato's readers—look to different kinds of misleading things (perceptibles and images of perceptibles) in order to acquire beliefs of various qualities that are about abstract objects or Forms.

The Cave

What is perhaps the most popular image in Plato's dialogues, the allegory of the cave, opens *Republic* VII.[7] Here, too, we will find that even the

---

τε καὶ νοητοῦ θεωρούμενον ἢ τὸ ὑπὸ τῶν τεχνῶν καλουμένων, αἷς αἱ ὑποθέσεις ἀρχαὶ καὶ διανοίᾳ μὲν ἀναγκάζονται ἀλλὰ μὴ αἰσθήσεσιν αὐτὰ θεᾶσθαι οἱ θεώμενοι, διὰ δὲ τὸ μὴ ἐπ' ἀρχὴν ἀνελθόντες σκοπεῖν ἀλλ' ἐξ ὑποθέσεων, νοῦν οὐκ ἴσχειν περὶ αὐτὰ δοκοῦσί σοι, καίτοι νοητῶν ὄντων μετὰ ἀρχῆς. διάνοιαν δὲ καλεῖν μοι δοκεῖς τὴν τῶν γεωμετρικῶν τε καὶ τὴν τῶν τοιούτων ἕξιν ἀλλ' οὐ νοῦν, ὡς μεταξύ τι δόξης τε καὶ νοῦ τὴν διάνοιαν οὖσαν.

7. There is a large body of literature that discusses the similarities and differences between elements of the line and the cave, with many arguing that they cannot be mapped directly onto one another. I do not propose to engage in this debate, as it has no relevance to my interests here; I only propose to show that both are about what the various epistemic agents *set* their capacities *over* (primary objects) rather than what the beliefs that are derived from these epistemic exercises are *about* (secondary

lowliest prisoners in the cave make unwitting reference to such things as beauty itself and equality itself and entertain beliefs that are about them.[8] The unfettering and subsequent movements of the prisoners in the cave can illustrate either the same person, or different groups of people, encountering and becoming aware of progressively different kinds of things to which to look during epistemic contemplation that is about Forms. The prisoners' appreciation of what creates these shadows and why they exist will be enhanced to the degree to which they realize that each one is understandable only in reference to that first principle that allows it to be. In the allegory of the cave, the shadows, puppets, and reflections of actual men and other things in water, all must be referred to actual men and other actual things—which are the analogues for things such as human itself (*Rep.* 514b7–515a3).[9]

At the beginning of the parable we find the prisoners in the lowest, darkest, part of the cave where they see only shadows of puppets that are moving behind them, illuminated by a fire that they cannot see. Presumably these prisoners will be in the worst epistemic condition. If anyone gets to be called "ignorant," it should be these poor deluded people. But we notice right away that they do not set their capacity upon nothing at all: they look at shadows of puppets. Further, they do not acquire nothing at all, they acquire beliefs or even systems of belief. Also, their beliefs are not about nothing; their beliefs aspire toward what-is:

> And if the men below had praise and honors from each other, and prizes for the man who saw most clearly the shadows that passed before them, and who could best remember which usually came earlier and which later, and which came together and thus could most ably prophesy the future. . . . (516c7–d2, Grube's translation)[10]

---

objects). Further, I will show that the images are exhausted by *doxa* and knowledge, there is no separate notion of ignorance in either of these images despite what seems to have been set out concerning ignorance at *Rep.* 477a9–10. How parallel they actually are has no bearing on these two claims.

8. We have already looked at this unwitting reference in chapter 4 (103–104) following Harte (2007).

9. None of the analogues from line to cave are clean, there seem to be a different number of levels in the two images (see Schindler 2012).

10. τιμαὶ δὲ καὶ ἔπαινοι εἴ τινες αὐτοῖς ἦσαν τότε παρ' ἀλλήλων καὶ γέρα τῷ ὀξύτατα καθορῶντι τὰ παριόντα, καὶ μνημονεύοντι μάλιστα ὅσα τε πρότερα αὐτῶν καὶ ὕστερα

Even those in the worst epistemic situation are trying to connect their beliefs to things that can make those beliefs true or false or better or worse, they hypothesize that there are such things even if they don't know that this is what they are doing and even if they cannot imagine what those truth-makers would have to be like. They intentionally refer to whatever these truth-makers *actually* are even if they are clueless as to where that reference lands.

Once they are unfettered, the prisoners will be able to turn their heads and will see the puppets, which were casting the shadows, and the fire that allowed them to see the shadows earlier and now allows them to see the puppets themselves. Traveling upward and emerging from the cave, the former prisoner will first see shadows and reflections "of men and other things" in water and then will see "the things themselves." The things themselves are presumably the Forms.

The prisoner entertains *doxa* from the very lowest point in the cave until long after he emerges from it and sees the living horse rather than shadows and images of it. Perhaps once he looks at the living horse (here the analogue for the horse itself), he has the opportunity to gain knowledge. Still, up until then, he casts his eyes on images and reflections but his thoughts are appropriately cast upon the things themselves (such as the living horse), which play the role of the Forms. He has an impoverished epistemic relationship to the living horse via all of its shadows and images. Nonetheless, this relationship still consists in beliefs, the truth and falsity of which is governed by the living horse (the analogue for the horse itself). Once again, ignorance is not mentioned in the parable and the worst-case scenario for an epistemic state in the cave is one that consists in *doxa*. No ignorance that is mutually exclusive with *doxa* can be found in this allegory. Furthermore, even the most feeble attempts at believing something based on the shadow of the unseen puppet of the unseen horse, where the shadow is created by the illumination by the unseen fire, are made true and false by the horse itself.

To put it another way, the prisoners in the cave continually mistake something that is other than the object they are trying to come to know for the object they are trying to come to know, just as the lovers of sights and sounds at *Republic* 475e4–476c9 mistake beautiful sights and sounds for beauty itself (they mistakenly think that this is where their intended

---

εἰώθει καὶ ἅμα πορεύεσθαι, καὶ ἐκ τούτων δὴ δυνατώτατα ἀπομαντευομένῳ τὸ μέλλον ἥξειν. . . .

reference to actual beauty lands). The slave in the *Meno* (82c4), in contrast, does *not* mistake the square in the sand for the square itself. He and the lovers of sights and sounds are the same in that they intend to investigate (and love) beauty itself and the diagonal itself whatever they are. However, the slave seems a bit more advanced in that he does not mistake the drawing in the sand for the square itself or the diagonal itself, despite the fact that he does not yet know what they are.[11] On the other hand, the lovers of sights and sounds mistake beautiful things for beauty itself.

Nevertheless, even the prisoners and the lovers of sights and sounds are more than happy to look to something else once they realize that they are gaining an inconsistent doxastic structure by mistaking the perceptibles for that which they are trying to understand. They learn that they can improve the integrity of their doxastic structure by looking beyond the perceptibles. The lovers of sights and sounds are happy to move farther along the path from E2 to E3 once they come to see that they are in E2 (see chapter 3, 71–76). The prisoner mistakes first the shadow of the puppet of a horse, then the puppet of the horse, and then the image of an actual horse in water, for the horse itself, on the way to discovering the horse itself (516a5–b2).

Resonance between the Cave and *Pheadrus* 248a1–249c4

As anticipated in chapter 6, *Phaedrus* 248a also shows that even those in the worst epistemic state—who we can assume are the utterly ignorant—have beliefs and opinions (*doxa*).

> [The soul of the god] in its circuit sees justice itself, sees self-control, sees knowledge—not that knowledge to which coming to be attaches . . . but that which is in what really is and which is really knowledge (247d6–e3). . . . [O]f the other souls, the one that follows god best and has come to resemble him most raises the head of its charioteer into the region outside

---

11. At least in answering Socrates's questions about the square being a figure like this and being able to be bigger or smaller than it is (*Men.*, 82b9–c4), the slave's epistemic capacities seem *epi* what-is, like someone who is a bit farther on the path from E2 to E3 than are the lovers of sights and sounds, who deny that "beauty is one" (see chapters 3, 71–76 and 4, 91–95).

and is carried round with the revolution, [even] while being disturbed by its horses and scarcely seeing the things that are; while another now rises, now sinks and because of the force exerted by its horses sees some things and not others. The remaining souls follow them, all straining to reach the place above but unable to do so. . . . (248a1–a7, Rowe's translation)[12]

Thus, the *Phaedrus*, the cave, the divided line, and the *Symposium*, all provide reasons for resisting an interpretation of *Republic* 477a5–b1 that takes the epistemic state labeled "ignorance" to consist in nothing at all rather than beliefs and opinions or to be about nothing at all rather than what-is.[13] That is, the claim that ignorance is set upon nothing at all should not be taken to assert that the contents of ignorant states and doxastic states are mutually exclusive. Nor should it be taken to indicate that ignorant people have no relationship to the Forms.

Also anticipated in chapter 6 was the resonance between *Phaedrus* 249b and these two images from the *Republic*:

> For the soul which has never seen the truth shall not enter this shape of ours. A human being must comprehend what is said universally, arising from many sensations and being collected together into one through reasoning: and this is recollection of those things which our soul once saw when it travelled in company with god and treated in contempt the things we now say are, and when it poked its head up into what really is. (249b6–c4, following Rowe's translation)[14]

Recall that *Phaedrus* 249b also makes it clear that the philosopher ("the one who uses the reminder of these things 'correctly,'" and "stands outside of human concerns" 249c6–d1) nevertheless uses perceptibles as a means, but does so while understanding that the point is to look beyond the perceptibles at the unities that they represent. Here, in the images of the line and cave in the *Republic*, we also see that the difference between lovers of sights and sounds and philosophers is not determined by that

---

12. See chapter 6, n. 3 for Greek and comments on Rowe's translation.

13. Hackforth readily compares this part of the *Phdr.* to the *Rep.*'s cave and the divided line (1952, 81).

14. See Greek and comments in chapter 6, 140–141, and n. 9.

upon which they cast their senses. They are different because lovers of sights and sounds take those things upon which they cast their senses to be identical with such things as beauty itself, but philosophers consciously use them as a means for improving the preestablished contact between their intelligence and beauty itself.

Conclusion

Republic 475e4–479d5 appears to represent ignorance as distinct from, and mutually exclusive with, every kind of *doxa*. In contrast, *Symposium* 201d1–212c3 begins by pretending to set a framework that separates at least some kinds of *doxa* from ignorance and rank them hierarchically only to provide numerous counterexamples to this possibility within the discussion in which the characters in that same passage engage. The *Phaedrus* and the midsection of the *Theaetetus* help to clarify how it is best to understand *doxa*'s richness and messiness in the *Symposium*. In keeping with this contrast, the *Republic*'s images of the cave (514a–518b) and the divided line (509d–511d) clearly represent even the lowest, most degraded, epistemic states—and therefore, those that are to count as ignorance—as composed of *doxa*. In our discussion of the *Symposium*, we even saw evidence to suggest that some of the *doxa* that ignorance consists in is on the higher end when it comes to quality: some of the *doxa* that ignorance consists in can be reasoned, some can be true, and some might even be true and relatively well reasoned. Passages from the *Phaedrus* confirm that Plato represents people in the worst epistemic conditions as being in those conditions *in virtue of* their *doxa* and the way it does or does not line up with what it is about—with what-is.

This supports my observation in chapters 5 and 6 that no linear ranking can be made of all human epistemic states, or even of all doxastic states, due to their inherent complexity. It further shows that this is recognized by Plato and lends support to a reading of *Symposium* 201d1–212c3 that argues that Plato is trying to rub our noses in the absurdity of conceiving of any kind of epistemic state as representable by an individual proposition that possesses any combination of truth-value and level of justification.

Furthermore, it lends support to the reading of *Republic* 475e4–479e5, described in chapter 7, above. That reading recognizes any perceived separation of what *doxa* and ignorance are "set upon" as a distinction made in order to appease the lovers of sights and sounds. Socrates is showing the lovers of sights and sounds that, while both they and others are mistaken about beauty itself, they are in a better position than those who are even more ignorant than they are. They, the lovers of sights and sounds, at least attempt to allow external criteria to organize their doxastic structures. They don't succeed because they misidentify the appropriate criteria—beauty itself and equality itself—with beautiful sights and sounds and equal sticks and stones, respectively. Thus, the lovers of sights and sounds are consoled that their beliefs (while still about—taking as their secondary objects—beauty itself and other such abstract objects) are at least "set upon" *something* (478b9), whereas the beliefs of those more ignorant (while also *about*—taking as their secondary objects—beauty itself and other such abstract objects) are "set upon"—take as their primary objects—nothing at all. This is not to say that Plato was not serious about the three-part distinction in *Republic* V. He did think that each "power" had a unique primary object and that setting this power on nothing at all destined the ignorant toward total failure, while setting it on perceptibles afforded the lovers of sights and sounds a confusion that could be improved, and setting it on what-is presented the philosophers the opportunity for knowledge. The cave and line show us that the lovers of sights and sounds' predicament is not terminal. The lovers of sights and sounds are far more remediable and far more able to become more like philosophers and have something more like knowledge (whatever that turns out to be) than those who are referred to as ignorant at *Republic* 475e4–479d5. Those who opine (and that's nearly everyone), opine beauty itself.

Conclusion

What *Doxa* Opines and What Ignorance Is

My First Major Thesis: *Doxa* Opines What-is

In this book, I have defended two major theses. The first is that Plato assumes that all cognizing that can be better or worse or true or false is ultimately about the only things that can be truth-makers, those things that *are*. These are the only objects that have determinate and immutable identities: things such as beauty itself, also known as his Forms. This is because Plato assumes that when we inquire or when we try to answer our inquiries and those posed by others, we intend to think about whatever will actually satisfy those inquiries by making our hypotheses and judgments true or false. The fact that there are things that are determinate and unchanging is what makes our judgments and hypotheses *about* what-is be more accurate or less accurate and, in turn, better or worse ways to think about the aspects of the world that we cannot control simply by choosing to think about them in a certain way.

Thus, Plato believes that everyone has a cognitive relationship with the Forms whether they realize it or not. Plato also tells us that those who do not have knowledge have *doxa*—they do not "know," they only "opine." It would be a stretch to argue that Plato ever gives us a named example of a human being with knowledge. Socrates is never represented as knowledgeable.[1] Those who have knowledge are generally referred to as "Philosophers" or "Philosopher Kings." But we are never introduced

---

1. His wisdom is limited to knowing that when it comes to anything of consequence any "wisdom" he has is useless (*Apol.* 23b). I will leave it to those who do struggle to uncover Plato's theory of knowledge to struggle with what, if any, kind of knowledge Socrates possesses.

to such an individual in the dialogues, and there is conflict over whether Plato imagined that any actual person could come to merit this title. So, Plato must think that just about everyone opines, and opines such things as beauty itself. This "everyone" includes ordinary people: lovers of sights and sounds, Meno's slave, the prisoners in the cave, and Plato's readers.

Plato gives us the resources to recognize ourselves as lovers of sights and sounds in *Republic* V and to conceive of ourselves in the image of the slave in the *Meno*. The lovers of sights and sounds cannot imagine that beauty itself is something other than the individual beautiful sights and sounds taken as a collection, yet they are sufficiently committed to the thesis that beauty itself ≠ ugliness itself that they cannot maintain all of their beliefs consistently when they reason through, and reflect upon, their *doxa*. Their inability to stick to a consistent story is due to the fact that they really do want to speak truly (even if what is true seems false to them at first blush) and to allow the reference of their use of "beauty itself" to land on whatever beauty itself actually is, even if they cannot yet imagine what it is. The Slave does not know what the diagonal is but he does not limit his reference to the square to the properties of the particular physical one that Socrates has drawn for him. His responses to Socrates do allow that his reference to a "shape like this" lands on something that he has not yet fathomed and might currently think unfathomable.

Outside of *Republic* V, the dialogues clearly point to beauty itself and those abstract objects that are akin to it—Plato's Forms—as that *about* which ordinary people, whether ignorant or experts, opine. Inquiry, *doxa*, and true and false judgments are all what they are because they are about what-is. The things that are—the Forms—are the truth-makers that are "out there" making our inquiries be answerable, our doxastic structures be decomposable into veridical propositions, and our true and false judgments, hypotheses, or conclusions be true or false.

Every dialogue that we have examined, including *Republic* V, makes it clear that human beings do not—while in human Form—set their epistemic capacities *directly* upon the Forms. Our capacities are always set upon perceptibles (when they are set upon anything).[2] Even the souls

---

2. We can "choose" to take nothing at all into consideration, although it will be hard to find a pure Protagorean who completely resists the urge to open her eyes and get at least a bit of external feedback regarding the internal model she is forming. Plato shows how readily even a diehard Protagorean will look to external expertise in his argument from the future (*Theaet.* 178c–179c), and Aristotle comments that Cratylus,

of philosopher kings use perceptibles to access the Forms once they are forced into physical bodies that can only interact with external, independent objects through perception.

In this book, I examined two kinds of passages to substantiate Plato's contention that those with *doxa* think about the Forms. First, I looked to discussions of the theory of recollection. The theory of recollection is a response to the paradox of inquiry. The paradox of inquiry can be divided into two problems: the beginning problem {B}, which deals with how we can begin an inquiry regarding something we do not know; and the ending problem {E}, which asks how we will know when we have found that about which we inquired (since we do not know what it is). I isolated the beginning problem as the one that Plato needed to solve in order to get his epistemology off the ground. Inquiry is a first step in the long journey that might lead to knowledge. Part of this journey is to recognize that we don't already know that concerning which we inquire and to rid ourselves of any misconceptions we are currently entertaining about the object of our inquiry. None of this can be done unless we assume that we are inquiring in a context that makes some answers to our inquiry better than others. That means we must be inquiring against the background assumption that there is a way that things *are* and that when we are inquiring, we are inquiring about the way things *are*. We intend to inquire about what-is and assume that there is a way that things *are*. When we ask some version of "What is x?" we want "x" to refer to whatever x actually is and thus, also to the *kind* of thing that x actually is, even if it is a kind of thing that we never imagined existed—even if it is something incorporeal.

I suggested that Plato advanced recollection because he felt that that he needed a mechanistic theory that overcame {B}. In order to overcome {B}, one first needs to overcome a paradox of reference {R}: How can I refer to something I don't know in order to "point an inquiry" at it? I analyzed recollection as Plato's attempt to resolve {R} in order to solve {B}. I did not address {E}, speculating that once Plato solved the beginning problem, he developed the rest of his epistemology throughout the rest of the dialogues in order to resolve {E}.[3]

---

in his effort to be a pure Protagorean, is reduced to eschewing language and only wiggling his finger by the end of his life (*Met.* IV. 5. 1010a).

3. I differ with many scholars who take Plato to solve both problems at the same time via recollection (see ch. 1 n. 25). Nothing regarding the ending problem is relevant to the aims of this book.

Plato resolves the paradox of reference by assuming that we are born with an unwitting connection to the Forms that we rely upon when we pose inquiries and make hypotheses that we intend to be about whatever will actually be their most appropriate targets whether or not the true natures of those targets comport with the beliefs we already have about them. The prenatal elements of the theory of recollection would make it the case that everyone is born with the fortunate pre-epistemic endowment that I labeled E2 in chapter 3. Being in E2, having this pre-epistemic, "pre-" or "non-" doxastic relationship with the Forms, affords all humans at least the opportunity to come to know what-is and move toward what I labeled E3, although not all lovers of sights and sounds take advantage of this opportunity. I hypothesized that rather than celebrating this aspect of recollection as the solution to his efforts to get epistemology off the ground, Plato became a bit more interested in it for its suggestion that the soul is immortal. As a result, his full-blown theory of recollection overreaches the goal of solving the paradox of reference in favor of developing sophisticated arguments for the immortality of the soul.

Either Plato felt he could not give a sufficient explanation for why we are born in E2, or he came to think it was unnecessary to account for it. In any case, when Plato returns to discuss inquiry and epistemology in dialogues such as the *Republic*, *Theaetetus*, and *Cratylus*, he does so in the absence of any overt reliance on recollection. I claim that the remainder of Plato's epistemology overtly assumes that we can refer to what-is in our inquiries and that we (nonphilosophers) rely upon this successful reference in our efforts to understand the perceptible world even though we rarely recognize that we are relying upon a reference to abstract objects (and even though we might claim—as the lovers of sights and sounds do—that there are no such things as abstract objects). Plato demonstrates that our confusion regarding our reference to whatever beauty itself actually is can be exploited in a positive manner. It plays a key role in the ability of nonphilosophers to advance toward the point where they can accept the existence of the Forms. Plato is attempting to perform this conversion for his reader in Socrates's demonstration with the slave at *Meno* 82b–85e and in Socrates's conversation with Glaucon regarding the lovers of sights and sounds at *Republic* 475e4–479d5.

My Second Major Thesis: Ignorance is *Doxa*

My second major thesis is that Plato holds that anything that falls short of knowledge is a kind of *doxa*. There is no epistemic condition that can be called "ignorance" that is not also *doxa*.[4] In chapter 5, I reviewed some assumptions that need to underlie Diotima's comments on love at 201d1–212c3 of the *Symposium*. Plato treats *doxa* as a complex structure of interwoven and interdependent (and often inconsistent) thoughts about what-is that might be best represented as a mass or "cloud" of thinking. He does not treat it as individual propositional beliefs. The illusion that there are individual propositional beliefs results from a subject's deliberations regarding her own beliefs. Once she has engaged in deliberation that allows her to artificially individuate a "judgment," a thinker can attempt to justify that judgment and deem it true or false. Plato illustrates this process when he distinguishes something like generic thinking from individual judgment making at *Theaetetus* 189e7–190a4. Whatever knowledge might turn out to be, it is hard to put together a model upon which Plato would claim that there can be knowledge of an *individual* judgment or proposition. The overall integrity of a person's doxastic structure must be considered when evaluating the quality of their *doxa*. This suggests that, whatever knowledge is, there cannot be an individual "piece" of knowledge in a sea of, for example, false or unjustified beliefs. We saw that this is also suggested at *Symposium* 207e1–208a5, when Diotima says that both we and every piece of our epistemic state are constantly changing.

The recollection passages in the *Phaedrus* and the discussion of false judgment at *Theaetetus* 187c7–200a10 bolster both of my major theses. The discussion of recollection in the *Phaedrus* makes it clear that Plato took people's *doxai* to vary in quality due to the degree to which their soul was able to see and appreciate "what-is" before it was born into its present body. Anyone able to be born into a human body must have had some contact with what-is. This is true even of those who are most "crippled," which presumably corresponds to being most ignorant (248a1–249c4). With regard to the puzzle over false judgment in the *Theaetetus*, I argued that it makes most sense to interpret Plato's dichotomy between knowing and not-knowing as a clean (law of excluded middle type) distinction between everything that counts as *doxa* (and thus falls short of knowledge) and everything that counts as knowledge. Thus, anything that counts as false judgment is on the *not knowing* (the *doxa* side) of the knowledge versus

---

4. Unless it is possible to be a cognitive blank, but even if it is possible to be a cognitive blank at other times, when one is inquiring, one at least intends one's inquiry to be about whatever will actually answer it. This involves some cognition, namely, intending (whether wittingly or unwittingly) for one's reference to land on that into which one actually wants to inquire.

not-knowledge dichotomy. Further, the *doxa* side can range (nonlinearly) from structures that represent the absolute worst kinds of ignorance to ones that are almost as useful as knowledge when applied in appropriate circumstances. The things on the *doxa* side vary in integrity due to the degree to which they capture what-is and are justified. So their epistemic evaluation can only result from the fact that they are about, and are trying to capture, what-is.

Focusing on my second thesis alone, these same passages in the *Phaedrus* and *Theaetetus* attest to the notion that people in the worst epistemic states—those that most deserve to be labeled ignorant—possess *doxa*. In fact, it would be hard to make sense of the epistemological discussions in the *Apology*, *Symposium*, *Phaedrus*, *Theaetetus*, and *Republic* VI and VII without assuming that ignorance is a kind of low-quality *doxa*. Ignorance, in all of these dialogues appears to be a doxastic structure whose contents suffer from inconsistency and lack of deliberative evaluation. But even once some deliberation has been done, one can remain ignorant. One can, for example, have the kind of ignorance that Socrates has, as opposed to the kind that he attributes to his interlocutors at *Apology* 21b–22e (see chapter 5, 117–118, above).

This leaves *Republic* 475e4–479d5 as the sole evidence to which anyone might point in order to disagree with these two theses. Here, Plato appears to make ignorance and *doxa* mutually exclusive. This is also the only place in the dialogues where Plato says anything to suggest a lack of relationship between *doxa* and what-is, or ignorance and what-is. I argued in chapter 7 that this is an artifact of Socrates's consolation of the lovers of sights and sounds: he is contrasting their situation with that of philosophers, to encourage them to aim to improve their understanding of perceptibles, but he also wants to console them by reassuring them that they are better off than they might be. As I argue in that chapter, neither Socrates's evaluation nor his consolation of the lovers of sights and sounds would even make sense if he did not assume that those with knowledge, *doxa*, and ignorance were trying to capture what-is and were better and worse than one another at capturing the *same* thing.

To reiterate what I've already said in chapters 7 and 8, I am not asserting that Plato was not serious about the three-part distinction. He intends it in the straightforward way that I have described it in chapter 7 (180). He did think that each "power" had a unique primary object and that this is what led the ignorant to total failure, the lovers of sights and sounds to a confusion that could be improved upon, and gave philosophers the opportunity for knowledge. Far from thinking that the primary objects were the "norms" by which these powers operated but that they *could* "overlap" with other powers to access something other than their own unique objects,[5] Plato has all people trying to reach for the same secondary object (whatever is actually the case: what-is). Unfortunately, both ignorance and *doxa* have fatal flaws that restrict the person practicing them from accessing what-is, unless that person arrives at a game-changing realization that alters their epistemological strategy changing the actual power that they deploy. In contrasting the lover of sights and sounds with the ignorant person, Plato suggests that only those entertaining *doxa* can be brought to alter their epistemological strategy.

The Three-part Distinction in *Republic* V and Plato Scholarship

When we look at matters this way, the profound focus that centuries of scholars have had on the three-part distinction as the centerpiece of, and litmus test for, the remainder of Plato's epistemology can strike one as myopic. There does not seem to be any Platonic, philosophical, or commonsense reason to resist my two theses. My view is classically Platonic in that it makes the possibility of knowledge revolve around the object that one is trying to come to know. Even though I have not discussed knowledge directly, my claims that every epistemological condition is ultimately *about* abstract objects and that knowledge (or even good *doxa*) is only possible because there are such objects as the Forms, attributes an object centered epistemology to Plato.[6] Plato thought our ability to know hinged on our engagement in an epistemological project with a know*able* object. Forms are the only knowable objects because they alone are determinate and unchanging. If the world did not have these kinds of objects, no person could have knowledge, no matter how much they attempted to curate and justify their beliefs.

While I have alluded to my suspicion that Plato thinks that those who know the Forms will also know the perceptibles, this is not because I think Plato thought perceptibles were also knowable objects. As I said

---

5. See Moss's (2021, 18–26) use of these terms to describe the views of Smith (2000, 2009), Kamtekar (2009), Szaif (2009), Vogt (2012), and Harte (2017).
6. I agree with Gerson (2009, 7) and Moss (2021, 65) that this is the mark of Platonist epistemology.

in chapter 8 (196–200), for Plato, perceptibles are not objects and are, therefore, not knowable. But, I don't see how we could be infallible about a Form without also knowing where it is partaken in. For someone who knows all of the Forms this will be tantamount to knowing what we think of as perceptible objects. This is an additional reason for why I think of my view as Platonic and object-centered, but as inconsistent with a two-world theory.

Regarding my first thesis, while it might sound jarring placed in this Platonic context, the notion that we have some way to refer to aspects of the external world that are independent of the way we conceive of and speak about them is the attitude that has come to counter many of twentieth-century analytic philosophy's more linguistically dependent theories of reference. These more linguistic theories of reference appear to be the ones embraced by those who attribute to Plato the notion that recollection solves the beginning problem by endowing us with true belief (see chapter 1, 34–35).

In my introduction to this book, I aligned Plato's goals as described in my first thesis with Kripke's goals as he attempts to find a way to describe a notion of what some call "direct reference" that is produced by a subject's intentions to get at what-is by somehow willing their reference to navigate around whatever the content of their thoughts might have gotten wrong.[7] Plato shows us that this is a necessary and commonsense assumption that must underwrite any notion of inquiry: things are what they are independent of some way that human beings have conceived of or constructed them and our inquiries and hypotheses must be about them as they actually are.[8] This is a presupposition of the assumption that we can entertain individual propositional judgments that are true or false, or where at least some of those judgments are better at capturing the way things are than others. That is, we must assume that the qualities that make these judgments better and worse are independent of our own assessments of the truth of those judgments. Otherwise, we couldn't be

---

7. I also pointed out (Introduction, n. 12) that this type of reference to an *actual* good is already commonplace among at least one group of Plato scholars when they discuss reference to the good in both the Socratic dialogues and at *Rep.* 505a–506b.

8. As I also noted in the introduction (n. 8 and 10), this ultimately departs from what Strevens (2019) is after. He is trying to make it possible for us to refer to a concept, but not the one we happen to have. He wants us to refer to the concept that will endure, which is easily not the one that any given person, or group of persons, has at a given time. But it is still a *concept* and not a human-independent abstract object.

wrong about them (as a result, we would be like the "ignorant" people that Socrates is warning the lovers of sights and sounds not to imitate). In short, it is not surprising to have Plato tell us that our inquiries and our *doxa* get to be about what-is even when our doxastic structure is of low integrity and quality and even when it completely mischaracterizes what-is, or even when we don't know the nature of what-is.

There is nothing earth-shattering about my second thesis. What counts as ignorance is almost always analyzed with respect to the beliefs—the *doxa(i)*—of the ignorant person in question. Further, it makes sense to think that the difference between being ignorant and possessing valuable, useful, and effective doxastic structures is a matter of degree and one that is impossible to sort out along a linear spectrum. Virologists might be good at figuring out how to identify a virus, but experts on fluid dynamics might be better at figuring out how it is spread, and neither will be the best at figuring out how to get a vaccine to the most vulnerable parts of the population. No one is infallible at any of these things (as we've noted, infallibility appears to be a requirement for knowledge, according to Plato).[9]

So why the preoccupation with the three-part distinction in *Republic* V? Scholars of Plato have a tendency to treat the *Republic* as the centerpiece of Plato's philosophy. As a result, many of the philosophical views in the *Republic* are treated as the standard against which one should measure one's interpretation of views regarding similar issues in other works. When it comes to political philosophy, or the psychology of the soul, this tendency is understandable (even if not obviously correct). But scholars have this same tendency with respect to Plato's epistemology. The three-part distinction between the capacities of knowledge, belief, and ignorance and their respective, apparently distinct, targets together with the striking images of the cave, the sun, and the divided line are treated by many as paradigms. The strategy toward which one is tempted is to interpret these passages first, and in the order in which they appear, and only then to judge one's understanding of other passages that deal with epistemological capacities and their objects in other dialogues by attempting to map them back onto the three-part distinction, and the images of the cave, the sun, and the divided line.

As I've already noted, the claims made at *Republic* 475e4–479d5 are often anomalous when taken in the context of the rest of the dialogues. This includes several singular claims and uses of terminology that contradict

---

9. *Euthd.* 280a6–8; *Rep.* 477e6–7; *Theaet.*152c5–6.

other claims and uses that are found in multiple places in other dialogues. There are many examples. The positive and optimistic characterization of human knowledge in the *Republic* is at odds with the celebration of human ignorance contained in the so-called Socratic dialogues (particularly, *Apol.*, *Euthd.*, *Charm.*, *Prot.*) and also the more pessimistic and aporetic conclusions reached in the *Cratylus*, *Theaetetus*, and *Sophist*. Further, the *Republic* professes this optimism without making any obvious use of recollection, which is the major mechanism furnished to provide the capacity for human knowledge in the *Meno*, *Phaedo*, and *Phaedrus*.

On a smaller scale, as we have rehearsed, at *Republic* 476e4–479d5, Socrates appears to separate the object of knowledge from the object of belief, saying that they are not identical and that, whereas the object of knowledge is *what is,* the object of belief is what *both is and is not*. However, in the *Meno* (97a6–98a8) and the *Theaetetus* (187b4–c5, 202b8–210b2), Socrates asserts (or examines the hypothesis) that knowledge is some sort of enhanced true belief, thereby implying that knowledge and belief *can* be about the same thing. To put the same point slightly differently, in the *Sophist* and *Timaeus*, Plato reduces perceptible objects to conglomerations of Forms, which, if they are to be the objects of belief as he implies, would show belief to have the same object as knowledge—the Forms—rather than a different one.

In this same *Republic* passage, all beliefs are equally oriented toward objects with the same degree of veridicality, with no apparent distinction in value between true beliefs and false beliefs. In contrast, the *Meno* celebrates true belief as better than false belief and the *Theaetetus* and *Sophist*, while treating true belief as straightforward, dedicate long passages to the struggle to find a coherent account of false belief and false statement (*Theat.* 187d–201a; *Soph.* 259d–261e).

Also, while *Republic* 477a appears to claim that the object of ignorance is *nothing at all,* the *Meno* and *Phaedo* develop a theory of recollection that allows people who are ignorant to inquire, hypothesize, and entertain false beliefs about the existent things concerning which they are ignorant.[10] In addition, in the *Sophist* (259d–261e), Plato finally shows the object of false speech and, by assimilation,[11] false belief to be about the same existent Forms that are the objects of knowledge. Even within the middle books of the *Republic*, the three-part distinction among epistemological

---

10. See Nehamas (1999, 5–10) and White (1976, 17) for arguments to this effect.
11. Berman (1996, 24–26).

capacities is at odds with the images of the cave and line as it treats what *doxa* and ignorance are *epi* as mutually exclusive, while neither the cave nor the line mention ignorance and both appear to regard ignorance as a kind of *doxa*, and the cave portrays ignorant prisoners as possessing *doxa*.

In chapter 7, I examined the three-part distinction among the epistemological capacities found at *Republic* 476e4–479d5 and their so-called objects. In order to do so, I brought forward some notable elements of the passage that are important to interpreting the passage in the context of Plato's metaphysics, including the *epi*-locution and the fact that the distinction is presented in the context of the consolation of the lovers of sights and sounds. As a result, I interpreted this passage in light of the notions of knowledge, *doxa*, and ignorance found in the rest of the dialogues, rather than the other way around.

The Two-World Theory and Its Opponents

My thesis in this book has been orthogonal to the projects of either those vindicating the two-world theory or those many contemporary authors who have sought to debunk it in recent times. I am discussing only epistemological states that fall short of knowledge, which I have contended all consist in *doxa*. Those other views are polarized over the object of knowledge versus the object of *doxa*. The two major points I am making depart from both poles of these interpretations. I am claiming that *doxa* is connected to what-is and that this connection is intentional and therefore cognitive, but *doxa* can be, at the same time, clueless regarding the object that it actually intends to be about and to which it is actually connected, and thus, this aboutness can be unwitting. The two-world theory and its opponents only discuss what each power is *epi* (what I call the first degree object of each power)[12] and that answers a different question than the one that I am asking and answering.[13]

---

12. See chapter 7, 176–181.

13. I am tempted to diagnose these two kinds of *Rep.* V centering views of Plato's epistemology as follows: each carries with it an agenda from its own time period that is foreign to Plato. Those who argue against the two-world view are enamored of many elements of contemporary analytic epistemology and see themselves as helping to recover a Platonic view that coheres with them and as such carries at least some of the validity that they associate with those contemporary theories. On the other hand, the two-world theory that these commentators argue against originated in Aristotle's

My efforts to revisit the three-part distinction, refocus Plato's theory of *doxa*, and to argue that Plato thinks we opine beauty itself contrasts with these two common trends in Plato scholarship regarding this passage. I claim that the three-part distinction was never intended to be a paradigm that eternally separated *doxa* from ignorance or kept *doxa* and ignorance from trying to be about what-is. It is intended by Plato as part of an analysis concerning what is wrong with the professed ontology of the lover of sights and sounds, to whom this speech is directed in absentia.

In my view, both the "two worlds" camp and those who depart from it have overemphasized the three-part distinction, treating *Republic* V as the centerpiece of Plato's philosophy and *Republic* VI–VII as the *origins* of Plato's epistemology rather than some iconic and summarizing images of what he has presented elsewhere in the dialogues.[14] I contend that the point of the three-part distinction is to show that being a lover of sights and sounds is worse than being a philosopher but better than being ignorant. Plato is encouraging and inspiring his readers (who he assumes are—at least mostly—nonphilosophers) that there is something to be gained from seeing themselves in the lovers of sights and sounds and attempting to go through the transition enabled by the concurrent argument I discuss in chapter 4. I suggest that Plato is cautioning the lovers of sights and sounds not to fall into ignorance, a position even worse than that of the lovers of sights and sounds (and which I suggest

---

condemnation of Plato's metaphysics. Aristotle says that Plato's view cannot be right because he "separates" the Forms from the particulars and turns them into independent ontological entities that can only be known as things in themselves. Aristotle argues that "universals" can only be comprehended as predicates of "primary substances" (*Met.* III. 6.1003a5–17). While Aristotle made the view look very unattractive to those who followed his more anthropocentric approach to metaphysics, once Aristotle characterized Plato's metaphysics this way, the two-world theory became very attractive to the monotheist Neo-Platonists who went on to influence Plato scholarship for generations to come.

14. Moss (2021, 17) calls her project an "experiment" in which she centers Plato's epistemology around the three-part distinction between knowledge, *doxa*, and ignorance at *Rep.* 475e4–479d5 and then interprets the rest of the dialogues that mention these terms in light of the "very clear and explicit instructions about how to define and understand cognitive kinds" that she takes him to give there, while granting that these take place "alongside of" Plato's "various claims and characterizations." But, these instructions, I would caution, are only explicit if we take them with a "read these first" implicitly attached to them. I sympathize with some of what she says about Plato and knowledge, but depart from her view of *doxa*.

Plato thinks is occupied by followers of Protagoras). The lovers of sights and sounds are at risk of becoming Protagoreans, but, given the proper attention and celebrated for what they already do, they can be redeemed. Plato wants his readers to heed this advice.

My thesis in chapter 7 is that Plato holds that what-is (i.e., the Forms) are the secondary objects of all three epistemological capacities and that this is evidenced by, and is consistent with, this *Republic* passage. Taken in the context of Plato's metaphysics, *Republic* 476e4–479d5 supports Plato's conviction that knowledge, belief, and ignorance are all *of* Forms. He did not see this passage as creating any sort of puzzle for that view, and certainly did not use it to propose that there was a second world other than—and distinct from—the Forms. We should assume that this secondary object—the Form—is what allows inquiry to succeed because each inquiry is already oriented toward what will answer it. I argued that this connection is pre-doxastic and unwittingly determines the intended reference of the inquiry. This is important because it allows the work done by this mode of reference to be ubiquitous and to stay in the background. It is important that it contribute nothing to the content of *doxa* other than allowing its cognizer to intend it to be about what-is. It is possible that Plato came to regard this referential connection as trivial and that is why he left it tacit and in the background both during his discussions of recollection and once he moved away from advancing the theory of recollection. Perhaps that is why he thought that simply showing that the slave can learn is enough to answer the beginning problem {B}.

My concern is that interpreters of Plato have overlooked this important—even if ubiquitous to the point of being trivial—connection. In so doing they have attempted to use doxastic states themselves (such as true belief) to fulfill this pre-doxastic requirement and solve {B}. This affects our interpretation of Plato's epistemology negatively in two ways. First, using *doxa* to resolve {B} does not work; *doxa* cannot be true or false unless its cognizer already holds this connection to its truth-maker. Second, once one has employed some notion of *doxa* in this way, one has already gotten off on the wrong foot. By misusing *doxa* in this way, we bias any subsequent theory of *doxa*. As a result, we make it harder to distinguish *doxa* from knowledge because knowledge also requires this same "non-" or "pre-" doxastic connection. For those who are in a debate over whether Plato thought that knowledge and *doxa* were distinct or might overlap—this stacks the deck in favor of the overlap view in a way that makes the arguments that are made in favor of either view irrelevant.

If we think that {R} is solved by true belief and that solving {R} is also necessary before knowledge is possible, then, if we use true belief to solve {R}, knowledge will inevitably ride piggyback on true *doxa*. As a result, knowledge and true belief will have to overlap.

Once we recognize this unwitting but cognitive connection between inquirers and *x* itself, we might indeed come to see it as trivial and condone its ubiquitous assumption. However, once we recognize it as the solution to {B}, we will also realize that it does very important work. It allows for cogent Platonic theories of *doxa* and, hopefully, knowledge to flourish. Only once we have connected *doxa* to what-is with something that is non-doxastic, do we give *doxa* a fighting chance at fulfilling an inquiry's mission. This is because *doxa* has to be about beauty itself before it can be more true, more reasoned, or better at capturing what-is than it would be otherwise. The point of inquiry and *doxa* is to allow us to be in the best epistemic situation that we can with respect to what-is, even if that situation falls short of affording us knowledge. Plato's epistemological theories allow for ordinary people to investigate what actually *is* and to make useful progress in their appreciation of it.

Bibliography

Ackrill, J. 1955. "ΣΥΜΠΛΟΚΗ ΕΙΔΩΝ." *Bulletin of the Institute of Classical Studies* 2: 31–35.
Ackrill, J. 1973. "*Anamnesis* in the *Phaedo*: Remarks on 73c–75c." In *Exegesis and Argument, Phronesis Supple. I*, edited by E. Lee, A. Mourelatos, and R. Rorty, 177–95. Assen: Van Gorcum.
Anagnostopoulos, M. 2003. "Desire for the Good in the *Meno*." In *Desire, Identity, and Existence*, edited by N. Reshotko, 171–91. Edmonton: Academic Printing and Publishing.
Annas, J. 1981. *An Introduction to Plato's* Republic. Oxford: Oxford University Press.
Baima, N. and Paytas, T. 2021. *Plato's Pragmatism: Rethinking the Relationship between Ethics and Epistemology*. New York: Routledge.
Benson, H. 1990. "Misunderstanding the 'What-is-Fness?' Question." *Archiv für Geschichte der Philosophie* 72: 125–42; reprinted in Benson, H., ed., *Essays on the Philosophy of Socrates*. New York: Oxford University Press.
———. 2000. *Socratic Wisdom*. New York: Oxford University Press.
———. 2015. *Clitophon's Challenge: Dialectic in Plato's* Meno, Phaedo, *and* Republic. New York: Oxford University Press.
Berman, S. 1996. "Plato's Explanation of False Belief in the *Sophist*." *Apeiron* 29, no. 1: 19–46.
———. 2003. "A Defense of Psychological Egoism." In *Desire, Identity, and Existence*, edited by M. Reshotko, 143–57. Edmonton: Academic Printing and Publishing.
———. 2020. *Platonism and the Objects of Science*. London: Bloomsbury Academic.
Bett, R. 2011. "Socratic Ignorance." In *The Cambridge Companion to Socrates*, edited by D. Morrison, 215–36. Cambridge: Cambridge University Press.
Bluck, R. 1955. *Plato's* Phaedo. London: Routledge and Kegan Paul.
———. 1962. *Plato's* Meno. Cambridge: Cambridge University Press.
Bobonich, C. 2002. *Plato's Utopia Recast*. Oxford: Oxford University Press.
Bostock, D. 1986. *Plato's* Phaedo. Oxford: Clarendon Press.
Brickhouse, T., and N. Smith. 2010. *Plato's Moral Psychology*. Cambridge: Cambridge University Press.

Brown, L. 1986. "Being in the *Sophist*: A Syntactical Enquiry." In *Plato I*, edited by G. Fine, 455–78. Oxford: Oxford University Press, 1999.
———. 2008a. "Review of Scott: *Plato's* Meno." *Philosophical Review* 117: 468–71.
———. 2008b. "The *Sophist* on Statements, Predication, and Falsehood." In *The Oxford Handbook of Plato*, edited by G. Fine, 437–62. Oxford: Oxford University Press.
Burnyeat, M. 1990. *The Theaetetus of Plato*. Translated by M. J. Levett. Indianapolis: Hackett.
Campbell, L. 1883. *The Theaetetus of Plato*. Oxford: Clarendon Press.
Caplan, B. 2006. "On Sense and Direct Reference." In *On Sense and Direct Reference: Readings in the Philosophy of Language*, edited by M. Davidson, 2–16. Boston: McGraw-Hill.
Chadwick, H., trans. 1991 Augustine, *Confessions*. Oxford: Oxford University Press.
Cherniss, H. 1957. "The Relation of the *Timaeus* to Plato's Later Dialogues." *American Journal of Philosophy* 78, no. 3: 225–66.
Cooper, J., ed. 1997. *The Complete Works of Plato*. Indianapolis: Hackett.
Cornford, F. 1935. *Plato's Theory of Knowledge*. London: K. Paul.
Dancy, R. M. 2004. *Plato's Introduction of the Forms*. Cambridge: Cambridge University Press.
Descartes, R., 1960. *Meditations*. Translated by L. Lafleur. Indianapolis: Bobbs-Merrill.
Devereux, D. 1995. "Socrates' Kantian Conception of Virtue." *Journal of the History of Philosophy* 33: 381–408.
Devitt, M. 1981. *Designation*. New York: Columbia University Press.
Dimas, P. 2003. "Recollecting and Forms in the *Phaedo*." *Phronesis* 48, no. 3: 174–214.
Donnellan, K. 1966. "Reference and Definite Descriptions." *Philosophical Review* 75, no. 3: 281–304.
Ferejohn, M. 2006a. "Knowledge and the Forms in Plato." In *A Companion to Plato*, edited by H. Benson, 146–63. Malden, MA: Blackwell.
———. 2006b. "Knowledge, Recollection, and the Forms in *Republic* VII." In *The Blackwell Guide to Plato's* Republic, edited by G. Santas, 214–23. Malden, MA: Blackwell.
———. 2013. *Formal Causes: Definition, Explanation, and Primacy in Socratic and Aristotelian Thought*. New York: Oxford University Press.
Ferrari, G., ed., and T. Griffith, trans. 2000. *Plato's Republic*. Cambridge: Cambridge University Press.
Fine, G. 1992. "Inquiry in the Meno." In *The Cambridge Companion to Plato*, edited by R. Kraut, 200–26. Cambridge: Cambridge University Press.
———, ed. 1999. *Plato 1: Metaphysics and Epistemology*. Oxford: Oxford University Press.
———. 2003. *Plato on Knowledge and Forms*. Oxford: Oxford University Press.

———, ed. 2008. *The Oxford Handbook of Plato*. Oxford: Oxford University Press.
———. 2014. *The Possibility of Inquiry: Meno's Paradox from Socrates to Sextus*. Oxford: Oxford University Press.
Franklin, L. 2005. "Recollection and Philosophical Reflection in Plato's *Phd.*" *Phronesis* 50, no. 4: 289–314.
———. 2009. "Meno's Paradox, the Slave-Boy Interrogation, and the Unity of Platonic Recollection." *Southern Journal of Philosophy* 47, no. 4: 349–77.
Furth, M. 1968. "Elements of Eleatic Ontology." *Journal of the History of Philosophy* 6, no. 2: 111–32.
Geddes, W. 1885. *The Phaedo of Plato*. London: MacMillan.
Gerson, L. 2009. *Ancient Epistemology*. Cambridge: Cambridge University Press.
Gettier, E. 1963. "Is Justified True Belief Knowledge?" *Analysis* 23, no. 6: 121–23.
Gonzalez, F. 1996. "Propositions of Objects? A Critique of Gail Fine on Knowledge and Belief in *Republic* V." *Phronesis* 41, no. 3: 245–75.
———. 1998. "Nonpropositional Knowledge in Plato." *Apeiron* 31, no. 3: 235–84.
———. 2007. "How Is the Truth of Beings in the Soul? Interpreting *Anamnesis* in Plato." *Elenchos* 28, no. 2: 275–301.
Gosling, J. 1965. "Similarity in the *Phaedo* 73b seq." *Phronesis* 10: 151–61.
Grgic, F. 1999. "Plato's *Meno* and the Possibility of Inquiry in the Absence of Knowledge." *Bochumer Philosophisches Jahrbuch für Antike und Mittelalter* 4: 19–40.
Grube, D., trans. 1974. *Plato's Republic*. Indianapolis: Hackett.
———, trans. 1992. *Plato's Republic*, with revisions by C. D. C. Reeve. Indianapolis: Hackett.
Gulley, N. 1954. "Plato's Theory of Recollection." *Classical Quarterly* N.S. 4: 194–213.
———. 1962. *Plato's Theory of Knowledge*. London: Methuen.
Hackforth, R. 1952. *Plato's Phaedo*. Cambridge: Cambridge University Press.
Hamilton, E., and H. Cairns, eds. 1961. *Plato: the Collected Dialogues*. Princeton: Princeton University Press.
Harte, V. 2006. "Beware of Imitations: Image Recognition in the *Phaedo*." In *New Essays in Plato: Language and Thought in Fourth Century Greek Philosophy*, edited by F. Herrman, 21–42. Swansea: Classical Press of Wales.
———. 2007. "Language in the Cave." In *Maieusis: Essays in Ancient Philosophy in Honour of Myles Burnyeat*, edited by D., Scott, 195–214. Oxford: Oxford University Press.
———. 2017. "Knowing and Believing in *Republic* V." In *Rereading Ancient Philosophy: Old Chestnuts and Sacred Cows*, edited by V. Harte and R. Woolf, 141–62. Cambridge University Press.
Irwin, T. 1977. *Plato's Moral Theory*. Oxford: Clarendon Press.
Jones, R. 2013. "Felix Socrates?" *Philosophia* 43: 77–98.
———. 2016. "Socrates' Bleak View of the Human Condition." *Ancient Philosophy* 36: 97–105.

Kamtekar, R. 2009. "The Powers of Plato's Tripartite Psychology." *Proceedings of the Boston Area Colloquium in Ancient Philosophy* 24: 127–50.
Kelsey, S. 2001. "Recollection in the *Phaedo*." In *Proceedings in the Boston Area Colloquium in Ancient Philosophy*, edited by J. Cleary and G. Gurtler, 91–121. Leiden: Brill.
Kirk, G., and J. Raven. 1957. *The Presocratic Philosophers*. Cambridge: Cambridge University Press.
Kripke, S. 1980. *Naming and Necessity*. Cambridge: Harvard University Press.
MacDonald, S. 2008. "The Paradox of Inquiry in Augustine's *Confessions*." *Metaphilosophy* 39, no. 1: 20–38.
Matthews, G. 1999. *Socratic Perplexity and the Nature of Philosophy*. New York: Oxford University Press.
McCabe, M. M. 1994. *Plato's Individuals*. Princeton: Princeton University Press.
McDowell, J. 1973. *Theaetetus*. Oxford: Clarendon Press.
Moravcsik, J. 1971. "Learning as Recollection." In *Plato I*, edited by G. Vlastos, 53–69. South Bend: University of Notre Dame Press.
Moss, J. 2014. "Plato's Appearance-Assent Account of Belief." *Proceedings of the Aristotelian Society* 114: 213–38.
———. 2021. *Plato's Epistemology: Being and Seeming*. Oxford University Press.
———, and W. Schwab. 2019. "The Birth of Belief." *Journal of the History of Philosophy* 57, no. 1: 1–32.
Nails, D. 2012. "Compositional Chronology." In *Continuum Companion to Plato*, edited by J. Press, 289–92. London: Continuum.
Nathan, M. 2021. *Black Boxes: How Science Turns Ignorance into Knowledge*. Oxford: Oxford University Press.
Nehamas, A. 1985. "Meno's Paradox and Socrates as a Teacher." *Oxford Studies in Ancient Philosophy* 3: 1–30.
———. 1999. *Authenticity of Virtue*. Princeton: Princeton University Press.
Owen, G. 1957. "A Proof in the *Peri Ideon*." *Journal of Hellenic Studies* 57: 103–11.
———. 1971. "Plato on Not-Being." In *Plato I: Metaphysics and Epistemology*, edited by G. Vlastos, 223–67. South Bend: University of Notre Dame Press.
Penner, T. 1987. *Ascent from Nominalism*. Dordecht: Kluwer.
———. 1991. "Power and Desire in Socrates: The Argument of *Gorgias* 466466e that Orators and Tyrants Have no Power in the City." *Apeiron* 24: 147–202.
———. 2003. "The Forms, the Form of the Good, and the Desire for the Good in Plato's *Republic*." *Modern Schoolman* 80, no. 3: 191–233.
———. 2006. "The Forms in the *Republic*." In *The Blackwell Guide to Plato's Republic*, edited by G. Santas, 234–62. Oxford: Blackwell.
———. 2007. "The Good, Advantage, Happiness and the Form of the Good: How Continuous with Socratic Ethics is Platonic Ethics?" In *Pursuing the Good*, edited by D. Cairns, F. Herrman, and T. Penner, 93–153. Edinburgh: Edinburgh University Press.

———, and C. J. Rowe. 1994. "The Desire for the Good: Is the *Meno* Inconsistent with the *Gorgias*?" *Phronesis* 39, no. 1: 1–25.
Prior, W. 2012. "Developmentalism." In *Continuum Companion to Plato*, edited by J. Press, 288–89. London: Continuum.
Pugh, A. 1976. *An Introduction to Tensegrity*. Berkeley: University of California Press.
Quine, W. V., and J. S. Ullian. 1970. *The Web of Belief*. New York: Random House.
Reshotko, N. 1994. "Heracleitean Flux in Plato's *Theaetetus*." *History of Philosophy Quarterly* 11, no. 2: 139–61.
———, ed. 2003. *Desire, Identity, and Existence*. Edmonton: Academic Printing and Publishing.
———. 2006. *Socratic Virtue: Making the Best of the Neither-Good-nor-Bad*. Cambridge: Cambridge University Press.
———. 2011. "Beyond *De Re*: Toward A Dominance Theory of Desire Attribution." In *Socratic, Platonic and Aristotelian Studies: Essays in Honor of Gerasimos Santas*, edited by G. Anagnostopoulis, 125–43. Dordecht: Springer.
———. 2013. "Socratic Eudaimonism." In *The Bloomsbury Companion to Socrates*, edited by J. Bussanich and N. Smith, 156–84. London: Bloomsbury.
———. 2014. "Plato on the Ordinary Person and the Form." *Apeiron* 47, no. 2: 266–92.
———. 2021. "Cosmology and *Ananke* in the *Timaeus* and Our Knowledge of the Forms." *Apeiron*, 2021, pp. 000010151520200080. https://doi.org/10.1515/apeiron-2020-0080.
Rowe, C., ed. and trans. 1998. *Plato* Symposium. Exeter: Aris and Phillips Classical Texts.
Rowe, C. 2004. "Plato on Knowing and Merely Believing." In *Ideal and Culture of Knowledge in Plato*, edited by W. Detel, A. Becker, and P. Scholz. Stuttgart: Steiner Verlag.
———. 2005a. "What Difference Do Forms Make for Platonic Epistemology?" In C. Gill, *Virtue, Norms, and Objectivity*, 215–32. Oxford: Oxford University Press.
———, trans. 2005b. *Plato* Phaedrus. London: Penguin.
Rowett, C. 2018. *Knowledge and Truth in Plato*. Oxford: Oxford University Press.
Rudebusch, G. 1985. "Plato on Sense and Reference." *Mind* 94, no. 376: 526–37.
———. 1990. "Does Plato Think False Speech Is Speech?" *Noûs* 24, no. 4: 599–609.
Russell, B. 1912. *The Problems of Philosophy* Oxford: Oxford University Press; all references are to the seventeenth edition.
Ryan, P. 2012, *Plato's Phaedrus: A Commentary for Greek Readers*. Norman: University of Oklahoma Press.
Ryle, G. 1976. "Many Things Are Odd about Our *Meno*." *Paideia* 5: 1–9.
Santas, G. 1979. *Socrates*. London: Routledge and Kegan Paul.
Scerri, E. 2007. *The Periodic Table*. Oxford: Oxford University Press.

Schindler, D. 2012. "The Allegory of the Cave." In *The Continuum Companion to Plato* edited by J. Press, 145–47.
Schwab, W. 2015. "Explanation in the Epistemology of the *Meno*." *Oxford Studies in Ancient Philosophy* 48: 1–36.
———. 2016. "Understanding *Epistêmê* in Plato's *Republic*." *Oxford Studies in Ancient Philosophy* 51: 41–85.
Scolnicov, S. 1976. "Three Aspects of Plato's Philosophy of Learning and Instruction." *Paidea* 5: 50–62.
Scott, D. 1995. *Recollection and Experience*. Cambridge: Cambridge University Press.
———. 2006. *Plato's Meno*. Cambridge: Cambridge University Press.
Sedley, D. 2006. "Form-Particular Resemblances in Plato's *Phaedo*." *Proceedings of the Aristotelian Society* 106, no. 1: 311–27.
Sharples, R. 1985. *Plato: Meno*. Warminster: Aris and Phillips.
Smith, N. 1996. "Plato's Divided Line." *Ancient Philosophy* 16: 25–46.
———. 2000. "Plato on Knowledge as Power." *Journal of the History of Philosophy* 38, no. 2: 145–68.
———. 2012. "Plato on the Power of Ignorance." In *Oxford Studies in Ancient Philosophy* Supplementary Volume, edited by R. Kamtekar, 51–73. Oxford: Oxford University Press.
———. 2019. *Summoning Knowledge in Plato's Republic*. Oxford: Oxford University Press.
Strevens, M. 2019. *Thinking off Your Feet: How Empirical Psychology Vindicates Armchair Philosophy*. Cambridge: Harvard University Press.
Szaif, J. 2007. "*Doxa* and *Epistêmê* as Modes of Acquaintance in *Republic* V." *Etudes Platoniciennes* 4: 253–72.
Taylor, C. 2008. "Plato's Epistemology." In *The Oxford Handbook of Plato*, edited by G. Fine, 165–70. Oxford: Oxford University Press.
Thomas, J. 1980. *Musings on the Meno*. Boston and The Hague: Springer.
Vlastos, G. 1954. "The Third Man Argument in the *Parmenides*." *Philosophical Review* 64, no. 3: 438–48.
———. 1965. "Degrees of Reality in Plato." In *Platonic Studies*, 58–75. Princeton: Princeton University Press.
Vogt, K. 2012. *Belief and Truth: A Skeptic Reading of Plato*. Oxford: Oxford University Press.
Weiss, R. 2001. *Virtue in the Cave*. New York: Oxford University Press.
White, N. 1976. *Plato on Knowledge and Reality*. Indianapolis: Hackett.
———, trans. 1997. In *Plato Complete Work*, edited by J. Cooper, 235–93. Indianapolis: Hackett.
Williams, T. 2002. "Two Aspects of Platonic Recollection." *Apeiron* 35, no. 2: 131–52.
Woolf, R. 2013. "Plato and the Norms of Thought." *Mind* 122: 171–216.

Index Locorum

Apology
  21b–22e, 228
  22d3–e1, 117
  22e6–23b4, 183
  23b, 117, 170n9, 223n

Charmides
  161d1–4, 189n

Cratylus
  383a–390e, 11n
  385d7–e3, 202
  385e4–386a4, 202
  386c2–d1, 202
  388b7–389a3, 203n
  389a5, 204
  389a6–8, 204
  389a7–8, 204
  389b1–3, 204
  389b3, 204
  389b5–6, 204n17
  389d8–390a3, 203
  390d9–e5, 203

Euthydemus
  280a6–8, 45n40, 128n27, 134n36, 231n
  280e5–6, 182n33
  291d7–e1, 189n

Euthyphro
  5d, 94n6
  5d8, 11
  7a, 102

Gorgias
  466a–468e, 122n16
  466b, 102

Lysis
  217a–218c, 122n17, 126n21
  218b, 122
  218d7–8, 189n

Meno
  71a3–7, 46
  71a5–7, 28, 46
  71a6, 46n43
  71b4, 46
  71e, 94n6
  77b3–78c2, 122n16
  79e7–80b7, 46, 54
  80a6, 118
  80b4, 46n44
  80b–d, 28
  80c6, 118
  80d5–6, 47
  80d5–8, 28
  80e1–5, 29, 31, 47

Meno (continued)
  80e2–5, 28
  81c5–d5, 30
  81c5–e2, 37
  81d, 34
  81d4–5, 81n30
  82b9, 79
  82b9–c4, 219n
  82b–85e, 226
  82b–86c, 78–81
  82c4, 80, 219
  82e, 78n22, 79
  82e12–13, 81
  83b7, 78
  84a1, 78
  84a2–b1, 118
  84a3–b1, 46, 54
  84e4–85a1, 78
  85b2, 78
  85c6–7, 47n46
  85c9–d1, 45, 183n34
  85c–d, 78
  86a3–4, 30
  86b6–c2, 29
  86b7–c2, 29
  96d, 119
  97a3–98d2, 125n20
  97a6–98a8, 170n10, 232
  97a9, 134n36
  97a–98a, 128n27, 130–31
  97a–98b, 114n4, 115
  97a–b, 115
  97c11–98b6, 45n40
  97c–d, 119
  98a, 2, 5, 30n
  98a3–4, 119
  98a5–6, 119n

Parmenides
  132b3–c7, 189n

Phaedo
  65–66, 78n21

  72–77, 28n3, 70
  72e2–73a2, 39
  73c1–3, 70
  73c5–d1, 70
  73c6–d1, 39
  73d–74a, 63
  73e5–10, 70
  74a5–7, 40, 67, 70, 83n
  74a6–7, 71n7
  74a11–12, 77
  74a12, 189n
  74b3, 77
  74b4–6, 77
  74b6–7, 77
  74b7–c5, 40, 67–69, 70, 77
  74b–c, 78n21
  74c3–4, 57
  74c7–9, 57
  74c7–12, 71
  74d4–8, 57
  74d4–75a4, 69
  74d8–10, 71
  74d9–e4, 68, 71
  74d9–e8, 57
  74d10–e1, 71
  74e9–75a2, 71n7
  74e9–75a3, 71
  75b1, 58
  75b4–8, 43–44
  75c6–e8, 30
  75c10–d3, 77n20
  75c–76c, 45
  75d7–76d6, 77
  75e–76d, 34
  76b, 58
  76d8–e1, 77n20

Phaedrus
  247d6–e3, 138, 219
  248a, 219
  248a1–7, 138–139
  248a1–249c4, 219–21
  248a1–a7, 219–20

Index Locorum | 245

248a–d, 138
248b3–5, 139
248b5, 139n4
249b, 220
249b6–c4, 139, 140–41
249c, 28n3
249c6–d1, 141, 220
249e4–250b1, 141–42
262c, 142
262c1–3, 143
265c8–266b2, 143–44
265c–e, 143–45
268d6–e6, 205–6
269b5–c2, 145
269b–d, 145–46
269c6–8, 145
269c9–d1, 146
269e4–270a1, 146
270b5–6, 146

Protagoras
330c1, 189n

Republic
249b6–c4, 220
338c, 102
345d1–353a11, 171n12
473c11–d3, 87
475–479, 12n
475b8–9, 88
475c6–8, 88, 98
475c9–d5, 184, 185
475e2, 88
475e4–476c9, 218
475e4–479d5, 59n17, 87–89, 113, 139, 140, 141, 166, 180, 183, 184, 188, 191, 194, 196, 200, 202, 205, 207, 208, 209–10, 211, 212, 221, 226, 228, 231, 234n14
475e4–479e5, 125n20, 221–22
475e6–7, 89, 90
475e6–479c5, 88
475e9–476a2, 89

476b, 87n
476b4–c8, 90, 91
476c, 102
476c2–3, 88
476c2–4, 106
476c2–7, 92, 96n7, 166
476c5–7, 175
476c5–9, 175
476d, 197n12
476d1–3, 176
476d5–6, 186
476e, 96n7
476e4–479d5, 232, 233, 235
476e5, 172
476e6–477a4, 96n8
476e7–8, 172
476e7–10, 175
476e10, 189n
476e–478e, 96
477a3–4, 173n17
477a3–5, 152
477a4, 195
477a5–479d5, 201
477a5–b1, 220
477a6–7, 173
477a6–b1, 147
477a7, 196
477a9–10, 146, 216n7
477a9–b1, 173
477a–479a5, 201
477b, 212
477b3, 173
477b5–6, 96n8
477b–478d, 173
477c1–d1, 168, 175
477c9–d5, 176–77
477e6–7, 45n40, 134n36, 167, 231n
478b1–2, 195
478b6–c1, 189n
478b7–8, 195
478b9, 195, 222
478c4–5, 173
478c13–14, 167

Republic (continued)
  478d5–9, 173–74
  478d6–7, 195
  478d10–e1, 88
  478e1–5, 96n8
  478e3, 174
  478e7–479a1, 97
  478e7–479b2, 90, 95, 97
  479–480, 75n18
  479a5–b2, 176
  479a–b, 98n
  479b, 94n6
  479b3–4, 98, 165
  479b3–10, 90
  479c3, 167
  479c3–5, 172, 174
  479c6–7, 172
  479c6–d1, 174
  479d2–4, 176
  479d3–5, 174
  479d7, 174
  479d9, 167
  505a–506b, 230
  505d, 101
  505d7–9, 102
  505d11–e3, 102
  509, 170n9
  509c9, 210
  509d–511d, 139, 210, 221
  509d–511e, 152n
  510b4–9, 213, 214
  510c2–d1, 214
  510e1–511a1, 215
  510e2–3, 214
  511c3–d5, 215
  511d5–7, 215
  514a1–517a7, 103–4
  514a–517b, 106
  514a–518b, 139, 210, 221
  514b7–515a3, 217
  516a5–b2, 219
  516c7–d2, 103, 217
  516e3–6, 17
  518a1–519a6, 184
  518a2–3, 185
  518c4–10, 186, 186n
  518c6, 184
  518c7, 185
  518d3–e3, 185
  518e2, 185
  518e3–519a1, 185
  519b4–5, 185
  519c10–11, 106
  520c6–7, 106
  523a, 105
  523a–525a, 59n17
  523c11–e2, 105
  523d3–5, 107, 183n35
  523e3–524a4, 105, 170n8, 183n35, 187
  523e–524a, 165
  533e3–534a8, 167, 171n12

Sophist
  237a3, 189n
  259d–261e, 54n7, 232
  262e5–6, 147n
  263e–264b, 152n

Symposium
  98a3–4, 115
  199d1–2, 189n
  199e6–7, 189n
  200–212, 12n
  201d1–212c3, 111–35, 210, 221, 227
  201e6–7, 120
  201e10–11, 120
  201e10–202a9, 33
  202–212, 36
  202a, 120
  202a2–3, 120
  202a2–212a7, 113
  202a5–9, 115, 116–17, 123, 133, 200–201, 207

202a9, 36n20, 114
202b6–7, 121
202b6–c1, 121
202c1–4, 122
202c5, 120
202c6–9, 122
202c10–12, 122
203c–212e, 201, 207
203c–d, 126
204–212, 125n20
204a4–7, 126
205e7–206a1, 126
207e1–208a5, 126–27, 227
207e1–208a7, 126
207e5, 126n22
207e5–211a7, 133
208a2, 126n22
208a3, 127n25
208a5, 129n28
208a6, 127n24
209a–b, 126
210e4–211a7, 127–28
210e6–211b2, 127
211c, 126
211c1–d1, 129
211c3, 129
211d2–212a1, 130
211d3–5, 129
211d8–e2, 129

Theaetetus
142a–186e, 146–47
146d, 94n6
152c5–6, 45n40, 128n27, 134n36, 231n
152d2–e1, 197
156a–157c, 75n17
163e4–7, 189n
166e9, 189n
178c–179c, 224n
187a4–6, 147
187a4–199d8, 54n7

187b4–5, 149, 150
187b4–c5, 170n10, 232
187b6, 148
187c7, 150
187c7–200a10, 227
187c–200d, 27n
187d1–4, 149
187d1–200c7, 137
187d–201a, 232
188a, 154
188a1–2, 147, 149, 150n27
188a1–4, 150
188a1–195b8, 195n5
188a7–8, 151n28
188a–b, 156
188b2–5, 151
188b7–10, 151
188c2–3, 151
188d3–e2, 152
188e5, 189n
189d7–8, 152
189e1–3, 152
189e7–190a4, 153, 227
189e–190a, 152n, 188n
189e–194d, 207
191b, 154
192a, 155
192a5–6, 155n32
192b, 155
192b2–5, 155–56
192d, 156, 162
192e5–6, 156
192e6, 158
193a, 162
193b9–d2, 157
194b, 159
194b1, 158n
194b1–4, 157
194b4–6, 159–60
194c5–d4, 159n
194c5–d7, 158
194c6, 160

Theaetetus (continued)
  194e1–195a9, 158
  196d8–197a4, 162
  197a7–9, 147
  199d, 163
  199d4–8, 163
  201c7–d3, 114n4
  201c–d, 115n7
  201d, 2, 131, 132n33

202b6, 131
202b8–210b2, 232
202c–210d, 170n10
203a1–d6, 131
248a1–249c4, 227
269b7–8, 146n18

Timaeus
  37b, 197n12

Subject Index

aboutness, 4–8, 13, 56, 147, 233. *See also* reference
acquaintance, knowledge by, 49–50, 148
agnôsia, 22n28, 57n13, 211
Anagnostopoulos, M., 10n12
anamnêsis, 39
Annas, J., 209n
aporia, 1, 28, 37, 46, 54, 56, 78, 118–19
Aristotle, 11n, 224n, 233n13
Augustine, 51–53
aviary, 162–63

Baima, N., 35n14
beauty: beautiful perceptibles mistaken for beauty itself, 87–101, 105–6, 174, 175–76, 219, 221–22; knowledge of Form of Beauty, 125–30; ordinary people opine beauty itself, 2, 6, 17, 188, 208, 222, 223–26. *See also* Forms
beginning problem {B}: and brute evidence for ability to inquire, 37–39, 48; cannot be resolved by using *doxa*, 33, 235; compared to Augustine's paradox, 51–53; and ignorance, 31–33, 35–36, 47; introduced by Meno's paradox, 28–31; recollection proposed as solution for, 27–39, 48, 51, 53, 77, 85–86, 225–26; relation to resolution of ending problem, 29–30, 38–39, 41–42, 48, 65, 225n3; resolved by resolving problem of reference, 53, 57, 65, 75, 86, 225; resolved by unwitting cognitive contact, 29, 31, 36–37, 41–42, 48–50, 81n28; true belief proposed as solution for, 32n12, 46–49, 230, 235
belief. See *doxa*; false belief; true belief
Benson, H., 8n7, 29, 32n11, 38n25, 94n6
Berman, S., 10n12, 11n, 232n11
black box, 15–16, 85–86, 86n
Bluck, R., 46n43, 59n16
Bobonich, C., 68n4
Bostock, D., 40n29, 42n32, 55, 152n
Brickhouse, T., 10n12
Brown, L., 14
Burnyeat, M., 152n, 160n40

Campbell, L., 160n40
Caplan, B., 48n47
cave, allegory of the, 17, 103–4, 216–21
Cherniss, H., 18n
cognitive blankness, 32, 36n18, 143, 148, 151n29, 158, 161, 163, 227n

249

complexity, 131–32
Cornford, F., 148n23, 152n, 169n2

Daedalus's statues, 30n, 119, 128n27, 132n33. *See also* true belief
Dancy, R. M., 4n2, 32n11, 47n46, 65n23, 68n4
desire: for beauty, 122; for the good, 10n12, 102, 103n17, 122, 124, 126
Devereux, D., 10n12
Devitt, M., 8n8, 9
diagonal, 16, 38–39, 78–79, 81n27, 82, 219, 224. *See also* Forms
dialectic, 215–16
dianoia (δ), 141, 152n, 170n9, 184, 211–15
Dimas, P., 68n4
Diotima's speech: on *doxa* as a system rather than individuated beliefs, 120–24, 126–27; on *doxa* as between knowledge and ignorance, 36n19, 114–15, 117, 134–35, 201, 207; on *doxa* as constantly changing, 127–28, 133, 227; on impossibility of a doxastic hierarchy, 116–17, 119, 200, 207, 210, 221; on upward path to knowledge, 125–30
divided line, 141, 170n9, 184, 210–16, 220–21
doxa: about what-is (second-degree object), 138–40, 146–47, 165–81, 209–22, 223–26, 233–36; can be improved, 170, 181–84, 187, 219; cannot be arranged into a hierarchy, 112, 116–19, 120, 123, 126, 134, 200, 207, 210, 221, 231; as a "cloud," 116, 120, 121, 125, 187, 201; constitutes all cognitive states that fall short of knowledge, 6, 11–12, 13, 226–29; contrasted with notion of individual propositional beliefs, 2–3, 17, 112–17, 125, 130, 135, 170–71, 182, 194, 227; and *dianoia*, 141, 152n, 170n9, 184, 213–15; English translations of, 3n, 27n, 113, 125n20, 152n; ignorance is poor quality *doxa*, 11–12, 116, 133–34, 139, 142–43, 145–46, 188, 200–201, 205–8, 226–29; on ignorance side of knowing/not-knowing dichotomy, 147–58, 160–61, 227–28; inferior to knowledge, 126–30, 133–34, 150, 168, 173, 179, 181, 182, 188; instability of, 126–30, 142, 227; integrity of doxastic structure, 128–35, 142, 153, 158–61, 219, 227; and justified true belief theories, 115–16, 117, 125, 130, 132n33; in between knowledge and ignorance, 36n19, 114–16, 117, 134–35, 201, 207; mixture of reasoned/unreasoned, true/false beliefs, 120–23, 128–30, 187, 200–201, 221, 227; opines the Forms, 2, 6, 17, 188, 208, 222, 223–26; process of individuating beliefs, 124, 153, 227; "set over" what both is and is-not (first-degree object), 138–40, 165–81, 200–201, 209–22, 232, 233–36; "thinking" vs. judgment, 6, 152–54, 161, 188n, 227; usefulness of various doxastic systems, 6, 133, 161, 228, 231. *See also* false belief; three-part distinction (ignorance, *doxa*, knowledge); true belief

eikasia (ε), 211, 212, 213
elenchos, 37, 47n46
ending problem {E}, 27, 28–29, 52, 53n5, 64n, 225; relation to resolution of beginning problem, 29–30, 38–39, 41–42, 48, 65, 225n3

epi-locution, 167, 171–72, 177, 185, 186n, 202, 206, 211–12
epistêmê, 17, 127, 168n, 170n9, 185, 187n, 191, 207, 209–12
equality/inequality, 40–41, 43–45, 52n2, 53, 70–78
Erôs, 120–24, 126
eye of the soul, 184–86

false belief: about the good, 101; and *aporia*, 54; aviary model, 162–63; cannot involve knowledge, 151, 154–63; *doxa* is a mixture of true and false beliefs, 120–23, 128–30, 187, 200–201, 221, 227; has unwitting cognitive contact with what-is, 48–49, 146–47, 154, 156, 158, 161; as heterodoxy, 152–54, 158–62; and judgment, 152–63; and knowing/not-knowing dichotomy, 147–58, 160–61, 227–28; portrayal across the dialogues, 232; as result of successful inquiry, 38n24; and suboptimal doxastic structures, 158–61; three impossibilities, 151, 155–57, 161–63; and types of ignorance, 57; wax block model, 154–61
Ferejohn, M., 131n, 209n, 211n3
Ferrari, G., 184n39, 210n
Fine, G., 4–5, 4n3, 5nn4–6, 13–14, 13n17, 28n2, 30n, 31n, 32, 32nn10–12, 35n15, 35n17, 36nn18–20, 37, 38n23, 38n25, 45n39, 45n41, 46n42, 47n46, 55n8, 64n22, 68n4, 94n6, 96n8, 99n, 118n, 148–49, 151n29, 158n, 169n3, 172n13, 178n, 194
finger example, 105–8
first-degree objects. *See* three-part distinction (ignorance, *doxa*, knowledge)
Forms: accessed by prisoners in the cave, 103–4, 217–19; all human beings have cognitive contact with, 16–17, 223–26; conscious access to, 68; and dialectic, 215–16; and *dianoia*, 212–15; *doxa* opines, 2, 6, 17, 188, 208, 222, 223–26; identified with what-is, 138, 168, 169–70; knowledge of Form of Beauty, 125–30; make knowledge possible, 229; and ordinary concept formation, 41–44, 57n14, 68–69; ordinary people's ability to reference, 68–69, 70–82, 86, 99–100, 103–8, 217–19, 224, 226; perceptibles partake in temporarily, 196–200, 206; philosophers look beyond perceptibles to, 141, 181–82, 185–86, 202, 204–5, 212–16, 220–21, 224–25; recollection supplies unwitting cognitive contact with, 43–44, 140; true propositions about, 199–200; as truth-makers, 2, 18, 20, 37n21, 223, 224. *See also* what-is
Franklin, L., 20, 41n, 44, 48n47, 68n5, 72n10, 75n15
Frege, G., 100, 149n24

Geddes, W., 59n16
Gerson, L., 17n23, 149n25, 150n26, 169n4, 170n9, 229n6
Gettier, E., 115n7
gnôsis, 211–12, 213
Gonzalez, F., 47n46, 194n4
good, 10n12, 101–3, 122, 124, 126
Gosling, J., 71n9
Griffith, T., 184n39, 210n
Grjic, F., 4n2
Grube, D., 125n20, 210n
Gulley, N., 45n41, 59n16, 60n18
Guthrie, W. K. C., 125n20

Hackforth, R., 45n41, 59n16, 138n2, 139n6, 220n13

Harte, V., 20, 43n34, 44nn36-37, 68-78ff, 94n5, 104n, 169n4, 170n7, 171n12, 217n8, 229n5
heterodoxy, 152-54, 158-62

ignorance: about what-is (second-degree object), 165-81, 184-89, 202-5, 209-22, 232, 233-36; and attempt to create hierarchy of doxastic states, 116-19; as cognitive blankness, 32, 36n18, 143, 148, 151n29, 158, 161, 163, 227n; composed of poor quality *doxa*, 11-12, 116, 133-34, 139, 142-43, 145-46, 188, 200-201, 205-8, 226-29; double ignorance, 116-19, 120, 123, 126, 130; *doxa* in between knowledge and ignorance, 36n19, 114-16, 117, 134-35, 201, 207; and knowing/not-knowing dichotomy, 147-58, 160-61, 227-28; lovers of sights and sounds are better off than the ignorant, 89, 96, 101, 181, 186, 202, 204-5, 206, 222, 234-35; recollection begins from, 46-47; reference possible even if ignorant, 55-57, 60; "set over" nothing at all (first-degree object), 140n, 146-47, 152, 165-81, 184-89, 202-5, 209-22, 232, 233-36; Socratic ignorance, 116-19, 120; types of, 56-57; ways of not knowing, 31-33, 35-36. See also *aporia*; three-part distinction (ignorance, *doxa*, knowledge)
intelligence, 185-86
Irwin, T., 46, 46n42, 47n46, 65n23, 96n8

JTB theories. See justified true belief
judgment, 6, 152-63, 188n, 227
justified true belief, 2-3, 112, 114n4, 115-18, 125, 130, 132n33, 170, 182, 221

Kamtekar, R., 106n, 229n5
Kelsey, S., 20, 43-44, 48n47, 68n5, 72n10, 74n14
Kirk, G., 195n6
knowledge: by acquaintance, 49-50, 148; and attempt to create hierarchy of doxastic states, 116-19; *doxa* in between knowledge and ignorance, 36n19, 114-16, 117, 134-35, 201, 207; false belief cannot involve, 151, 154-63; of Form of Beauty, 125-30; Forms make possible, 229; has what-is as both its first and second-degree objects, 165-81, 209-22, 233-36; knowing/not-knowing dichotomy, 147-58, 160-61, 227-28; knowledge of perceptibles derived from knowledge of the Forms, 17, 191n, 197, 229-30; no character in the dialogues has, 223-24; and *noêsis*, 215-16; philosophers' capacity for, 176, 178n29, 179; stability of, 128-30, 142; superior to *doxa*, 126-30, 133-34, 150, 168, 173, 179, 181, 182, 188; and varied prenatal experiences, 138-42; whether recollection results in, 38-39, 44-45. See also justified true belief; three-part distinction (ignorance, *doxa*, knowledge)
Kripke, S., 8n8, 9-11, 48n47, 75n18, 230

Larissa, road to, 119, 130, 134n36, 135n
lovers of sights and sounds: better off than the ignorant, 89, 96, 101, 181, 186, 202, 204-5, 206, 222, 234-35; can be converted from their inconsistent beliefs, 89-101, 105-8, 174, 224; compared to

philosophers, 87–89, 141, 175–76, 181–82, 185–86, 201–5, 220–21; consolation of, 89, 96, 139–40, 166, 172, 181–82, 185, 201–2; have unwitting cognitive contact with beauty itself, 99, 224; identified with prisoners in the cave, 103–4, 185; potential to become philosophers, 88, 90, 187, 219, 226; represent ordinary people, 87–89, 197; set their epistemic capacities upon perceptibles, 175–76, 181–82, 185–86, 197, 202, 204–7, 212–14, 216, 220–21

MacDonald, S., 52n2
matching, 13–15, 55n9, 64n, 188n. *See also* mismatching
Matthews, G., 4n2
McDowell, J., 148n23, 152n
meaning, 100
Meno's paradox, 15, 16, 27–39, 52n2, 78, 147–48. *See also* beginning problem {B}; ending problem {E}
mismatching, 149n24, 155n32, 155n33, 158–62
Moravcsik, J., 4n2, 38n25, 47n45, 55n8
Moss, J., 17n23, 17n24, 27n, 114n3, 114n5, 149n25, 150n26, 168n, 169n4, 170n8, 171nn11–12, 182n32, 229nn5–6, 234n14

names, 202–5
Nathan, M., 15–16, 85, 134n36
Nehamas, A., 46, 47n46, 94n6, 125n20, 232n10
noêsis (v), 184, 211, 212, 213, 215–16
nonphilosophers. *See* ordinary people
nothing at all, 140n, 146–47, 152, 165–81, 184–89, 202–5, 209–22, 232, 233–36

opinion. *See doxa;* false belief; true belief
ordinary people: epistemological abilities of, 3, 7, 10; objects of beliefs of, 82–83; opine beauty itself, 2, 6, 17, 188, 208, 222, 223–26; and ordinary concept formation, 41–44, 57n14, 68–69; potential to become philosophers, 75n15, 88, 90, 139n5, 187, 219, 226; provoking them to reflection, 105–8, 183n35; represented by lovers of sights and sounds, 87–89, 197; represented by Meno's slave, 41, 78–81; souls of, 75; whether their recollection results in knowledge, 38–39, 44–45

paradox. *See* beginning problem {B}; ending problem {E}; Meno's paradox; reference, problem of {R}
Parmenideanism, 189, 193–200
Paytas, T., 35n14
Penner, T., 10n12, 11n, 40, 50n49, 59n16, 87n, 96n8, 103n17, 105n20, 194n3, 196n, 198n
perceptibles: cannot be known directly, 169, 176, 214, 230; and *dianoia,* 212–15; identified with what both is and is-not, 145–46, 169, 176, 188, 196, 204; knowledge of derived from knowledge of the Forms, 17, 191n, 197, 229–30; lovers of sights and sounds mistake beautiful perceptibles for beauty itself, 89–101, 175–76; and Meno's slave, 78–82; partake in Forms temporarily, 196–200, 206; perception cannot deal with on its own, 187, 196; philosophers look beyond, 141, 181–82, 185–86, 202, 204–5, 212–16, 220–21, 224–25; and problem of reference, 59–65;

254 | Subject Index

perceptibles *(continued)*
provoke reflection, 105–8; and Pythagoreanism, 188; sticks and stones, 40, 43, 73, 75–76; wax block, 154–61

perception. *See* perceptibles; wax block

philosophers: capacity for knowledge, 176, 178n29, 179; compared to lovers of sights and sounds, 87–89, 141, 175–76, 181–82, 185–86, 201–2, 204–5, 220–21; Erôs as, 126; look beyond perceptibles to the Forms, 141, 181–82, 185–86, 202, 204–5, 212–16, 220–21, 224–25; no character in the dialogues is one, 223–24; ordinary people's potential to become, 75n15, 88, 90, 139n5, 187, 219, 226; as rulers, 87, 106, 139n5, 223; souls of, 75; study that which provokes reflection, 105–8

phronêsis, 185

pistis (π), 141, 184, 211, 212, 213

propositional beliefs, 2–3, 17, 112–17, 125, 130, 135, 170–71, 182, 194, 227

Protagoras/Protagoreanism, 44n36, 202–5, 224n, 235

Pugh, A., 132n32

Quine, W. V., 22n27

Raven, J., 195n6

recollection: *aporia* often triggers, 54–55; as a "black box," 15–16, 85–86; dogs analogy for, 61–64; Harte's interpretation of, 70–78; implausible explanation for learning and inquiry, 30, 34–35, 51, 56; not mentioned outside of *Meno, Phaedo,* and *Phaedrus*, 15–17, 85–86, 226, 232; and ordinary concept formation, 41–44, 57n14, 68–69; prenatal knowledge, 4, 12, 30, 33–35, 39, 55–56, 63, 79, 137–42, 219–20, 226–27; prerequisites for, 4, 46–47; proposed by Plato to resolve beginning problem, 27–39, 48, 51, 53, 77, 85–86, 225–26; Scott's interpretation of, 42n32, 68–78 passim, 81nn27–29, 82–83; and slave demonstration, 16, 37–39, 44–45, 78–83; and sticks and stones argument, 40–41, 43–45, 52n2, 70–78; supplies ability to refer, 13, 33–34, 51–65; supplies unwitting cognitive contact, 11–12, 34, 43–44, 48–49, 140; triggers of, 39–40, 42, 70–72; whether it results in knowledge, 38–39, 44–45

reference: "direct reference," 9–10, 48n47, 53n5, 230; and matching and stepping stone prerequisites, 13–15; and meaning, 100; and nonidentity of discernibles, 57–64; ordinary people's ability to reference the Forms, 68–69, 70–82, 86, 99–100, 103–4, 105–8, 217–19, 224, 226; possible even if ignorant, 55–57, 60; prerequisite for all epistemic states, 27, 33, 35–37; prerequisite for inquiry, 8–12, 53–54, 64–65; recollection supplies ability to refer, 13, 33–34, 51–65; as unwitting cognitive contact, 7–12. *See also* reference, problem of {R}; unwitting cognitive contact with what-is

reference, problem of {R}: in Augustine's paradox, 51–53; dogs analogy for, 61–64; and nonidentity of discernibles, 57–64; resolved by unwitting cognitive contact, 65, 226; resolving it resolves beginning

problem, 53, 57, 65, 75, 86, 225; and true belief, 54n7, 56, 236
Reshotko, N., 10n12, 11n, 56n11, 75n17, 103n17, 146n20
Rowe, C., 10n12, 138n2
Rowett, C., 35n16, 50n48
Rudebusch, G., 149n24, 155nn32–33
Russell, B., 50
Ryan, P., 138n2
Ryle, G., 38n25

Saunders, R., 132n33
Scerri, E., 183n37, 184n38
Schindler, D., 217n9
Schwab, W., 17n23, 17n24, 27n, 114n3, 114n5, 149n25, 150n26, 169n4, 170n8, 171nn11–12, 182n32
Scolnicov, S., 47n45
Scott, D., 4n2, 10n13, 20, 28, 29, 30n, 32, 32n10, 41n, 42n33, 43–44, 45n38, 47n46, 57n14, 68–78 passim, 81nn27–29, 82–83, 87n, 118n
second-degree objects. *See* three-part distinction (ignorance, *doxa*, knowledge)
Sedley, D., 68n4
Sharples, R., 38n25
slave demonstration, 16, 37–39, 44–45, 78–83, 118–19, 219, 224
Smith, N., 10n12, 169n4, 171n12, 178n, 184n39, 210n, 229n5
soul: and desire for the good, 101–3; dialogue with itself, 153–54; eye of, 184–86; immortality of, 12, 15, 16, 44n37, 70, 75, 86, 226; investigates from hypotheses, 213–14; and prenatal knowledge, 4, 12, 30, 33–35, 39, 55–56, 63, 79, 137–42, 219–20, 226–27; varied prenatal experiences of what-is, 138–42, 227
square, 39, 78–81, 215, 219, 224

stepping stone, 13–15
sticks and stones argument, 40–41, 43–45, 52n2, 70–78
Strevens, M., 8–9, 50n49, 230n8
Szaif, J., 169n4, 186n, 187n, 191n, 197n12, 229n5

Thomas, J., 47n45
three-part distinction (ignorance, *doxa*, knowledge): analogies to the physical senses, 175–79; anomalous in context of everything but *Rep.* V, 209–10, 231–33; contrasted to console lover of sights and sounds, 172–74, 179n, 185–87, 208, 210, 221–22, 228–29, 234; and *epi*-locution, 167, 171–72, 177, 185, 186n, 202, 206, 211–12; first and second-degree objects of epistemic capacities, 165–81, 209–22, 233–36; not seen in cave allegory, 216–21; not seen in charioteer image, 219–21; not seen in divided line, 210–16, 220–21; in Plato scholarship, 168–69, 229–36; and two-world theory, 233–36
true belief: *doxa* is a mixture of true and false beliefs, 120–23, 128–30, 187, 200–201, 221, 227; falls short of knowledge, 45n40, 130–34; justified true belief, 2–3, 112, 114n4, 115–18, 125, 130, 132n33, 170, 182, 221; Meno's slave arrives at, 37–38, 47n46; not a prerequisite for inquiry, 32n12, 64; portrayed differently across dialogues, 232; prenatal possession of, 34–35; proposed solution for beginning problem, 32n12, 46–49, 230, 235; and resolution of problem of reference, 54n7, 56, 236; "tethered" or "tied-down," 5n4, 30n, 45n40,

true belief *(continued)*
  115, 119, 130–32; and types of ignorance, 57; usefulness of, 119
truth-makers, 2, 10, 11, 18, 20, 34, 36, 37n21, 53, 223–24. *See also* Forms
two-world theory, 17, 26, 96n8, 168n, 178n, 230, 233–36

Ullian, J. S., 22n27
universal literal self predication, 191n, 199n
unwitting cognitive contact with what-is: all human beings have, 16–17, 223–26; even the ignorant have, 137–46, 208; and false belief, 48–49, 147, 154, 156, 158, 161; and false judgment, 154, 156, 158, 161; by lovers of sights and sounds, 70–82, 89–104, 224; by Meno's slave, 78–82, 219, 224; other than knowing and not knowing, 13, 32–33; prerequisite for all *doxa*, 7, 11–12, 15–17; by prisoners in the cave, 103–4, 217–19; recollection as "black box" for, 15–17, 85–86; recollection supplies, 11–12, 34, 43–44, 48–49, 140; reference as, 7–12; resolves beginning problem, 29, 31, 36–37, 41–42, 48–50, 81n28; resolves problem of reference, 65, 226; by souls pursuing the good, 101–3; in sticks and stones argument, 70–78; and varied prenatal experiences of what-is, 137–38, 142, 226
upward path, 106, 125–30, 133

virtue, 28, 37–39, 46
Vlastos, G., 47n46, 193–94, 199n
Vogt, K., 17n23, 27n, 114n3, 149n25, 150n26, 169, 170nn7–9, 171n12, 172n13, 182nn31–32, 183n35, 229n5

wax block, 154–61
Weiss, R., 4n3, 30n, 46n44
what both is and is-not: first-degree object of *doxa*, 138–40, 165–81, 200–201, 209–22, 232, 233–36; identified with perceptibles, 145–46, 169, 176, 188, 196, 204; ontological, predicational, and veridical readings of, 193–94, 199–201
what-is: identified with Forms, 138, 168, 169–70; second-degree object of ignorance, *doxa*, and knowledge, 138–40, 146–47, 165–81, 209–22, 233–36; and something or nothing dichotomy, 193–200; varied prenatal experiences of, 138–42, 227. *See also* unwitting cognitive contact with what-is
White, N., 4n2, 38n25, 46, 232n10
Williams, T., 20, 35n14, 44nn36–37, 57n14, 65n24, 68n5, 75n15, 81n27

www.ingramcontent.com/pod-product-compliance
Lightning Source LLC
Chambersburg PA
CBHW020328240426
43665CB00044B/891